# LITERARY CRITICISM
# AND CULTURAL THEORY

*Edited by*
William E. Cain
Wellesley College

A ROUTLEDGE SERIES

# Literary Criticism and Cultural Theory

William E. Cain, *General Editor*

"Keeping Up Her Geography"
*Women's Writing and Geocultural Space in Twentieth-Century U.S. Literature and Culture*
Tanya Ann Kennedy

Contested Masculinities
*Crises in Colonial Male Identity from Joseph Conrad to Satyajit Ray*
Nalin Jayasena

Unsettled Narratives
*The Pacific Writings of Stevenson, Ellis, Melville and London*
David Farrier

The Subject of Race in American Science Fiction
Sharon DeGraw

Parsing the City
*Jonson, Middleton, Dekker, and City Comedy's London as Language*
Heather C. Easterling

The Economy of the Short Story in British Periodicals of the 1890s
Winnie Chan

Negotiating the Modern
*Orientalism and Indianness in the Anglophone World*
Amit Ray

Novels, Maps, Modernity
*The Spatial Imagination, 1850–2000*
Eric Bulson

Novel Notions
*Medical Discourse and the Mapping of the Imagination in Eighteenth-Century English Fiction*
Katherine E. Kickel

Masculinity and the English Working Class
*Studies in Victorian Autobiography and Fiction*
Ying S. Lee

Aesthetic Hysteria
*The Great Neurosis in Victorian Melodrama and Contemporary Fiction*
Ankhi Mukherjee

The Rise of Corporate Publishing and Its Effects on Authorship in Early Twentieth-Century America
Kim Becnel

Conspiracy, Revolution, and Terrorism from Victorian Fiction to the Modern Novel
Adrian S. Wisnicki

City/Stage/Globe
*Performance and Space in Shakespeare's London*
D.J. Hopkins

Transatlantic Engagements with the British Eighteenth Century
Pamela Albert

Race, Immigration, and American Identity in the Fiction of Salman Rushdie, Ralph Ellison, and William Faulkner
Randy Boyagoda

Cosmopolitan Culture and Consumerism in Chick Lit
Caroline J. Smith

# Cosmopolitan Culture and Consumerism in Chick Lit

Caroline J. Smith

First published 2008
by Routledge
270 Madison Ave, New York, NY 10016

Simultaneously published in the UK
by Routledge
2 Park Square, Milton Park, Abingdon, Oxon OX14 4RN

*Routledge is an imprint of the Taylor & Francis Group, an informa business*

Transferred to Digital Printing 2009

Copyright © 2008 Taylor & Francis

Typeset in 11 pt. Adobe Garamond by IBT Global.

All rights reserved. No part of this book may be reprinted or reproduced or utilised in any form or by any electronic, mechanical, or other means, now known or hereafter invented, including photocopying and recording, or in any information storage or retrieval system, without permission in writing from the publishers.

**Trademark Notice:** Product or corporate names may be trademarks or registered trademarks, and are used only for identification and explanation without intent to infringe.

*Library of Congress Cataloging in Publication Data*
Smith, Caroline J., 1974-
Cosmopolitan culture and consumerism in chick lit / by Caroline J. Smith.
p. cm. — (Literary criticism and cultural theory)
Includes bibliographical references and index.
ISBN 0-415-95662-5
1. American fiction—Women authors--History and criticism.  2. English fiction--Women authors—History and criticism.  3. Chick lit—History and criticism.  4. Cosmopolitanism in literature.  5. Consumption (Economics) in literature.  6. Women--Books and reading—English-speaking countries.  7. Single women in literature.  8. Young women in literature.  I. Title.

PS374.W6S65 2007
813'.6099287—dc22

2007024395

ISBN10: 0-415-95662-5 (hbk)
ISBN10: 0-415-80626-7 (pbk)
ISBN10: 0-203-92914-4 (ebk)

ISBN13: 978-0-415-95662-8 (hbk)
ISBN13: 978-0-415-80626-8 (pbk)
ISBN13: 978-0-203-92914-8 (ebk)

*This book is dedicated to my parents,
who have always given the best advice.*

# Permissions

From THE GIRLS' GUIDE TO HUNTING AND FISHING by Melissa Bank, copyright © 1999 by Melissa Bank. Used by permission of Viking Penguin, a division of Penguin Group (USA) Inc.

Reprinted with permission of the author: THE GIRL'S GUIDE TO HUNTING AND FISHING by Melissa Bank, Viking 1999.

From SEX AND THE CITY by Candace Bushnell. Copyright © 1996 by Candace Bushnell. By permission of Warner Books (US).

From SEX AND THE CITY by Candace Bushnell. Copyright © 1996 by Candace Bushnell. By permission of Grove/Atlantic, Inc.

From BRIDGET JONES'S DIARY by Helen Fielding. Copyright © 1996 by Helen Fielding. By permission of Pan Macmillan.

From BRIDGET JONES'S DIARY by Helen Fielding, copyright © 1996 by Helen Fielding. Used by permission of Viking Penguin, a division of Penguin Group (USA) Inc.

From GETTING OVER IT by Anna Maxted, published by Arrow. Reprinted by permission of The Random House Group Ltd.

From THE CIGARETTE GIRL by Carol Wolper, copyright © 1999 by Carol Wolper. Used by permission of Riverhead Books, an imprint of Penguin Group (USA) Inc.

From ANIMAL HUSBANDRY by Laura Zigman, copyright © 1998 by Laura Zigman. Used by permission of The Dial Press/Dell Publishing, a division of Random House, Inc.

From ANIMAL HUSBANDRY by Laura Zigman, published by Hutchinson/Arrow. Reprinted by permission of The Random House Group Ltd.

# Contents

Acknowledgments — ix

*Chapter One*
Introduction — 1

*Chapter Two*
One Simple Step to Becoming a V.G. Consumer:
Read Women's Magazines — 20

*Chapter Three*
The Girls' Guide to Breaking *The Rules* — 45

*Chapter Four*
Down with Marriage: The Search for Romantic Alternatives — 74

*Chapter Five*
Living the Life of a Domestic Goddess: "It's a Good Thing" — 101

*Chapter Six*
Afterword — 134

Notes — 145

Bibliography — 163

Index — 177

# Acknowledgments

A project on the topic of advice literature would not be complete without acknowledging those people who provided me with their words of wisdom along the way. I would like to thank Peter X. Feng, Maria Frawley, Sherrie Inness, Margaret Stetz, and Julian Yates for not only showing their support for this project in its early stages but for also continuing to show their support as the project grew and developed. A sincere thank you to my official editor, Max Novick, and to my unofficial editor, Devin Harner. Thank you to my students at both the University of Delaware and The George Washington University who read and discussed various chick lit texts throughout these past few semesters. Lastly, I would like to extend thanks to my family, Dad, Mom, Clay, Amy, Frank, Maddie, and Ruby.

# Chapter One
# Introduction

> Who needs a book of etiquette? Everyone does.
> —*Amy Vanderbilt's Complete Book of Etiquette:*
> *A Guide to Gracious Living* (1952)

In British author Helen Fielding's 1996 popular novel *Bridget Jones's Diary*, the author describes the primping and prepping that her heroine undergoes before her first date with her boss Daniel Cleaver. Bridget reflects:

> Ugh. Completely exhausted. Surely it is not normal to be revising for a date as if it were a job interview? . . . Since leaving work I have nearly slipped a disc, wheezing through a step aerobics class, scratched my naked body for seven minutes with a stiff brush; cleaned the flat; filled the fridge; plucked my eyebrows, skimmed the papers and the *Ultimate Sex Guide*, put the washing in and waxed my own legs, since it was too late to book an appointment. Ended up kneeling on a towel trying to pull off a wax strip firmly stuck to the back of my calf while watching *Newsnight* in an effort to drum up some interesting opinions about things. My back hurts, my head aches, and my legs are bright red and covered in lumps of wax. (59)[1]

Though in the paragraph that follows Bridget acknowledges "Daniel should like me just as I am," she also notes, "I am a child of *Cosmopolitan* culture . . . traumatized by supermodels and too many quizzes and know that neither my personality nor my body is up to it if left to its own devices" (59). Bridget's observation, along with her pre-date actions, reveals the pervasive hold that women's magazines have upon her life. As a "child of *Cosmopolitan* culture," Bridget subscribes to advice that encourages women to perfect their bodies through such beauty regimens as exercise, exfoliation, and waxing. Only after perfecting her body according to *Cosmopolitan* magazine standards will she be acceptable for her date.

Bridget's remarks in this passage reveal just how heavily she relies on the advice of others. Not only does she consult *Cosmopolitan*, but she also reads *The Ultimate Sex Guide* as well as the papers and watches *Newsnight*, hoping to glean information that will perfect both her body and mind. Bridget cannot seem to believe that Daniel will like her just as she is because she consistently consults texts that tell her he cannot. Being "a child of *Cosmopolitan* culture," then, becomes metaphoric for the hold that consumer culture mediums from magazines to self-help books have upon Bridget's life. Bridget struggles to determine what advice she should follow and what advice she should disregard, and subsequently, a central theme of *Bridget Jones's Diary* becomes Bridget's (in)ability to navigate these controlling texts. In this passage and throughout her novel, Fielding creates a complicated and contested representation of the reader/text relationship and comments, ironically, on both women characters and readers as consumers.

*Bridget Jones's Diary* is just one of many texts from the recent literary phenomenon popularly known as chick lit which dialogues with consumer culture mediums, particularly women's advice manuals.[2] Loosely defined, chick lit, which arguably began with Fielding's text, consists of heroine-centered narratives that focus on the trials and tribulations of their individual protagonists.[3] At its onset, the genre was narrowly defined in that the protagonists depicted in these texts were young, single, white, heterosexual, British and American women in their late twenties and early thirties, living in metropolitan areas. Very often, these protagonists not only mirror the authors of these texts, but they also reflect the demographic of their reading audience, connecting the texts directly to their readers. Additionally, chick lit seeks to unite readers across genre lines, by both grounding themselves in nineteenth-century, heroine-centered literature and by dialoguing with various twenty-first century consumer culture mediums, particularly women's advice manuals. For these reasons, among others, the genre, as Suzanne Ferriss and Mallory Young note in the introduction to their collection of essays, *Chick Lit: The New Woman's Fiction*, has experienced "amazing commercial success. [It] has been called a 'commercial tsunami'" (2).[4] They continue, referencing Heather Cabot's 2003 article for abcnews.com entitled "Chick Lit: Genre Aimed at Women Is Fueling Publishing Industry" which indicated that "In 2002, for instance, chick-lit books earned publishers more than $71 million" (2). Largely, because of this commercial viability, the demographic for chick lit has grown; it now chronicles the lives of women of varying ages, races, and nationalities.[5] And, not only has the demographic expanded, but also chick

*Introduction* 3

lit texts have been adapted for television, the film industry, and the World Wide Web. For instance, Candace Bushnell's *Sex and the City* was adapted for television; running on HBO from 1998–2004, and in America, it is currently re-running on the CW network. Helen Fielding's novel was released as a feature film of the same title in 2001. And, Sherrie Krantz's *The Autobiography of Vivian Livingston* (2002) began as a website, Vivianlives.com.

Despite this immense popularity with readers, however, chick lit texts have been heavily criticized by reviewers of the individual novels and literary critics alike. In her review of *Bridget Jones's Diary* for the *New York Times* entitled "Dear Diary: Get Real," Alex Kuczynski declares, "Bridget is such a sorry spectacle, wallowing in her man-crazed helplessness, that her foolishness cannot be excused" (6) while Scarlett Thomas wrote in the *Independent*, "Chick lit is not just bad for the reader—it is bad for the author too." In the most highly publicized criticism of the genre, author Doris Lessing echoed Beryl Bainbridge's sentiments and pronounced chick lit "'instantly forgettable'" on the BBC Radio 4's *Today* program which aired on August 23, 2001 ("Bainbridge denounces chick-lit as froth"). Bainbridge, the six-time, Booker Prize shortlist recipient, declared that the genre represents "a froth sort of thing," and she asked, "'What is the point in writing a whole novel about it? . . . As people spend so little time reading, it is a pity they perhaps can't read something a bit deeper, a bit more profound, something with a bit of bite to it'" ("Bainbridge denounces chick-lit as 'froth'"). Three-time, Booker Prize shortlist recipient Doris Lessing concurred, "It's a pity that so many young women are writing like that. I wonder if they are just writing like this because they think they are going to get published . . . It would be better, perhaps, if they wrote books about their lives as they really saw them and not these helpless girls, drunken, worrying about their weight and so on'" ("Bainbridge denounces chick-lit as 'froth'").

Bainbridge and Lessing's conversation spurred subsequent, sensational media headlines that explored the state of contemporary women's popular fiction. The *Times* asked, "Be Honest With Me, Do My Literary Pretensions Look Big in This?" while the *Guardian* announced "Real Lives: We Know the Difference Between Foie Grass and Hula Hoops, Beryl, but Sometimes We Just Want Hula Hoops."[6] The *Sunday Telegraph* decried, "No Wonder Beryl's Cross. Bainbridge, et al. Wanted Boadiceas. Instead They've Got Posh Spice."[7] Media critics and chick lit authors, in turn, rushed to the genre's defense. Jenny Colgan, author of such chick lit novels as *Amanda's Wedding* (1999) and *West End Girls* (2006), responded, criticizing Bainbridge for her comments which imply "that . . . young women are too: ditzy/fizzy/stupid/drunken/man-crazed to a) write books and b) read them" ("Real Lives: We

Know the Difference Between Foie Gras and Hula Hoops, Beryl, but Sometimes We Just Want Hula Hoops"). Author Matt Thorne agreed, "'People who are dismissive of chick lit are misogynistic and elitist . . . Chick lit is a perfectly acceptable genre, no different from 'literary fiction.' The best writers in the genre are producing some of the best writing around today'" (qt. in Thomas).

Though this critical discussion helped to bring chick lit to the forefront of public consciousness, the debate was reductive in so far as it preoccupied itself with what Jean Radford, editor of *The Progress of Romance: The Politics of Popular Fiction*, deems "the [critics'] same obsessive concern with the problem of value" (7). In the past, critics have been reluctant to take popular fiction seriously, and, as Radford and other feminist critics have concurred, all too often literary critics are quick to label women's fiction as low art, a term which, by default, often denies any thoughtful consideration of that art. Deemed "'feeble and tiresome'" by Nathaniel Hawthorne in 1852 (Massie and Francassini), "silly" by George Eliot in 1856 (Eliot), "'froth'" by Beryl Bainbridge in 2001 ("Bainbridge denounces chick-lit as 'froth'"), and "'garbage'" (Weinberg) by a random man that writer Anna Weinberg encounters on a train out of New York City in 2003, women's novels have been disparaged throughout the centuries.[8] Chick lit, then, becomes an easy target for the critics' derision, relegated to both subordinated spaces—the popular and the female.

As a result, chick lit, like the sentimental novels of the nineteenth century and the paperback romance novels of the 1980s, has not been a genre that literary critics have immediately embraced. While the mainstream media has been quick to take up the subject of these young, single, working women, the academic community has been slower to respond.[9] Of late, there has been increased scholarly interest, including articles such as Kelly A. Marsh's "Contextualizing Bridget Jones" from *College Literature* and Jessica Lyn Van Slooten's "A Truth Universally (Un)Acknowledged: *Ally McBeal, Bridget Jones's Diary*, and the Conflict Between Romantic Love and Feminism" from Elwood Watson's collection of critical essays, *Searching the Soul of Ally McBeal*. Additionally, Imelda Whelehan who wrote *Helen Fielding's Bridget Jones's Diary: A Reader's Guide* has also produced an article entitled, "Sex and the Single Girl: Helen Fielding, Erica Jong and Helen Gurley Brown" and has written *The Feminist Bestseller: From Sex and the Single Girl to Sex and the City*, which chronicles the history of women's popular fiction, focusing specifically on, and making connections between, the fiction of the 1960s and 1970s and the chick lit boom of today. Chick lit has also been the topic of several graduate theses in England, America, and Hong Kong, and

*Introduction* 5

it is finding a place in the undergraduate classroom as well.[10] In an article entitled "Chick Lit 101" for the Fall 2006 edition of *NWSAction*, Brenda Bethman notes that "both Harvard and Tania Modleski (at the University of Southern California) are offering courses that at least partially engage with chick lit, indication that the study of the genre is gaining more respectability" (12). Perhaps the most comprehensive study of the genre comes with the publication of Suzanne Ferriss and Mallory Young's collection of essays, *Chick Lit: The New Woman's Fiction*, which contains fourteen essays on chick lit texts such as *Bridget Jones's Diary*, Sophie Kinsella's *Shopaholic* series, and Candace Bushnell's *Sex and the City* (1996). The collection covers such common chick lit themes as eating, shopping, and female sexuality, and several of its essays engage with more recent chick lit sub-genres such as mommy lit and chick lit for teenagers.

Still, there has not been a single, comprehensive study of the genre to date, and, more specifically, one which examines the nuanced way that chick lit engages with consumer culture mediums, particularly women's advice manuals, such as women's magazines, self-help books, romantic comedies, and/or domestic-advice manuals, despite the fact that the genre references and responds to these manuals in varied ways.[11] In the passage above from *Bridget Jones's Diary*, we see how Bridget continually compares herself to the ideal offered by women's magazines while Melissa Bank's Jane Rosenal (*The Girls' Guide to Hunting and Fishing*, 1999) reads a dating, self-help book in the hopes of finding a man. Carol Wolper's narrator from *The Cigarette Girl* (1999), a screenwriter of action films, puzzles over the fact that her life does not follow the simple plotline of a romantic comedy. And, Helen Bradshaw, of Anna Maxted's *Getting Over It* (2000), consults home decorating magazines and catalogues in an attempt to construct the ideal home for herself. These consumer culture mediums, however, are more than just present in the text. Rather, these mediums heavily influence the protagonists of these texts, dictating to them expected feminine behaviors and ideals that they should attempt to achieve. In many of these novels, chick lit writers establish the behavioral guideline or standard for their protagonists to follow by including references to the explicit advice offered by women's magazines, self-help books, and domestic-advice manuals and the more implicit advice for women conveyed through romantic comedies. In doing so, chick lit authors present complex representations of young, single women as both readers and consumers.

*Cosmopolitan Culture and Consumerism in Chick Lit* demonstrates how these texts question the "consume and achieve" promise offered by these women's advice manuals and in doing so challenge the consumer industry to which they are closely linked. Through their narrative structure and their depictions of discerning female readers and consumers, chick lit authors create fictionalized instructional guides that problematize the ideologies offered by the advice manuals their characters read. Chick lit authors, then, respond in varied ways to the manuals they reference, and in doing so, complicate the readers' expectations about female consumption, women readers, women's writing, and popular fiction. More specifically, *Cosmopolitan Culture and Consumerism in Chick Lit* examines chick lit texts from the genre's early period, beginning with an analysis of Helen Fielding's novel (1996) and concluding with an examination of Sherrie Krantz's *The Autobiography of Vivian Livingston* (2002), pairing, in each chapter, these chick lit texts with the women's advice literature to which they respond.

Chick lit, like other literary movements, is a historically situated genre. In their introduction, Ferriss and Young cite Heather Cabot's 2003 article "Chick Lit: Genre Aimed at Young Women Is Fueling Publishing Industry" for abcnews.com. In the article, Cabot quotes Jennifer Weiner, author of chick lit texts such as *Good in Bed* (2001) and *In Her Shoes* (2002). Weiner comments that there is "'an authenticity frequently missing from women's fiction of the past... I think that for a long time, what women were getting were sort of the Jackie Collins, Judith Krantz books—sex and shopping, glitz and glamour, heroines that were fun to read about, but just felt nothing like where you were in your life'" (qt. in Ferriss and Young 4). Chick lit author Laura Zigman agrees that this need was historically situated as women writers and readers of the late 1990s were looking to write and read texts that validated women's experiences:

> "In my heartbroken, urban, single, postfeminist mood I felt like there was a lot going on with women that no one was really talking about... We had a lot of freedom and a lot of choices, but there was a price. People were lonely... But you would pick up these books and go, Okay, I am not mad, I am not the only loser in the world who feels lonely." (Weinberg)

This feeling of disconnect prompted women writers like Weiner and Zigman to begin writing chick lit narratives, which they felt more directly connected to their own experiences. The author bios at the back of chick lit texts serve as evidence of this fact; they emphasize the similarities between the authors, their characters, and their readers. Bank highlights her single status in her author biography, noting that she "lives in New York City with her Labrador retriever, Maybelline," while Sherrie Krantz emphasizes her own

*Introduction* 7

career achievements, a major focus of her protagonist's quest. Helen Fielding's author photograph for the hardcover, 1998 British edition of *Bridget Jones's Diary* even goes so far as to mimic the cover design.[12] Both Bridget Jones, on the cover of the novel, and Fielding, on the back of the inside flap, are photographed in profile, smoking cigarettes.

In turn, book publishers responded to this need; as Sarah Bernard explains in "Success and the Single Girl," they began publishing texts with protagonists whose experiences mirrored those of their real-life readers. Bernard quotes Morgan Entrekin, a Grover/Atlantic publisher: "'Without question, 30-to-45-year-old women are currently the core readers of the fiction market. They are the strongest buyers and readers . . . If publishers are interested in these girls as characters, it's because they are the ones who read these days'" (34). Bernard continues, noting that not only are the protagonists similar to the audience for these texts, but "many of the editors and agents acquiring the books are women in their thirties as well" (34). In fact, characters, readers, and authors are so similar that often, in defining the genre, critics collapse the genre's characters, readers, and writers. In her 1999 article "The Plight of the High-Status Woman: Recent Fiction, Essays, and Self-Help Books," Barbara Dafoe Whitehead simultaneously defines the demographics for the main characters and readers of chick lit texts when she writes, "It is written for and about the privileged members of a new generation" (120) while Alyson Ward, writer for the *Washington Post*, acknowledges the confused relationship between writers and characters when she notes that chick lit is "written by and about young women" (D5). These observations stress the similarities that exist between heroine, reader, and author thus blurring what we might have previously considered a fairly stable distinction.

Arguably, chick lit texts are enmeshed in the present. However, in many ways, these novels, and the approaches taken by chick lit novelists, are not remarkably new. Rather, their roots are in the heroine-centered novels of the nineteenth century, novels like Charlotte Brontë's *Jane Eyre* and Jane Austen's *Northanger Abbey*. Helen Fielding herself acknowledged her debt to such nineteenth-century authors such as Jane Austen in an interview for *Time* where she noted that she did indeed structure her novel after Austen's *Pride and Prejudice*: "'Yes. I shamelessly stole the plot. I thought it had been very well market researched over a number of centuries.'"[13] In "Mothers of Chick Lit: Women Writers, Readers, and Literary History," Juliette Wells discusses these connections between nineteenth-century women's fiction and chick lit while critic Stephanie Harzewski in "Tradition and Displacement in the New Novel of Manners" more specifically analyzes the structural similarities between chick lit and the novel of manners.[14] Harzewski also explores the connections between chick lit, prose romance, and popular romance, noting how the genre relies on the conventions of the romance but updates them for its present day setting. And, as noted earlier, chick lit also draws upon the female-centered fiction of the 1960s and 1970s. Imelda Whelehan's *The Feminist Bestseller: From* Sex and the Single Girl *to* Sex and the City connects the genre to Erica Jong's 1973 novel *Fear of Flying* as well as Marilyn French's *The Women's Room* (1977).

Chick lit authors are not the first women writers to connect their novels to contemporary popular culture mediums. In *Northanger Abbey* (1818), Austen explores the impact that Gothic fiction had upon her heroine Catherine Moreland; Edith Wharton mentions Tiffany & Co. in *The House of Mirth* (1905); American writer Sylvia Plath chronicles Esther Greenwood's summer spent interning for the fictional *Ladies' Day* magazine in *The Bell Jar* (1962); contemporary African American writer Toni Morrison's details her character Claudia's passionate hate for Shirley Temple in *The Bluest Eye* (1970); and author Diane Johnson, who "divides her time between San Francisco and Paris," concludes her novel *Le Divorce* (1997) with an action-packed scene set in EuroDisney.[15] Women writers have a long history of connecting their fiction with consumer culture, and in some ways, chick lit novels are merely continuing that trend with their direct references to magazines, self-help books, romantic comedies, and domestic-advice manuals. In these ways, then, chick lit is linked to the literary traditions that preceded it.

Yet, chick lit is fast becoming a new chapter in the history of the novel. The late twentieth and early twenty-first century has produced a cultural climate in which consumer culture plays an increasingly important role in the production and distribution of popular fiction, allowing texts to travel more easily than before. In an age where "Today's savvy authors hire their own manuscript consultants and their own publicists . . . go into the process knowing exactly when and where they'll compromise when the marketing department (not the editor) says they've got the wrong title, wrong protagonist gender, wrong plot," and where "agents and editors read a writer's marketing plan before they read the submitted manuscript," a more nuanced relationship between popular fiction and consumer culture has developed (Holt). Now, chick lit fiction not only directly references consumer culture mediums like women's magazines, other popular fiction texts, consumer products, movies, and television, but consumer culture mediums themselves publicize women's popular fiction.[16] For instance, women's magazines include women's fiction excerpts and recommended reading lists, the promotion of women's fiction through advertisements, and the mention of women's popular fiction heroines in articles. Websites like Vivianlives.com where Vivian Livingston, the protagonist of Sherrie Krantz's *The Autobiography of Vivian Livingston*, resides not only promote certain products but also encourage readers' consumption of particular television shows, movies, and books. Krantz's character even made appearances in magazines such as *Elle, InStyle, Glamour,* and *Marie Claire* promoting such products as Herbal Essences True Intense Color by Clairol and Betsey Johnson clothing.[17] Chick lit authors have frequently worked in the consumer industry about which they are writing. Anna Maxted wrote for British *Cosmopolitan* before publishing novels in which her protagonist works for a teen magazine.[18] Likewise, Carol Wolper was a screenwriter, and Sophie Kinsella was a financial journalist before turning to fiction writing.[19] More indirectly, contemporary women's popular fiction often mimics the writing style of the glossies and targets an audience demographically similar to the audience of women's magazines such as *Cosmopolitan, Glamour,* and *Marie Claire*. And, like women's magazines, which have consistently, and successfully, wooed women readers since the nineteenth century, chick lit has become wildly successful, spawning numerous publications and prompting such publishing giants as Harlequin Enterprises Inc. and Pocket Books, a division of Simon & Schuster, to launch their own lines of chick lit, Red Dress Ink and Downtown Press, respectively (Barrientos).[20]

Subsequently, chick lit texts have traveled across the globe. Though both British and American chick lit texts are often locally tied to a major city (London, New York City, Los Angeles, for instance), the books are still traded across the Atlantic and around the world. For instance, American *Vogue* published an excerpt of *Bridget Jones's Diary* under the title "Sex and the Single Girl" in their May 1998 edition, and the novel itself was published and became a bestseller in America that same year (Whelahan 67). The September 2001 American edition of *Glamour* magazine featured an article on actress Bridget Moynahan entitled "Bridget's Diary;" the subtitle reads, "No, not that Bridget" (Zanzinger 283), referencing Fielding's protagonist, and the subtext for the story in the table of contents reads "Mrs. Big," an allusion to Mr. Big from *Sex and the City* (20). And, as Whelehan notes in *Helen Fielding's* Bridget Jones's Diary: *A Reader's Guide*, the novel was not only embraced by the American public, but it also became an international bestseller, having been "translated into at least 33 languages" (33).

One of the major factors for chick lit's popularity rests with the television and film productions of chick lit texts, which have enabled an even larger audience to be exposed to the genre. The trajectory of *Bridget Jones's Diary* attests to this fact. Fielding's novel developed out of her newspaper column in the *Independent*, which first ran on February 28, 1995 (Whelahan 12). Two years after its publication in England, the novel traveled to the United States where it became a bestseller (Whelahan 67). In light of this favorable reception, Miramax films produced the film in 2001; Fielding wrote the screenplay herself while her friend Sharon Maguire directed and Renée Zellweger, Colin Firth, and Hugh Grant starred ("*Bridget Jones's Diary*"). Similarly, Candace Bushnell, author of *Sex and the City* transformed her newspaper column for the *New York Observer* into a collection that was then adapted into the HBO series, premiering in June of 1998 (Sohn 14–15, 26). In 2001, Laura Zigman's *Animal Husbandry* was developed into the film *Someone Like You* starring Ashley Judd, Greg Kinnear, and Hugh Jackman ("*Someone Like You*"). Currently, Melissa Bank's *The Girls' Guide to Hunting and Fishing* is being adapted into a feature length film, starring Sarah Michelle Gellar ("*Suburban Girl*"). According to the Internet Movie Database, the film is tentatively scheduled to be released in 2007 under the title, *Suburban Girl* ("*Suburban Girl*"). These adaptations have contributed to an even more wide-scale consumption of these texts and their transformation into popular culture relics. In "The Marriage Mystique," Daphne Merkin describes Fielding's novel as "the cultural artifact that is recognizably larger than itself" (70). As Merkin acknowledges, today *Bridget Jones's Diary* and Bridget Jones herself have become something other than what Fielding may have first conceptualized to both the British and American public. Merkin's description can just as readily be applied to *Sex and the City*, an equally influential twenty-first century cultural phenomenon.

The World Wide Web has also furthered this exchange of texts. Authors such as Jennifer Weiner include their web addresses at the end of their novels and encourage readers to visit their sites. Advancements in web technology allow booksellers such as Amazon.com to customize sites for their visitors. Registered users at Amazon.com who return to the website may receive suggestions for new books, or movies, that might interest them, and they can create their own reader/viewer lists that detail their favorite texts as well as read the lists of others. For instance, American reader Melissa Wilson, Senior Editor at Amazon.com, created the list entitled "The Singleton Life" which includes such books as *Getting Over It* (2000) by Anna Maxted and *Thirtynothing* (2002) by Lisa Jewell while on the Amazon.co.uk site, the list "great chick-lit for rainy afternoons" was created by leahy2j, final year student, and includes novels by Jenny Colgan and Marian Keyes. These features add to the way in which both reading and viewing material is exchanged. As fiction is increasingly adapted into visual productions and as writers and readers increasingly exploit the World Wide Web, national boundaries continue to dissolve, allowing for texts to travel even further and providing for more nuanced and direct connections between fiction and consumer culture.

Introduction                                                                 11

These connections further manifest themselves in the chick lit texts, as authors reference various consumer culture mediums. In the short passage from Fielding quoted above, we see four allusions alone to consumer culture mediums, and throughout Fielding's novel, she continually mentions products (Cadbury's Dairy Milk), television shows (*Eastenders*), books (*Backlash*), and media events (Prince Charles and Princess Diana's divorce). Likewise, other chick lit texts make similar references. Bushnell mentions movies (*Breakfast at Tiffany's* and *Disclosure*) while Kinsella consistently lists the stores that her protagonist frequents (Top Shop, Harvey Nichols, French Connection). And, chick lit authors often create fictional worlds in which their protagonists participate in the production of consumer culture mediums whether it be movies, as with Elizabeth West of *The Cigarette Girl*, television, as with Jane Goodall of *Animal Husbandry*, magazines, as with Helen Bradshaw of *Getting Over It*, or the music industry, as with Vivian Livingston in *The Autobiography of Vivian Livingston*.

Even more specifically, however, we see the protagonists engaging with advice manuals, specifically women's magazines, self-help books, romantic comedies, and domestic-advice manuals. For instance, Vivian Livington might turn to the pages of *Marie Claire* for fashion advice or Jane Rosenal from *The Girls' Guide to Hunting and Fishing* might consult a self-help book that eerily mirrors the 1995 dating manual, *The Rules: Time-tested Secrets for Capturing the Heart of Mr. Right*. Helen Bradshaw espouses that movies like *Pretty Woman* taught her good always triumphs over evil, and Bridget Jones consults a Marco Pierre White recipe in the hopes of impressing her friends and love interest, Mark Darcy. Consistently, these protagonists are found consulting these advice manuals as they navigate their everyday lives.

It is commonly accepted that such mediums as magazines and self-help books present their readers with prescriptive instructions regarding how to live their lives. The rhetoric of these texts is directive, using the second person to appeal to their readers and to incite those readers to action. Robina Dam's article "Love Bites" which appeared in the February 2000, British edition of *Marie Claire* reads:

> You've promised dinner to a man. It's the first time you've invited him to your home and, according to the rules of etiquette (OK, according to Ally McBeal), that means you're probably going to be the dessert. What you need are some ground rules to make the evening a perfect seduction scene. A combination of these plus some delicious food and he'll be (firmish) putty in your hands. (172)

The article continues to offer specific instructions such as "Think simple," "Keep it tactile," and "Candles are a must" (172). Readers of this article, then, are promised results, "(firmish) putty," and provided with instructions that, according to the magazine, guarantee this result. Self-help books adopt this instructional formula, too. Books such as Ellen Fein and Sherrie Schneider's *The Rules: Time-tested Secrets for Capturing the Heart of Mr. Right* promise readers that if they follow their instructions, which include such advice as "Don't Stare at Men or Talk Too Much" (33) and "Always End Phone Calls First" (45), they will obtain "A marriage truly made in heaven" (5–6). Again, female readers are encouraged to consume the advice offered in order to attain a desired result.

Like magazines and self-help books, domestic-advice manuals are explicitly prescriptive, sometimes even more so than other advice manuals. *Martha Stewart's Living* magazine contains articles detailing do-it-yourself projects, and cooking shows such as *Nigella Bites*, which first aired in England in 2000, provide viewers with step-by-step instructions for making the perfect meal. However, other domestic-advice manuals are less obvious in their attempts to guide their readers. A catalogue such as Williams-Sonoma does not offer readers much instructive text, rather the blurbs that accompany products are descriptive; however, its pages, filled with Jadite Waring 60th Anniversary Blenders and KitchenAid Artisan Stand Mixers, construct an ideal for its readers, visually encouraging them to reform their homes (*Williams-Sonoma: The Catalog for Cooks* Spring 2001). A properly equipped home, according to Williams and Sonoma, is one complete with all necessary accoutrements, ranging from monogrammed wine coasters to egg frying rings.

Romantic comedies, perhaps, offer the least obvious form of instruction to their readers. Unlike the other mediums mentioned, very few romantic comedies use direct address as a means of connecting with and encouraging their readers. Yet, though not explicitly instructive, romantic comedies can serve, as Gwendolyn Audrey Foster notes in *Troping the Body: Gender, Etiquette, and Performance*, as a form of conduct literature.[21] Foster notes the way in which many contemporary cultural mediums, including movies, offer advice in a way similar to that of conduct literature, and her work seeks to "redefine the boundaries of conduct literature through a theoretical examination of the gendered body as it is positioned in the conduct book, etiquette texts, poetry, fiction, and film . . . to develop an interdisciplinary approach to conduct literature and literature as conduct" (x). Like Foster, I wish to extend the consideration of texts that can be considered conduct literature. Though a romantic comedy's primary purpose may not be to instruct, these

*Introduction* 13

films nonetheless often deploy specific and scripted gender ideologies and have the potential to influence a person's conduct. For instance, a romantic comedy like the 1998 remake *The Parent Trap* reinforces in its construction certain gendered behaviors. As Mark D. Rubinfeld notes in *Bound to Bond: Gender, Genre, and the Hollywood Romantic Comedy*, the pursuit plot is an important element of that film, which makes the remake "significantly deviate from the original version of the movie" (9). Rubinfeld argues that the twins' mother, Elizabeth, reinforces gendered stereotypes when she explains how she felt upon leaving her ex-husband Nick. She says, "I packed. And you didn't come after me." Her response reinforces the idea that women wait to be pursued and men actively pursue. While Disney's remake might not have intended to instruct its viewers, the film indirectly encourages gendered behaviors. Romantic comedies, then, though not implicitly instructive, script expected, gendered behaviors for both readers and viewers.

What is interesting about the presence of such advice manuals in these chick lit texts is the way in which they operate. Some might argue that their inclusion contributes to the perpetuation of the gendered ideologies offered by these manuals. After all, how does referencing Top Shop, Calvin Klein, and Karen Millen *dis*courage consumer behavior? Doesn't Sophie Kinsella's descriptions of Becky Bloomwood's shopping sprees in Octagon actually *en*courage women readers to indulge, rather than curb, their spending? Don't these novels, then, become prescriptive in the same, often damaging, ways that these behavior manuals do? How, if at all, do these novels challenge readers' expectations about women's reading practices, their consumer behavior, and ultimately female agency?

In Melissa Bank's *The Girls' Guide to Hunting and Fishing*, we see an example of the complex relationship that can exist between a reader and her reading material. Bank's novel preoccupies itself with its main character's concerns about her unfulfilling job as an editor and her less than perfect romantic life. The novel becomes, on one level, a chronicle of Jane Rosenal's attempts to correct these unsatisfying situations. Directly connected to these struggles, however, is the role that behavioral guides, from etiquette books to dating manuals, play in Jane's life. Jane is consistently bombarded by advice from her mother, her father, *The Girl Scout Handbook*, and a self-help manual remarkably similar to the 1996 publication *The Rules: Time-tested Secrets for Capturing the Heart of Mr. Right*. Of equal importance to Jane's struggle to find happiness with her career and romantic life becomes her ability to successfully navigate these texts, particularly because Jane often blindly follows the advice offered to her, which consistently leads her to unhappiness. Only when she can successfully recognize which advice to follow and which advice to disregard, in other words only when she becomes a more discerning reader, does the reader of Bank's work feel as though Jane has found some fulfillment in her life. Bank creates a representation of female reader/consumer that challenges the idea of passive consumption and encourages women to become active and discriminating readers of the instructional manuals that they encounter.

In *The Secret Dreamworld of a Shopaholic*, Sophie Kinsella takes a different approach to critiquing consumer behavior; she satirizes her protagonist's extreme consumer behavior.[22] Unlike Jane Rosenal, Becky Bloomwood, Kinsella's heroine, makes little to no attempt to become a critical reader of the advice manuals that she reads. Rather, Becky represents what I deem the "ideal" reader of women's magazines—the woman who reads and abides by the advice offered no matter what the obstacles. Though Becky spirals into crippling consumer debt, she continues to purchase those items promoted by women's magazines in the hopes of achieving the lifestyle associated with them. Yet, Kinsella's narrative structure makes it clear that Becky's behavior is not one to be followed by readers. Rather, throughout the novel, Kinsella comments ironically on her behavior. For instance, in the American edition of the text, Kinsella depicts Becky observing a man seated near her on the tube. She writes:

> As the train finally gets going again I sink into my seat with a dramatic sigh and look at the pale, silent man on my left. He's wearing jeans and sneakers, and I notice his shirt is inside out. Gosh, I think in admiration, did he read the article on deconstructing fashion in last month's *Vogue*, too? I'm about to ask him—then I take another look at his jeans (really nasty fake 501s) and his sneakers (very new, very white)—and something tells me he didn't. (25)

The humor in this moment comes from the fact that Becky is not aware of the ridiculousness of her conjecture. She immediately jumps to the conclusion that the man's clothing reflects an article that he may have read in *Vogue* not that, perhaps, he just chose to dress that way for reasons that rest completely outside of the realm of women's magazines. Significant, too, is the fact that Kinsella chose to add this detail in her later, American edition of her text, further highlighting the exaggerated consumer behavior exhibited by Becky in the original, British edition. Kinsella crafts this moment in such a way that allows for the reader to laugh at the absurdity of Becky's hypothesis, and in doing so, Kinsella simultaneously acknowledges the hold that women's magazines can have on their readers if not kept in check and critiques the reader/consumer who is unable to maintain perspective on the role that these publications should have in her life.

The assumption that novels such as these cannot challenge the consumer industries that they reference is again indicative of the deeply rooted, historical bias against popular fiction—a bias that exists against women's fiction as well. As Jean Radford explains in *The Progress of Romance: The Politics of Popular Fiction*, a common presumption is that "Literature [operates] transformatively on ideology, producing a 'knowledge' of it, whereas popular fiction merely reproduces and transmits that ideology" (2). Therefore, it becomes common to assume that since chick lit is popular fiction it reiterates, rather than questions or challenges, dominant ideological discourse.[23] As Janice Radway notes in *Reading the Romance: Women, Patriarchy, and Popular Literature*, to believe that romances merely reiterate established ideologies is "troubling because its conception of ideology and domination seems to preclude the possibility of any kind of social change or resistance from the very start. It does so by reifying human process itself and by according extraordinary and preeminent power to the commodities produced and used within such processes rather than the human activities themselves" (6). Though Radford and Radway's comments apply to popular fiction generally, their scholarship examines women's cultural productions, specifically romance novels.[24] Their comments, then, resonate even more, revealing that historically rooted biases against both popular fiction and women's writing have existed and continue to exist even today, as evidenced by the heavy criticism aimed at chick lit.[25]

This study, then, is not unlike previous studies that have critically engaged with female cultural productions. Feminist critics in the 1980s and 1990s, writing about the genres of romance novels and soap operas, have acknowledged the bias toward women's cultural productions that exists in literary studies and have worked to shift the focus from value to an actual analysis of these important cultural texts. In her 1982 book *Loving With a Vengeance: Mass-Produced Fantasies for Women*, Tania Modleski opened by noting, "Although Harlequin Romances, Gothic novels, and soap operas provide mass(ive) entertainment for countless numbers of women of varying ages, classes, and even educational backgrounds, very few critics have taken them seriously enough to study them in any detail" (11). Modleski's study and Janice Radway's subsequent 1984 work *Reading the Romance: Women, Patriarchy, and Popular Literature* acknowledge the fact that women's cultural productions are often deemed less worthy of study than men's. Modleski and Radway then move on to discuss those cultural productions, often placing an emphasis, as in Radway's study, on the readers of these texts and showing the ways in which these readers can, and do, use mass produced texts subversively. These studies opened the door for a host of other critical analyses of women's cultural productions, all of which recognized the criticisms railed at their given genre of study, often deeming that criticism unnecessary, but then proceeding to analyze the texts regardless of the stigma that was often attached.[26]

Just like Modleski and Radway, I wish to examine female cultural productions, both chick lit and behavioral guides, that have been consistently marginalized and to begin a critical, scholarly consideration of these texts. As these critics have done, I argue that this literature is adept at revealing and/or reflecting the society that produced it, interfacing with the dominant ideologies of the time period, and challenging, rather than deploying, the ideologies transmitted by women's magazines, self-help books, romantic comedies, and domestic-advice manuals. Rather than taking a sociological approach as Radway has done, however, my study is grounded in the literature itself, concentrating on the way in which chick lit authors represent their characters as readers and consumers. This examination, in turn, has implications for our perception of chick lit writers and readers for their portrayals reflect upon and/or question dominant ideological discourse—a move that asserts agency and reverses the perception of women as unthinking, "passive" consumers, mindlessly "ingesting" messages imparted to them without further discrimination.[27]

I begin by examining two popular, British novels considered forerunners of the chick lit phenomenon, Helen Fielding's *Bridget Jones's Diary*, arguably the übertext of the genre, and Sophie Kinsella's *The Secret Dreamworld of a Shopaholic*. These novels present heroines who are obsessed with women's magazines such as *Cosmopolitan* and *Marie Claire*. Both authors satirize consumer behavior by creating protagonists who could conceivably be women's magazines "ideal" readers; Bridget and Becky blindly follow the advice of these publications, and in doing so, often find themselves conflicted. Fielding's protagonist contradicts herself from entry to entry (she's satisfied as a singleton, she's dissatisfied being alone; she's happy with her weight, she desperately wants to lose a few more pounds) while Becky struggles to control her compulsive shopping habit, encouraged by the glossy advertisements that grace the pages of her favorite magazines. Through their depictions of this exaggerated consumer behavior, Fielding and Kinsella mock the advice given by these publications and comment ironically on both women characters as readers and consumers.

In my third chapter, I examine two, American novels, Melissa Bank's *The Girls' Guide to Hunting and Fishing* and Laura Zigman's *Animal Husbandry*.

These books present protagonists preoccupied with their relationships and searching for emotional fulfillment. In order to better understand their past relationships, Jane Rosenal (*The Girls' Guide to Hunting and Fishing*) and Jane Goodall (*Animal Husbandry*) turn to self-help books as their guide. What they discover, however, is not the key to a successful relationship but a host of advice that is ill fitting for their personal circumstances. The concluding story of Bank's collection shows Jane rejecting the dating manuals that she has been so desperately trying to follow in exchange for her own set of "rules" while Zigman's Jane goes so far as to construct her own self-help book—an action that leads to her recovery from a badly broken heart. These protagonists serve as models for female readers suffering through emotionally draining relationships, and the novels, in turn, become "self-help" in and of their own right, providing readers with an alternative instructional guide. In their novels, Bank and Zigman present protagonists capable of critically reading the texts presented to them, accepting and rejecting self-help advice when it is appropriate and creating their own texts when the manuals they encounter fall desperately short.

My next chapter looks at *Sex and the City*, American author Candace Bushnell's collection of newspaper columns for the *New York Observer*, and Carol Wolper's *The Cigarette Girl*. In the opening pages of Bushnell's novel, she mentions another important consumer culture medium, the Hollywood movie, and her novel responds to contemporary, Hollywood romantic comedies in pointed ways. Bushnell's protagonists, like Elizabeth West of Carol Wolper's *The Cigarette Girl*, attempt to lead their lives in the face of the ideologies about female sexuality offered by these romantic comedies. In examining both the 1962 movie *Sex and the Single Girl* and the 2002 movie *The Sweetest Thing*, I argue that romantic comedies of the past and present posit that female sexuality is something that needs to be controlled; by emphasizing a "happily ever after" ending, these films imply that women can only be completely fulfilled if they enter into a monogamous, heterosexual relationship. Both Bushnell's characters and Elizabeth West find these definitions of female sexuality limiting, and they rebel against these sexual standards, finding romantic alternatives to what they have grown to expect from a classic Hollywood ending. These novels offer readers an option to the often times innocent and demure females depicted in romantic comedies and present readers with an additional, sexual-behavior model.

Chapter Five examines the multiple ways in which chick lit authors construct homes for their protagonists. Though chick lit characters are single women seemingly far removed from occupying a "traditional" domestic space, chick lit authors, from Helen Fielding to Candace Bushnell to Anna

Maxted, often preoccupy their characters with household tasks and the home. This preoccupation is thus informed by the characters', and ultimately their authors', familiarity with domestic-advice manuals, that, like women's magazines, present their readers with an "idealized mirror image" of what their home should contain and what their given behaviors within that private sphere should be (McCracken 13). These protagonists are often drawn to the goods and skills marketed to them by these domestic-advice manuals because these household goods signify something more to these women—the domestic sentiments that they currently lack. A reoccurring theme in many of these novels, then, is a longing for perceived domestic bliss. Characters such as Bridget Jones, Jane Goodall, and Carrie Bradshaw discover, however, that anxiety about what these goods and skills represent accompanies this longing. These characters are often shown questioning whether they will ever achieve the sentiments associated with domesticity if they choose to make untraditional life choices and create a home devoid of husband and family, as exemplified in particular by Elizabeth West of *The Cigarette Girl*. Though I examine multiple texts in this chapter, I organize this section around British author Anna Maxted's book *Getting Over It*—a book in which anxieties about the home play a key role. Following the death of her father, Maxted's main character, Helen Bradshaw, is forced to redefine what family, and in turn home, means to her, and as a result of this renegotiation, she struggles to understand who she is and how to make a home space for herself. In Maxted's novel, "moving on" has dual significance, for Maxted consistently realizes Helen's emotional recovery through her attempts to find and buy a flat. Displaced from her apartment and then from her mother's house, Helen finally "gets over" her intense grief when she purchases, furnishes, and finally inhabits her new flat alone. Like other chick lit authors, Maxted depicts her protagonist as struggling with the ideologies of domestic-advice manuals that offer particular constructions of family and home, yet she ultimately writes a heroine who finds an alternative that more adequately fits her lifestyle.

My afterword synthesizes my observations about female consumption and reading practices through the lens of Sherrie Krantz's *The Autobiography of Vivian Livingston*. I begin this chapter by discussing the various off-shoots and sub-genres that were inspired by such texts as *Bridget Jones's Diary* and *Sex and the City* before moving to discuss Krantz's text more specifically. All of the elements of my study converge in this text. Vivian Livingston, Krantz's character who began as a cartoon, web-based character and morphed into her own consumer culture icon, makes appearances in such publications as *Elle*, *InStyle*, *Glamour*, and *Marie Claire* to promote products such as Clairol Herbal Essences, Cingular Wireless, Betsey Johnson, and Audi TT® Roadsters

(Mack 6).[28] Much like other chick lit texts, Krantz's novel encourages women readers to simultaneously embrace and interrogate the advice being offered to them by women's magazines, self-help books, romantic comedies, and domestic-advice manuals. However, Krantz's text differs from early chick lit text in so far as it expands upon the connections to consumer culture previously made by chick lit authors and, in some ways, becomes representative of the direction that current chick lit texts are headed. As a result, Krantz's texts have obvious implications for the history of the novel, particularly in understanding the ways in which contemporary global society has altered the consumption of fiction.

Nancy A. Walker concludes her book *Shaping Our Mothers' Worlds: American Women's Magazines* with a paragraph that begins, "It would be disingenuous for me to pretend that my interest in women's magazines of this period is purely scholarly" (xvii). Walker's statement resonated with me as I embarked on this project. Throughout my life, I have continually felt drawn to women's magazines, purchasing several different publications each month ever since my junior year in high school when my mother bought me the back to school, August issue of *Seventeen* magazine, which is currently housed in a place of honor on my best bookshelf in my small, studio apartment. While I voraciously consume these magazines each month, I am simultaneously disturbed by and wary of the messages that they impart to their readers, and I see the negative effects that these images and articles can have upon their consumers when I teach *Bridget Jones's Diary* in my college classes. Many young women in my classes speak fervently about their identification with Bridget, and I worry that they, like Bridget, are unable to dissect or critique the messages conveyed to them everyday by consumer culture. In class, we discuss ways to become more discerning readers, and together, we work toward improving our critical reading skills. Mass media and all its components will not soon disappear, and I adamantly believe that it is extremely important to become informed consumers. I hope that this study further encourages readers to appreciate, yet at the same time interrogate, the products of consumer culture that we encounter each and every day.

## Chapter Two
# One Simple Step to Becoming a V.G. Consumer: Read Women's Magazines

> Constantly measuring your body, your relationship, your life against others can crush self-esteem completely. On the other hand, it may be just what you need for success.
>
> —From "How Do You Compare?" by Sarah Kennedy, *Cosmopolitan*, UK edition (November 1996)

The 2002, February edition of British *Cosmopolitan* boldly declares, "The single girl's man map[:] You know he's out there, we know where . . . find him tonight!"[1] The cover lines of women's magazines, like this contemporary example, have always been crafted in such a such a way as to entice readers, vying for the consumer's attention over the other magazines for sale around them, and they have served as a preview of the inside text, informing the reader as to what the magazine itself holds. More importantly perhaps, but less obviously, this particular cover line reveals the instructional nature of women's magazine. Here, *Cosmopolitan* implies that their magazine contains the information a single girl might need to acquire a man—a how to guide to finding Mr. Right. The cover line suggests that while a woman might realize what she needs (a man) she cannot figure out how to go about attaining one without reading the magazine first. By following these "rules," *Cosmopolitan* implies, readers can exchange their single status for a happily coupled existence.

Though women's magazines are seemingly straightforward in their intentions, it is important to recognize the contradiction upon which women's magazines are based. Admittedly, women's magazines purport to help readers make consumer decisions ranging from what to eat to what to wear. They offer advice on such matters as improving one's sex life while also endorsing particular products through both the advertisements that appear inside the magazine and the purchasing suggestions offered within individual articles. Yet, women's magazines are themselves a consumer product, one that continually relies on its readers/consumers to purchase them. So, while women's magazines can encourage women to improve themselves, if those women actually did achieve the ideal maintained by those magazines, the consumer market for such publications could be in jeopardy. As a result, the information offered by these publications from month to month is often inconsistent. Just as fashion trends change from season to season, so does the advice offered to women. While one month *Cosmo* may be celebrating the joys of being single, in a few months they may be discussing why every woman seems to be getting married.[2] This contradictory content may leave a reader confused, and when reading conflicting advice from month to month, she may begin to wonder which advice to follow.

Women's magazines have long been a topic of scholarly debate. Critics have documented the history of women's magazines as well as analyzed the genre in terms of content.[3] Additionally, some scholars have heavily criticized the medium for its problematic, gender representations. The first significant, twentieth-century criticism of the genre came in 1963 when Betty Friedan questioned the messages delivered to American housewives by such American publications as *Good Housekeeping*, the *Ladies' Home Journal*, *McCall's*, and the *Woman's Home Companion* in her book *The Feminine Mystique*. Later in the century, women's magazines, specifically those publications aimed at a demographic younger than those reading such magazines as *Good Housekeeping*, became the target of heavy criticism. Scholars began analyzing the negative effects that such publications had upon young women, particularly in regard to body image. Jean Kilbourne, a leading media critic, began exposing the negative effects that magazine advertising had upon readers with her series of films *Killing Us Softly: Advertising's Image of Women* (1979), *Still Killing Us Softly* (1987), and *Killing Us Softly 3* (2000). In these films, and in her book *Deadly Persuasion: Why Women and Girls Must Fight the Addictive Power of Advertising* (1999), Kilbourne addresses such issues as women and violence and women and addiction, but she also focuses on the pressure that such advertisements put on young women to be thin, a theme which she returned to and analyzed in more depth with her 1995 film *Slim Hopes*. Likewise, in 1991, Naomi Wolf released *The Beauty Myth: How Images of Beauty Are Used Against Women*. Wolf's book discussed the role that women's magazines play in constructing femininity, and, more specifically, *The Beauty Myth* exposed the harmful social pressure that the diet industry, cosmetic companies, and the plastic surgery industry can place on women. And, Susan Bordo addresses the negative impact that women's magazines have on women readers in her 1993 book *Unbearable Weight: Feminism, Western Culture, and the Body*.

Here, Bordo devotes a section to "The Slender Body and Other Cultural Forms," and she links women's desire to be thin with the media representations of women that are held up as an ideal. Both Kilbourne and Bordo level heavy criticism at a genre long popular with women readers.

More recently, however, the criticism of women's magazines has taken another form—that of popular fiction. In their texts, chick lit authors frequently refer to women's magazines like *Cosmopolitan* and *Marie Claire*, often depicting their protagonists reading these publications. Though many chick lit authors make reference to women's magazines, British authors Helen Fielding and Sophie Kinsella engage with women's magazines on another level; they play with the concept of the constructed reader in their respective novels, *Bridget Jones's Diary* (1996) and *The Secret Dreamworld of a Shopaholic* (2000).[4] Like other chick lit heroines, Fielding and Kinsella's protagonists are the target demographic for these publications, young, single, women in the late twenties and early thirties. And, these heroines are frequently depicted reading and referring to these women's magazines. Yet, both authors take these associations a step further by crafting heroines who not only read such publications and represent the target readership but who also devotedly adhere to the advice given by such publications. In other words, through the depictions of their protagonists, Bridget Jones and Becky Bloomwood, Fielding and Kinsella seem to posit what would happen if a woman were to blindly follow the consumer guidelines advocated by women's magazines.

In this chapter, I will examine the ways in which both Fielding and Kinsella construct their protagonists, exaggerating their consumer behaviors as a means of critiquing the problematic consumption practices endorsed by the publications that their heroines so devotedly read. As mentioned earlier, women's magazines encourage readers to consistently alter their consumption patterns, and they often present their readers with conflicting information about their expected behaviors. Both authors respond to the contradictory content of these magazines by depicting characters who struggle to follow the consumption guidelines offered by such publications. While Fielding concentrates primarily on Bridget Jones's relationship to her weight, Kinsella centers on her protagonist's shopping habits. Fielding exposes, as Kilbourne and Bordo do, the negative effects that women's magazines can have on a woman's relationship with her body. However, unlike Kilbourne and Bordo, Fielding deploys humor to highlight the ridiculous consumption patterns encouraged by women's magazines, exposing the unrealistic expectations they place on women. Though Kinsella's protagonist, Becky, does not have the weight issues that Bridget does, her shopping behaviors mimic that of a bulimic; she binges and purges regularly, buying ridiculous amounts of clothing, feeling guilty about her purchases, and then vowing vehemently to reduce.[5] Again, just as Fielding does, Kinsella exaggerates Becky's consumer behaviors in order to satirize publications like *Cosmopolitan* and *Marie Claire* that regularly encourage readers to replace their old wardrobes with entirely new ones. Additionally, I will examine the ways in which both Kinsella and Fielding's narrative style is similar to that of the glossies, a move which results in a multi-layered reading of their novels and which furthers this critique of women's magazines.

Fielding and Kinsella's use of women's magazines in their novels is not the first time that fiction and women's magazines have been paired. In fact, in both England and the United States, women, magazines, and fiction have long been closely associated; women's issues have played an integral part in the magazines produced, and likewise, women writers have long been contributors to this medium. In his book *Magazines in the United States*, James Playstead Wood notes that as early as April 1709 in England *The Tatler*, though not a magazine targeted specifically at women, devoted space to women's issues; Richard Steele, the magazine's initiator, wrote a column under the pen name of Jenny Bickerstaff that addressed those subjects that would be of concern to women.[6] Similarly, in America, early magazine publishers addressed women's issues in their publications; Noah Webster's first issue of *The American Magazine* in 1787 "provided the kind of Gothic and sentimental fiction considered appealing to feminine taste" while also "offer[ring] advice on female dress and behavior" (Wood 23). As Wood notes, during the nineteenth century, in both England and America, women proved to be a viable demographic and publications aimed specifically at women grew during this century with such British publications as the *Englishwoman's Domestic Magazine* (1852), the *Ladies' Treasury* (1858), and *Myra's Journal of Dress and Fashion* (1875) and American publications such as the *Ladies' Home Journal* (1883), *Good Housekeeping* (1885), and the *Women's Home Companion* (1873).[7] Particularly during the latter part of this century, there was "enormous growth in the magazine industry; in Britain alone, 48 new women's magazines were founded between 1880 and 1900, and the diversity of the new publications reflected the increasing diversity of women's lives" (Reed 205). At this time in America, magazines also began to have higher circulation rates, in part because of advancements in technology. Theodore Peterson, author of *Magazines in the Twentieth Century*, notes "By the last ten years of the nineteenth century, advances in printing trades were making possible magazines of large circulations" (5).

Many of the titles that came to be in the nineteenth century continued to prosper into the twentieth century, and despite two world wars, the magazine industry, in general, still flourished in the first half of the twentieth century on both sides of the Atlantic.[8] In *The Popular Magazine in Britain and the United States: 1880–1960*, David Reed observes, "The war . . . had stimulated a great demand for reading material and the British women's press exploited that need with great determination" (206). As demand increased so did supply. Magazine historian Mary Ellen Zuckerman, author of *A History of Popular Women's Magazines in the United States, 1792–1995*, explains that the nature of magazine production and purchase in America both during and after the war was complicated due mainly to the introduction of a new form of entertainment—television. While she notes that as women "were increasingly defined as consumers in American society" publications directed toward this demographic "emerged with . . . strength and popularity," she also acknowledges the important role that television began to play in American families' lives (xii). In many ways, television threatened to displace magazines to some extent, forcing the industry as a whole to rethink their purpose and compelling many individual magazines to revamp their publications.

Despite any minor setbacks that the magazine industry may have faced throughout the early twentieth century, women's magazines never faded out entirely; generally speaking, the industry on the whole continued to be prosperous. Post-1950 magazines began to revamp their publications, responding in part to the women's movement. The number of single, working women was growing, and the magazine industry saw the need to respond to that fact. Both British and American magazines began putting less stress on domestic issues. The forerunner of this "new magazine" was *Cosmopolitan*, which enlisted the help of Helen Gurley Brown, author of the 1962 best seller *Sex and the Single Girl*. Brown's advice manual, as Betsey Israel explains in *Bachelor Girl: The Secret History of Single Women in the Twentieth Century*, revamped perceptions of the single woman. Brown replaced the image of the spinster with:

> . . . a new variation of the single girl, this one a tornado of competence—pretty, slim, but also smart, "up" on the news, well-read, and given to sewing and cooking while at the same time cramming in some art history or Russian literature. She worked hard at a job in the arts and lived by herself in a sleek, sexy apartment. She was enormously popular but seemingly choosy, selective; very hard to get. (212)

When asked to serve as editor of *Cosmopolitan* magazine in 1965, Helen Gurley Brown revamped the magazine so that it appealed to the generation of women she described in her book—women who become known as *Cosmo* girls (McDonald 63). The success that followed proved to other publishers that *Cosmo*'s template could and should be followed. As a result, magazines such as *Glamour* applied Brown's principles to their publication and increased their revenues by responding to market demand. Publishers in Britain recognized the potential market for a magazine like *Cosmopolitan* in England, and in 1972, the British edition of *Cosmopolitan* was launched and enthusiastically received by the reading public. *Cosmopolitan*'s success sparked the first in a series of twentieth-century, transatlantic trades. Not only did *Cosmopolitan* travel to England in 1972, but also other publications, such as *Marie Claire*, a magazine which originated in France but which was extremely popular in England, made its way to the United States. With globalization relaxing national boundaries, the magazine industry responded.

Today, women's magazines continue to prosper. According to the Hearst Group's press kit for *Cosmopolitan* magazine, accessible through their website www.hearstcorp.com, at the end of 2006, magazines such as *Cosmopolitan* and *Marie Claire* reportedly had a rate base of 2,947,220 and 962,025 respectively; *Cosmopolitan* is currently published in 100 countries (*The Hearst Group*). Furthermore, the late nineties saw the emergence of a crop of new magazines, many directed toward the female population. *Teen People* (1998) (Pogrebin C1) led the way in the ever-expanding teen market with *Cosmo Girl!* (2001) ("The National Magazine Company" 11) and *Teen Vogue* (2003) (Caperton NA) to follow. Condé Nast launched the magazine *Lucky* in 2000, which vice president and publisher Alexandra Golinkin describes as "a hybrid of a magazine and Internet and catalog" (Handelman SR37). And, most recently, riding on the success of her daytime talk show, Oprah Winfrey began the magazines *O: The Oprah Magazine* (2001) ("The World According to Oprah" 43). Women's magazines, it is apparent, continue to be a powerful force in the consumer market, being bought and read by women and potentially affecting women's consumer decisions and behaviors.

Not only have magazines long been associated with women, but women writers have also been avid contributors to the magazine industry, writing articles, fiction, and poetry for their pages. Margaret Beetham and Kay Boardman acknowledge women's early contributions in their anthology *Victorian Women's Magazines*. Their book includes a section on prose fiction in which they note that both short fiction and serialized fiction appeared in many women's magazines from the nineteenth century. In nineteenth century England, magazine historian Cynthia White explains that publication such as *Woman's World* (1903) published "sensational fiction" often written by women (70). In America, too, well known women writers, such as Willa Cather and Ellen Glasgow, were contributing to magazine publications

(Tebbel and Zuckerman 99). And, into the twentieth century, women continued to write for these publications. David Reed notes that "Fiction dominated every issue of *Woman's Own* with over 41% of editorial space for the first half of 1950" (205). Nancy A. Walker's collection of articles from popular women's magazines, entitled *Women's Magazines 1940–60: Gender Roles and the Popular Press*, contains within it articles written by such well known twentieth-century, American women writers as Pearl S. Buck, M.F.K. Fisher, Mary McCarthy, and Joan Didion.

This association still continues today and has, perhaps, grown even stronger with not only the majority of the articles in women's magazines being written by women but also with the majority of editorial and staff positions at these magazines being occupied by women. The May 2007, British edition of *Marie Claire* reveals that of the sixteen positions available in the fashion and features department only one is occupied by a man. Likewise, in the June 2007, American edition of *Cosmopolitan*, six of the ten major features listed on the contents page of the magazine were written by women.[9] Furthermore, the association that women's magazines hold with popular fiction continues as well. Women writers often showcase their fiction in women's magazines; in fact, in the late nineties the British edition of *Cosmopolitan* consistently ran excerpts and short stories by leading writers—the majority of these writers profiled were women. Also, published, female authors may be contributors to these publications; both Anna Maxted (*Getting Over It*) and Jane Green (*Jemima J*, 1998) wrote articles for British *Cosmopolitan*.[10] Additionally, many women's magazines run recommended reading lists and advertise upcoming books, further strengthening the connections between these two genres.

As noted earlier, chick lit authors are also furthering these associations by referring to women's magazines in their novels, crafting characters who read and respond to the advice offered by these texts, and, more significantly, by critiquing this medium through their fictional representations. Central to this critique is the way in which both Fielding and Kinsella play with the concept of the constructed reader. Most consumer products need to have a clear sense of their audience in order to market their products successfully. Women's magazines are no different, so publishers often construct a reader who they posit as the ideal reader of their publication. The constructed reader is the imagined consumer that the publisher of a women's magazines envisions when conceptualizing a publication. Helen Gurley Brown perhaps best exhibited this concept when she revamped *Cosmopolitan* in 1965. Convinced that the magazine's low sales were due in part to the magazine's inability to imagine its audience, Brown overhauled the magazine, capitalizing on the sexual revolution of the 1960s and targeting the publication toward young, single women (Hantman). Her self-created "Cosmo girl" was clearly envisioned, and Brown and her staff constructed the magazine to appeal to this imagined reader, filling the publication with content (i.e. articles on sex, beauty, and shopping) targeted toward this perceived demographic (Hantman).

Today, women's magazines continue to follow the same formula; the concept of the constructed reader is evident in the promotional material that appears on the websites for such publications as *Cosmopolitan* and *Marie Claire*. For instance, *Cosmopolitan* defines themselves as "'Fun, fearless, female'" on their website, noting that their publication "inspires with information on relationships and romance, the best in fashion and beauty, the latest on women's health and well-being, as well as what is happening in pop culture and entertainment . . . and just about everything else fun, fearless, females want to know" (*"Cosmopolitan"*). *Marie Claire*, according to the magazine history section published on *iVillage* in 2004, purports to be "aimed at women encouraging them to consider their own autonomy, charm, and personal development," and additionally, the magazine aspires "to show readers a different view of the world and its people." In 2007, the magazine's website purports: "*Marie Claire* is more than a pretty face. It is the fashion magazine with character, substance, and depth, for women with a point of view, an opinion, and a sense of humor" (*"Marie Claire"*). The content of these publications is consistent with the way that these publications define themselves. For instance, the February 2002, American edition of *Cosmopolitan* includes a section entitled "*Cosmo's* Passion Package: A Raunchy Guide to Living Your Lust-Life to the Full" (86). The 1995 February, UK edition of *Marie Claire*, by contrast, not only contains articles on sex, health, and beauty ("Table of Contents" 3), but it also includes a feature on the abuse of young, Chinese gymnasts, an article consistent with its mission to expose readers to other cultures ("China's Child Sports Slaves" 140). In these mission statements and article content, each magazine attempts to define itself in such a way as to appeal to a particular segment of the female population. So, before a "real" reader even picks up the magazine, a great deal of work goes into imagining who that reader might be.

Like magazine publishers, Helen Fielding and Sophie Kinsella imagine readers of women's magazines in their works of fiction. Fielding constructs Bridget Jones, a fictional character who first appeared in her newspaper column for the *Independent* on February 28, 1995 (Whelehan 12). The column, which ran for two years in the *Independent* and which later moved to the *Telegraph* in 1997, was wildly successful with the *Independent's* readership, and Bridget was so well liked that Fielding decided to transform her columns into a novel (Whelehan 12). Published in England in 1996 and in the United States in 1998, *Bridget Jones's Diary*, which is written in diary form, tracks the daily, often hilarious, exploits of a young, thirty-something, unmarried British woman whose self-image is clearly influenced by the magazines that she reads. Throughout the course of the novel, Bridget attempts to make sense of what she perceives to be her disorderly life, reflecting on and lamenting about the (often times bad) choices that she makes. During the course of the year, she falls for her boss, quits her job, attempts to counsel her mother through a trial separation from her father, and gets her mother out of a legal jam with the help of her "'top human-rights lawyer'" friend who eventually becomes her lover (101). The novel begins at the start of the New Year, presumably the year 1995 because of the later mention of the breakup of Prince Charles and Princess Diana's marriage, and ends that December; a list that summarizes such vital statistics as weight lost and "Hangover-free days" follows the formal conclusion of the novel (310).

Integral to Fielding's novel are her numerous popular culture references; on nearly every page there is some mention of an event, a product, or a medium that characterizes the time period in which Fielding's protagonist lives. This narrative quality is due in part to the fact that Fielding adapted her newspaper column for her novel; naturally, her column relied heavily on being timely. In the novel, Fielding references such events as Prince Charles's affair with Camilla Parker-Bowles and the BBC's production of *Pride and Prejudice* which aired in 1995 to orient her novel historically. In particular, Fielding repeatedly makes mention of the popular culture medium of women's magazines, both overtly and covertly. She depicts Bridget searching for her latest issue of *Marie Claire*, and she refers to clothing brands like Calvin Klein and Ralph Lauren, two designers regularly featured in both *Cosmopolitan* and *Marie Claire*. More indirectly, she depicts Bridget engaging in such activities as "date-preparation" where Bridget exercises, exfoliates, plucks, and waxes—all activities encouraged by women's magazines—in order to be presentable for her date with Daniel Cleaver. Throughout her novel, Fielding signifies the importance that women's magazines play in Bridget's life by repeatedly alluding to them.

In addition to this referencing, the structure and content of Fielding's opening makes clear the significance that women's magazines play in Bridget's life. Before the formal narrative begins, Fielding presents the reader with two lists—one that is entitled "I WILL NOT" and the list on the facing page is entitled "I WILL." These lists call to mind the New Year's resolution lists that often appear in January issues of women's magazines. The January 1995 edition of *Cosmopolitan* includes an article by Phillip Hodson entitled "How to Change Your Life: New Year's Revolutions." This article offers suggestions to readers, noting that 1995 is the year to "Try and accept your feelings at each stage of the process" and "If you are quite stuck, it's probably best to make small changes that don't really count, to build your confidence" (20). This lists, and lists like it, are staples in January editions of women's magazines, and they can range from suggestions to improving your state of mind to more frivolous lists that encourage women to do outrageous things before the New Year is up. Immediately, Fielding connects her narrative to the narrative structure of women's magazines.

Fielding concentrates Bridget's New Year's resolution list primarily upon the transgressions of Bridget's body, and her "I Will Not" list directly addresses the ways in which Bridget will attempt to correct her perceived, disordered bodily practices. On her "I Will Not" list, she notes ceasing such practices as drinking alcohol, smoking, and overeating—negative habits often addressed by women's magazines. This theme is addressed in Mary Elizabeth Adams's "Female Fear: The Body, Gender, and the Burdens of Beauty," which details multiple consumer industries that influence women to feel alienated from their body—including tanning salons, day spas, and cosmetic counters. Adams's dissertation, however, also analyzes a few select popular culture texts, including *Bridget Jones's Diary*, where she discusses the fear that Bridget has of her body in a natural state. Adams cites the following passage from Fielding, an excellent example of the alienation that Bridget feels toward her body:

> Completely exhausted by entire day of date-preparation. Being a woman is worse than being a farmer—there is so much harvesting and crop spraying to be done: legs to be waxed, underarms shaved, eyebrows plucked, feet pumiced, skin exfoliated and moisturized, spots cleansed, roots dyed, eyelashes tinted, nails filed, cellulite massaged, stomach muscles exercised. The whole performance is so highly tuned you need only to neglect it for a few days for the whole thing to go to seed. Sometimes I wonder what I would be like if left to revert to nature—with a full beard and handlebars moustache on each shin, Dennis Healey eyebrows, face a graveyard of dead skin cells, spots erupting, long curly fingernails like Struwelpeter, blind as a bat and stupid runt of species as no contact lenses, flabby body flobbering around. Ugh, ugh. (30)

Here, Fielding's clearly expresses Bridget's disgust toward her body in its natural state by using such words as "blind," "stupid," and "flabby."

More importantly, Fielding focuses on the way in which Bridget attempts to overcome her body in its natural state—conforming to the guidelines offered by women's magazines. Magazines like *Cosmopolitan* and *Marie Claire* contain information vital to managing the body. Articles on the best ways to shave the body and the best ways to reduce the body are a staple of these magazines. In the February 1995 edition of *Marie Claire*, the table of contents indicates that there will be articles on the season's new looks in fashion, "Finding the Right Foundation," and solutions to tough hair problems ("Table of Contents" 3). All of these articles focus on helping the female reader, like Bridget, achieve a look similar to the models who grace the pages of women's magazines—women with clear complexions, carefully coifed hair, and toned bodies. As Ellen McCracken notes in her 1993 book *Decoding Women's Magazines: From* Mademoiselle *to* Ms., the photographs in women's magazines reflect "an idealized mirror image of the woman [reader] who gazes" (13). This idealized image, in turn, becomes the future self that the consumer hopes to achieve by managing her body as directed by these magazines. Bridget sees reflected on these pages the type of woman whom she aspires to be, and she attempts to achieve that by following the guidelines such publications offer.

The chief way in which Bridget attempts to manage her body is by controlling her weight. Throughout the novel, Fielding depicts Bridget struggling to lose weight; she obsessively records her calorie intake at the start of nearly every diary entry. Additionally, Fielding reveals Bridget's obsession with counting calories in a conversation with that Bridget has with her gay, male friend, Tom. When Bridget chastises Tom for being preoccupied with negative feelings about the shape of his nose, Tom attempts to expose Bridget's equally unhealthy preoccupation with her weight. He quizzes her on how many calories are in a variety of foods (including both large and small bananas), and although Bridget cannot immediately remember what letter of the alphabet comes before J, she can easily guess how many calories are in a black or green olive. Bridget's learned behavior seems to be connected to the body ideologies purported by women's magazines, one of the major mediums criticized for negatively affecting women's perceptions of their bodies and self-esteems.

This scene, however, is not a serious commentary on women's disordered eating patterns. Unlike Susan Bordo and Jean Kilbourne, who critically assess the effects that women's magazines have on readers, Fielding's chosen method of exposing the problematic nature of these magazines is to deploy humor to critique the role that these publications play in Bridget's life. For instance, in this scene, Fielding exaggerates Bridget's calorie counting habits. Like many women, Bridget counts calories, but unlike many women, she also knows the difference between a large and small banana and a black and green olive. Here, Fielding mocks the emphasis that some women place on their weight by making it, in Bridget's case, an absurd preoccupation. Additionally, in the scene where Bridget prepares for her date, Fielding humorously draws attention to the many ways that these magazines encourage women to alter and perfect their appearances. The numerous references to topics frequently discussed in these publications (waxing, shaving, plucking, pumicing, exfoliating, moisturizing, cleaning, dying, tinting, filing, massaging, exercising) in one small passage make the beauty rituals that Bridget undergoes seem ridiculous.

We can also see this humor built into Fielding's narrative structure. Fielding's novel relies heavily on the act of record keeping, one of the chief ways that women's magazines encourage readers to control their bodies. These publications encourage readers to keep lists, diaries, and charts as a first step to correcting disordered behavior. For instance, in the 1995 January edition of *Cosmopolitan*, there is an advertisement for the "essential *Cosmo* diary," which one can buy either as a pocket diary, desk diary, wallet, or pocket diary with wallet.[11] The advertisement copy reads:

> The *Cosmopolitan* diary is *the* guide to planning a happy and successful 1995. It's got the latest names and numbers for all your networking contact, crucial health and fitness advice, information on the best clubs, theatres, restaurants and shopping facilities, travel checklists, dates to remember and at-a-glance guides to great cities. So, start 1995 in style with the life-saving, life enhancing *Cosmopolitan* diary. (15)

This product reinforces to women the necessity of keeping their lives ordered through writing. Buying the *Cosmo* diary will provide the consumer with "crucial health and fitness advice," and reading this advice and recording your own habits will not only save your life but also enhance your life. The copy also implies that a healthy body is the type of body that can properly enjoy "clubs, theatres, restaurants and shopping facilities" and tour "great cities." Repeatedly, women's magazines stress this type of record keeping as a chief means of controlling one's body and, in turn, one's life.

*Cosmopolitan* advises readers to begin a diary in the New Year. And, Bridget does just that. Her diary becomes the first way that she attempts to control the transgressions of her body. As noted earlier, her "I WILL" and "I WILL NOT" lists concentrate on these transgressions and the ways in which she can correct them. Additionally, the italicized entries that start each entry become ways for Bridget to record her consumption patterns in a first attempt to correct them. Yet Bridget's diary, as Alison Case has noted in "Authenticity, Convention, and *Bridget Jones's Diary*," often "violate[s] the mimetic logic of the diary form" (178). Case goes on to record a number of instances Fielding records "minute-by-minute accounts of Bridget's efforts to get something done" (178). Her chief example cited is the scene in which Bridget prepares for her birthday dinner. Case notes numerous mimetic discrepancies in the text, observing that it would be unrealistic for a person to so excessively record each and every activity in which she engaged. While Case's essay suggests that this divergence from the "proper" diary format should not diminish the text's "authenticity," I would like to suggest that this excessive record keeping serves as another example of the way in which Fielding satirizes the ideologies offered by women's magazines. Again, Fielding crafts Bridget as an extreme reader of women's magazines; she exaggerates Bridget's behaviors, completely preoccupying her character with recording her daily habits. This form of narration, then, furthers Fielding's critique.

Bridget's exaggerated consumption habits structure Fielding's narrative. Each diary entry begins with an italicized section that details such behaviors as how many calories she has consumed, how many cigarettes she has smoked, and how many alcohol units she has drunk. Interestingly enough, the consumption habits noted in these sections—mainly eating, buying and sexuality—are the three consumption habits that women's magazines focus upon as well. And, like the cover lines on women's magazines, these italicized sections act as a preview of Bridget's mindset for the upcoming entry. As readers, we know that a drastic increase in calories recorded by Bridget at the start of a diary entry often indicates traumatic events while weight loss designates positive occurrences.

Frequently, these entries differ dramatically in tone. Fielding often will juxtapose an extremely positive entry with an extremely negative entry. These frequent shifts in tone are extremely obvious and serve to highlight Bridget's manic behaviors. Fielding also includes drastic shifts in tone within individual entries. For example, on Friday, January 6, Bridget shifts from elated to depressed. At 5:45 pm, she writes, "Could not be more joyous. . . . Yesssss!Yesssss! Daniel Cleaver wants my phone no. Am marvelous. Am irresistible Sex Goddess. Hurrah!" (26). However, on Sunday, January 8, Bridget writes, "Oh God, why am I so unattractive?" when Daniel fails to call (27). And, Fielding further reinforces these moods through the opening, italicized entries. On January 6, Fielding omits Bridget's normal record keeping while on January 8 Fielding includes the following note: "*9 st 2 (v. bloody g. but what is point?), alcohol units 2 (excellent), cigarettes 7, calories 3100 (poor)*" (27). Central to the construction of Fielding's character, and to her narrative, are these mood shifts. Not only does Fielding exaggerate Bridget's consumer habits, but she directly connects her exaggerated temperament to her consumption patterns.

Bridget's disposition reflects her perception of her body, as evidenced by the italicized sections that open each entry. On a good day, Bridget forgets to record her calorie intake; on a bad day, it's "poor." More interestingly, perhaps, is the way that Fielding links Bridget's relationship with her body to her relationship with men—a narrative move that conflates body image issues and men in a way similar to women's magazines. Women's magazines often imply that the audience for the managed, female body is the male. For instance, the article "Streets Ahead" in the December 2000 edition of *Marie Claire* magazines includes a pull-out quote which reads, "'This cowl-neck top and earrings make me feel sexy and feminine and very sophisticated'" (172). Though ostensibly the article is about the affordable clothing offered in London's high-street stores, "Streets Ahead" still implies that the performance of femininity is for the male gaze. Above, we see Bridget's perceptions of her body and her self directly linked to the successes and failures she has in her relationship with Daniel. Additionally, Fielding further critiques this tendency of women's magazines by repeatedly depicting Bridget's body management rituals as part of her "date-preparation" activity. While women's magazines *imply* that men are the audience for the managed, female body, Fielding *actualizes* that implication by having Bridget's major body management scenes, cited earlier, occur in preparation for her date with Daniel Cleaver. Fielding further mocks the excessiveness of this date-preparation when, in the first passage referenced, Daniel cancels his date with Bridget—"Entire waste of whole day's bloody effort and hydro-electric body-generated power" (31).

Though Fielding frequently depicts Bridget feeling frustrated at having to follow the body management techniques encouraged by women's magazines, at the same time, she infrequently portrays Bridget as straying from the advice offered by these publications, no matter how contradictory or at odds with her own lifestyle that advice may be. At one point, Bridget notes, "Today is a historic and joyous day. After eighteen years of trying to get down to 8 st 7 I have finally achieved it," yet "There is no reliable explanation. I have been to the gym twice in the last week, but that, though rare, is not freakish. I have eaten normally. It is a miracle" (105). Despite Bridget's own elation at having achieved her goal, her friends react negatively to her newfound figure. Though Bridget thinks she looks great, her friends find her to look sick, "'drawn'," or "'flat'" (106). Because she is so enmeshed in the body ideology (i.e. thinner is better) of women's magazines, she is unable to understand their reactions:

> Now I feel empty and bewildered as if a rug has been pulled from under my feet. Eighteen years—wasted. Eighteen years of calorie and fat-unit-based arithmetic. Eighteen years of buying long shirts and jumpers and leaving the room backwards in intimate situations to hide my bottom. Millions of cheesecakes and tiramisus, tens of millions of Emmenthal slices of cheese left uneaten. Eighteen years of struggle and sacrifice and endeavor—for what? Eighteen years and the result is "tired" and "flat." I feel like a scientist who discovers his life's work has been a total mistake. (107)

While Bridget is clearly upset at her discovery, Fielding again deploys humor as a means of critique in this passage. Bridget's sacrifice has not been that great a sacrifice because, throughout the novel, we see Bridget eating both cheesecake and Emmenthal slices. Additionally, her realization that her "life's work" has all been for naught does not last too long. She returns to counting calories two passages later.

Fielding's chief means of satirizing women's magazines, then, is through her portrayal of a character that is not unlike the constructed reader of magazines like *Cosmopolitan*. Demographically speaking, Bridget is the target audience of such publications; she exhibits many qualities of the "Cosmo girl;" and she devotedly follows the advice offered by these publications. However, what Fielding does throughout the novel is to develop a character that is not only the constructed, but also the ideal, reader of women's magazines. Bridget steadfastly follows the advice offered to her by these publications, no matter how contradictory or ill-fitting that advice might be, and in doing so, Bridget becomes a cautionary tale to real readers of women's magazines of reading gone wrong. Her exaggerated consumer behavior serves as a warning as to what could happen if one was to follow the advice offered by such publications too closely.

Published several years after *Bridget Jones's Diary*, Sophie Kinsella's *The Secret Dreamworld of a Shopaholic* bears narrative similarities to Fielding's text. As with Fielding's book, Kinsella's text contains stylistic similarities to women's magazines. The chapters are relatively short, as women's magazines' articles are, and the chapters are often broken up by the occasional letter from various banks and credit card companies demanding that Becky pay her past due bills, another strategy that emphasizes the episodic nature of the text. Furthermore, Kinsella's text, like women's magazines, contains a huge amount of product placement; Kinsella continually mentions shops that Becky frequents such as Top Shop, Boots, Oddbins, and Body Shop. Kinsella's deft weaving of product names into the narrative works in much the same way as covert advertising in women's magazines. As Ellen McCracken explains in *Decoding Women's Magazines*, covert advertising is "the promotions disguised as editorial material or hidden in some other form so that they appear to be non-advertising" (38). She goes on to write, "Covert advertising extends structural links to the purchased advertising, creating a harmonious, integrated whole. It can take specific forms such as the recommendation of brand name products in an editorial feature or be more generalized as in the broad, thematic correlation of editorial content to advertising" (38–39). Though, admittedly, Kinsella is not accepting money from these industries to advertise their goods, her novel does mention many consumer products and might affect Kinsella's reader in the same way that covert advertising might affect the readers of women's magazines.

Additionally, the paperback, British and American editions of the book use engaging visual images on their covers that draw the reader into the text. The paperback, British edition includes the title of the book, *The Secret Dreamworld of a Shopaholic*, in big, bold pink letters. Carrier bags dangle from an invisible line atop the book. The American edition includes the title of the book, *Confessions of a Shopaholic*, inside a large, pink price tag, and in the bottom right hand corner, there is a drawing of a high-heeled shoe, sticking out of a shoebox. Both the price tag and the shoe, however, are cut off, leading the eye beyond the right page to the inside cover. Here, the drawings continue; the high-heeled shoe is only a small part of the larger closet revealed on the endpapers. Inside, there are drawings of what appears to be Becky's closet; clothing is strewn about while shoes and hats clutter the floor. Many of the items shown still retain their original price tags. This immediate contact that the reader has with the visual is not unlike women's magazines, which as noted above, rely heavily on the interaction between text and image. Kinsella's covers work in much of the same way; the title clues the reader into what the text will be about while the visual images reinforce that assumption. The excessiveness that we encounter on the endpapers in the American edition, and the fact that Becky's closet is so overfilled that it spills out onto the cover, indicates that a shopping problem will most likely drive the narrative. Much like the cover lines on magazines, the cover design and endpapers of Kinsella's text preview the novel to come.

More specifically, Kinsella's protagonist, Becky Bloomwood, shares many traits similar to Fielding's protagonist—particularly in so far as the way in which women's magazines profoundly influence her. Becky, a financial journalist, is a twenty-five-year-old, single career girl, working in London and living, as the back of the paperback, American edition notes, in a "fabulous flat in London's trendiest neighborhood." Like Bridget Jones, Becky is a bit bumbling; she has the best intentions when it comes to putting her life in order, yet she cannot quite seem to follow through with her plans as she knows she is expected to. Becky's chief preoccupation, which the novel's title belies, is shopping, and her excessive spending habits get her into financial debt that she cannot quite seem to escape. The novel revolves around Becky's creative attempts to erase this debt; Kinsella constructs a financial mystery involving a cheating investment company, and despite the fact that Becky often seems inept, she deftly unravels the mystery, winning the respect of her friends, family, and the man whom she admires, Luke Brandon.

Kinsella's major critique of these publications lies in her depiction of her main character. Like Fielding, Kinsella exaggerates her protagonist's consumption patterns; although instead of concentrating on Becky's eating habits and weight issues, Kinsella concentrates on another popular consumption habit encouraged by women's magazines—shopping. In *The Secret Dreamworld of a Shopaholic*, Kinsella critiques women's magazines tendency to encourage women's continual, yet consistently changing, shopping habits by depicting the extreme shopper. And again, like Fielding, Kinsella consistently deploys humor as a means of deconstructing the consumer ideologies of women's magazines, particularly the way in which they encourage excessive spending habits of female readers.

Kinsella opens *The Secret Dreamworld of a Shopaholic* with a correspondence between her protagonist Becky Bloomwood and Endwich Bank. The first letter from Endwich Bank informs Becky that, as a recent college graduate, she is eligible for an account with £2,000 overdraft; the second letter informs her that she has significantly exceeded her given overdraft; the third sends condolences for her broken leg but encourages to pay her overdraft regardless; and, the four expresses sympathy over her glandular fever but again asks for the money owed. This early exchange, which becomes increasingly more ridiculous, sets the tone for the narrative to come as well as previews the major action. Here, Kinsella not only humorously critiques the tendency of financial agencies to offer lines of credit to inexperienced consumers, but she also critiques the consumer's excessive spending habits through Becky's increasingly desperate, yet inventive, attempts to evade her debt.

Kinsella's early exchange between Becky and Endwich Bank illuminates Becky's primary, problematic consumption pattern. In reading through the correspondence, it becomes clear that Becky overspends and, in turn, has difficulties managing her debt, and within the first few pages of the narrative proper, Kinsella reveals that this difficulty has arisen because of Becky's excessive shopping habit. At the start of Chapter 1, Kinsella depicts Becky trying to reconstruct the shopping list that has resulted in her £200 VISA bill. The list includes such items as a suit at Jigsaw, hypo-allergenic eyeliner, lingerie, and "that skin brusher thing" from the Body Shop (15).[12] The more she thinks about it, the more Becky's shopping list grows, and before long, the reader realizes that the term shopaholic is aptly chosen for Kinsella's protagonist.

Becky's VISA bill reads like a series of advertisements from a magazine; the list includes both clothing items and beauty products commonly advertised on the pages of *Cosmopolitan* and *Marie Claire*. In fact, Kinsella depicts her main character reading such publications, using their advice to guide her consumer decisions. Throughout the course of the novel, Becky mentions reading magazines such as *Marie Claire* and *Cosmopolitan*, and she also reads such publications as *Vogue* and *Elle Decoration*. Additionally, *Woman's Journal* and *Good Housekeeping* are mentioned in the text. These references indicate Becky's interest in women's magazines, but they also further support the fact that she is not a discerning consumer. Though the target audience is different for publications such as *Marie Claire*, *Vogue*, and *Good Housekeeping*, Becky purchases and reads these publications regardless of whether or not their content is relevant to her own life, a detail that further reinforces her passive approach to consumption. And, her VISA bill is not the only evidence that we see of Becky purchasing brands commonly advertised in women's magazines. Kinsella's novel is rich with references to such shops as Jigsaw, French Connection, and Agnés B—brands that often appear in the fashion spreads of magazines like *Cosmopolitan* and *Marie Claire*.[13] Immediately, Kinsella portrays her narrator as being deeply affected by these publications.

Kinsella satirizes Becky's consumer behavior throughout her text. Like Bridget, Becky is completely devoted to women's magazines; she buys into their consumer ideologies almost as much as she purchases actual items. Early in the novel, Kinsella reveals her devotion. She writes:

> It's a habit of mine, itemizing all the clothes I'm wearing as though for a fashion page. I've been doing it for years—ever since I used to read *Just Seventeen*. Every issue, they'd stop a girl on the street, take a picture of her, and list all her clothes. "T-Shirt: Chelsea Girl, Jeans: Top Shop, Shoes: borrowed from friend." I used to read those lists avidly, and to this day, if I buy something from a shop that's a bit uncool, I cut the label out. So that if I'm every stopped in the street, I can pretend I don't know where it's from. (21)

Becky consistently imagines herself as a woman in a fashion magazine, and the only way that she can achieve that ideal is to purchase those items of clothing that are up *to Just Seventeen*'s standards. Terrified of being caught in an item of clothing that is not up to par, Becky goes so far as to cut certain labels out of her clothes. Her actions are extreme, as Kinsella subtly, and not so subtly, indicates in this passage. Though many readers of women's magazines might turn to the fashion spreads in these publications for advice on which fashion trends are in and which are out, Kinsella depicts Becky taking this consumption advice to the extreme. Becky turns to these manuals for suggestions on what to wear, and she fears straying from their advice so much that she cuts the labels out of clothing that would not be up to the magazine's standards. Not only does Kinsella mock Becky's unwavering concern with the guidelines offered by these publications, but she also subtly chides her for this devotion in her reference to *Just Seventeen*. Though Becky is in her late twenties, she still structures her life around the guidelines offered by a magazine directed at teenagers, and she still holds onto the belief that she might be stopped in the street and asked to share where her clothing is from. Here, Kinsella critiques the pervasiveness that women's magazines can have in consumers' lives through Becky's unwavering and absurd devotion to them.

Additionally, Kinsella's novel critiques women's magazines for the "consume and achieve" promise that they make to readers. Frequently, women's magazines imply to readers that buying and reading their publication, buying the products mentioned within, and buying into the advice offered by such publications will enable readers to achieve an enhanced lifestyle—usually the lifestyle that the constructed reader of their publication purportedly lives. Ellen McCracken notes this tendency in *Decoding Women's Magazines: From* Mademoiselle *to* Ms. In her chapter "Codes of Overt Advertisements," McCracken deconstructs a series of advertisements, noting the way in which these ads use both image, text, and image and text together to offer readers a better appearance or a more affluent lifestyle. McCracken's observations are easily seen in contemporary magazines. For instance, the special advertisement section for the Jaeger London Collection included in the April 1995 edition of *Marie Claire* uses a variety of techniques that McCracken mentions to convince readers that purchasing this clothing will lead to an improved existence. The title of the spread, "Cool and Collected," denotes the qualities that one can gain by purchasing the clothing advertised; the text included bolsters this promise by professing that "Immaculate tailoring is the look of the moment" and "the perfect fabric for spring and summer" (102). The implication here is that the reader, too, can be "Immaculate" and "perfect" if they obtain these items. The photograph underneath further supports this claim; it presents readers with what McCracken deems the "idealized mirror image of the woman who gazes," in other words, the reader (13). The model in this photograph gazes out over her left shoulder, hands in her pockets, stance wide. Her posture exudes confidence; like the spread promises, she is cool and collected. This fashion spread, then, subtly works to convince the reader that they, too, could achieve this look and these qualities if they purchase the clothing shown.

*The Secret Dreamworld of a Shopaholic* satirizes these consumer behaviors encouraged by these publications by, again like Fielding, depicting the ideal—and often times extreme—reader of these magazines. Repeatedly, Kinsella depicts Becky buying a particular item of clothing because it becomes, for her, a way to define herself. After shopping at Benetton, she sees "The most perfect cardigan in the world" and then convinces herself to buy it using the rationale that if she owns it "people will call me the Girl in the Grey Cardigan" (67). Just as Becky desires to be outfitted in the clothing acceptable to *Just Seventeen*, here she imagines people noticing and defining her by the cardigan that she wears. Even more interesting than her tendency to identify herself solely by her clothing is Kinsella's justification of Becky's actions. At this point in the novel, Becky is desperately trying to reduce her spending; however, the cardigan upsets her plans. She reflects:

> David E. Barton [author of *Controlling Your Cash*] says I should act as naturally as possible. So really, I *ought* to act on my natural impulses and buy it. It would be false not to. It would ruin the whole point.
> And it only costs forty-five quid. And I can put it on VISA.
> Look at it another way—what's forty-five quid in the grand scheme of things? I mean, it's nothing, is it?
> So I buy it. The most perfect little cardigan in the world. People will call me the Girl in the Grey Cardigan. I'll be able to *live* in it. Really, it's an investment. (67)

Kinsella's passage deploys humor to mock Becky's excessive spending habits and the psychology of a shopaholic. Though Becky knows she should not spend anymore, her desire for the grey cardigan and the promises the piece of clothing holds become too much for her to resist. In this passage, Kinsella critiques these impulsive shopping behaviors often encouraged by women's magazines.

When Becky spends money it is not just with the intention that this spending will lead to an overall improvement in her lifestyle. She also hopes that these purchases will help to give her the appearance of a more affluent lifestyle. As Ellen McCracken notes, this consumer ideology is often conveyed by women's magazines, which capitalize upon consumers' desire for upward mobility by encouraging them to purchase products that give them the appearance of affluence. A model follower of women's magazines, Becky cultivates this affluent lifestyle despite the fact that it is against her own best financial interests to live in such a way. Becky frequently shops at high-end stores; she drinks champagne; she reads publications like *Vogue*; and she table hops at Terrazza, a fashionable, high priced restaurant and bar. Furthermore, she lives in a section of London that her boss Philip deems "Trendy Fulham," a neighborhood "Full of It-girls, all living on trust funds" (147). To those that surround her, she gives the impression of being rich, though her bank account indicates otherwise. Implicit in this portrayal of Becky is Kinsella's critique of the consumer manuals which promise that excessive consumption will result in a more desirable, and upscale, lifestyle. Ironically, but not surprisingly, Kinsella indicates, Becky's excessive spending habits result in her being broke as opposed to rich.

Readers of women's popular fiction on both sides of the Atlantic greeted the publication of *The Secret Dreamworld of a Shopaholic* and *Bridget Jones's Diary* favorably. As A. Rochelle Mabry writes in "About a Girl: Female Subjectivity and Sexuality in Contemporary 'Chick' Culture," "Although sales figures . . . can't always tell us *how* readers and viewers read a book or a film, they do clearly indicate that these works have caught on with their intended audience(s)" (193). Reader reviewers from America and England gave Kinsella's novel four and a half out of five stars, deeming the book "a thrilling and easy read" ("*The Secret Dreamworld of a Shopaholic*") and declaring it "light, clever, and totally disarming . . . a quick fun read" ("*Confessions of a Shopaholic*"). Fielding's novel was even more successful. After the profitable launch of the novel in England, where it already had a strong fan base due to the popularity of Fielding's column in the *Independent*, the novel traveled to America, where it was greeted with an equally favorable reception. Soon, plans were made to publish the novel more widely, and by 2001, *Bridget Jones's Diary* "had sold about two million copies in the UK and in excess of eight million copies worldwide" (Whelehan 67). Furthermore, Fielding's work achieved not only commercial success, but it also received critical acclaim, winning the book of the year award at the British Book awards in 1998 (Whelehan 67). In 2001, two years after the novel was released in America, the film version of *Bridget Jones's Diary* premiered, starring American actress Renée Zellweger and British actors Colin Firth and Hugh Grant ("*Bridget Jones's Diary*"). While the book itself launched a literary phenomenon, the movie seemed to further catapult the text into popular culture with allusions to Bridget Jones appearing in women's magazines and even the *Oxford English Dictionary*.[14]

Yet, despite their popularity, both novels faced some harsh criticisms. Many critics disliked the novels' tendencies to erase their protagonists' troubles with a rapid, tying up of the narrative. While readers responded positively to Kinsella's text, *The Secret Dreamworld of a Shopaholic* was not heavily reviewed by critics. The few reviews that were published were fairly dismissive of the novel, relegating it to an easy read meant for the beach.[15] In one of the only scholarly examinations of Kinsella's text, Jessica Lyn Van Slooten, in "Fashionably Indebted: Conspicious Consumption, Fashion, and Romance in Sophie Kinsella's Shopaholic Triology," targets the ending of Kinsella's texts, in particular, noting, "Throughout the series, however, Becky never *really* suffers privation because off her spending habits. Instead, her problems almost miraculously disappear, suggesting to readers that there are no real consequences to Becky's behavior and providing readers with a 'safe' consumerist fantasy world" (219).

Fielding's novel, unlike Kinsella's received a great deal of press. Yet, in both England and America, critics' reception of the novel was mixed. Generally, critics agreed that the book was funny, but a caveat often ensued. Any praise for the novel was usually followed by concerns about what Bridget represents or the harmful affects such a character might have upon the world's women. Penny Perrick of the *Sunday Times* warned, "*Bridget Jones's Diary* is a gloriously funny book, not a heavy tract on the plight of contemporary spinsters. But while you are wiping tears of laughter from her [sic] eyes, you can't help thinking that for young women to be so fixated on being something other than themselves is one of the unforeseen consequences of feminism." American reviewers were perhaps even harsher in their judgments of the novel, adamant about the harm that a character like Bridget might cause. Michiko Kakutani writes her review, "It's Like Really Weird: Another Bad-Luck Babe," in the form of a letter to Bridget Jones from Ally McBeal, the American icon to whom many critics have compared Fielding's protagonist. The tone of Kakutani's review seems to be sarcastic; she writes, "It's that . . . it's that we seem to have unwittingly become targets of the same critics, all these mean, awful, nasty naysayers who complain that we're some kind of pre-feminist throwbacks—Stone Age women who just want to be hauled off to a nice warm cave by some cute, dishy guy" (E8). Her comment seems less about the naysayers and more about the pre-feminist throwbacks, and her review seems to question just how healthy it is to identify with Bridget Jones and just how wise it is to hold her up as a "feminist icon."

Perhaps the harshest criticism of Fielding's text comes from American reviewer Alex Kuczynski. Her title "Dear Diary: Get Real" for her column in the *New York Times* sets the tone for a scathing review. She writes, "That's what 'Bridget Jones's Diary' is about: the learned helplessness thrust upon women by advertisers, popular entertainment and, yes, women's magazines," going on to conclude:

> At the end of the book, Bridget is carried away by an inscrutable character who has magically metamorphosed from the dull boor he was for the first 250 pages into a dashing knight, sweeping her out of her family's dysfunctional home on Christmas Day. The pair have never even been on a date, but she gamely joins him in a hotel suite where he makes love to her on—someone call Barbara Cartland! Her material is being ripped off!—a four poster bed. She is surrounded by the trappings of long-sought material comfort, secure in the arms of a faceless Prince Charming who has saved her day.
> 
> But not mine. (6)

Though Kuczynski attempts a concession toward the end of this scathing review, noting that she understands the novel can be read as "satire, a sassy spoof of urban manners," she ultimately rejects that reading, following with "But Bridget is such a sorry spectacle, wallowing in her man-crazed helplessness, that her foolishness cannot be excused" (6). Kuczynski's assessment of Fielding's novel makes a dangerous assumption about both Fielding's novel and the nature of women's popular fiction. To Kuczynski, *Bridget Jones's Diary* merely functions as a fairytale, providing a happily ever after ending for its supposedly single, love hungry, female reader.

Both Kuczynski and Van Slooten favor a reading of the novels which deny the potential to affect positive change for female readers. Van Slooten concludes her essay with the assertion, "[The *Shopaholic* series] allow[s] readers a safe haven to explore their own anxieties and assuage their fears with decadent fantasies. For a mere $10.95, readers can vicariously experience Becky's exploits and create their own fantasies with these alluring, fashionable books" (237). Her conclusion, then, is that Kinsella creates novels which serve as a form of escapism rather than as a cultural critique. Likewise, though Kuczynski nods toward the possibility that Fielding's novel might serve as a critique, she fails to seriously entertain the idea. Rather, she concludes that Fielding merely reproduces the ideologies purported by texts with fairytale endings—from Cinderella to romance novels to romantic comedies.

Van Slooten's criticism of *The Secret Dreamworld of a Shopaholic* and Kuczynski's criticism of *Bridget Jones's Diary*, however, seems a bit short sighted. Admittedly, both novels end happily. Kinsella's novel ends with Becky's discovery of foul play on the part of Flagstaff Life, an investment company that encouraged investors to switch funds, offering the incentive of a carriage clock for doing so. The promotional campaign cheated investors out of a huge windfall that they could have gained if they had remained with their initial investment. Becky writes an expose for the *Daily World*, and her story attracts the attention of the talk show *Morning Coffee*. Becky goes on camera to defend her position and triumphs; she not only gets investors their money back, but she wins the affection of Luke Brandon, her love interest, and a permanent position on the television show as their financial advisor, which provides her with the means to resolve her debt. Bridget's tale ends equally as well. Bridget's mother inadvertently gets herself involved in a scheme which defrauds her friends and family of money; she flees to Portugal with her accomplice, Julio. Mark Darcy, however, rights the situation, and he and Bridget fall in love. The narrative proper ends with Bridget's assertion, "'Don't say 'what', say 'pardon', darling, and do as your mother tells you" (307).[16]

However, as seen above, *The Secret Dreamworld of a Shopaholic* and *Bridget Jones's Diary* can be read as cleverly engaging with contemporary consumer culture mediums, particularly women's magazines. If one reads these texts, then, through this lens, both Fielding's and Kinsella's conclusions further critique this popularly consumed medium. In their endings, Fielding and Kinsella have rewarded their protagonists with the ultimate accessories for their lives—men. A surface reading of the texts would imply both women have actualized the ideal lifestyle purported by women's magazines by following these prescriptive texts. But, as noted throughout this chapter, Fielding's and Kinsella's novels are not to be taken at face value; rather, there is an ironic undercurrent to their texts. While on the surface, Bridget Jones and Becky Bloomwood seem to have achieved a happily ever after ending, reminiscent of the conclusions of Jane Austen's novels or the endings of Hollywood romantic comedies, as readers, we may wonder exactly how long these women will be able to maintain such an existence.[17] Consistently, throughout their novels, Fielding and Kinsella rely on the reader's ability to distance herself from the main characters in order to achieve their comedic effects. While we may be able to identify with Bridget Jones and Becky Bloomwood on some level, at the same time, we are able to acknowledge the absurdity of their actions. Because of this fact, at the end of the novel, it is hard to passively accept that Bridget has made "an *excellent* year's progress" or that

Becky Bloomwood will remain free of debt (310). In reading over Bridget's final summary of the year's vital statistics, we still see Bridget once again stressing her weight. She writes, "*Weight gained 5st 2 lb*" and "*Weight lost 5st 3lb (excellent)*" (310). Though technically, she has lost only one pound more than she has gained all year, ending up the year not much worse off than she began it, she still feels the need to praise herself for her hard work. Though Bridget claims progress, Fielding's closing indicates otherwise in such a way that makes us wonder just how long Bridget's relationship with Mark Darcy will be able sustain itself. Likewise, as readers, we wonder if Becky has indeed "changed" by the end of the novel, as she promises to her roommate Suze when she swears off shopping (304). Kinsella undercuts this declaration with the final letter included in the novel to Becky from Endwich Bank. Though only pages before Becky vowed to visit the bank manager and resolve her debt, the concluding letter reads very much like the opening letter of the novel, "I am sorry to hear you are still suffering from acute agoraphobia;" Becky postpones her meeting in exchange for spending the day with Luke (320). Though as readers we may root for the main characters to make positive changes in their lives, at the same time, both Fielding and Kinsella make it hard to believe that these changes will actually occur. Like the women's magazines that offer us surface appearances, we wonder if the substance of either Bridget's or Becky's lives can be maintained.

Despite this negative press by contemporary critics, *Bridget Jones's Diary* and *The Secret Dreamworld of a Shopaholic* do offer serious critiques of contemporary consumer culture mediums—particularly women's magazines. In crafting protagonists addicted to following the advice offered by these publications and by portraying heroines who exhibit exaggerated consumer behaviors, both *Bridget Jones's Diary* and *The Secret Dreamworld of a Shopaholic* deconstruct the consumer ideologies encouraged by such publications. These texts, then, serve as a warning to real life readers of the pitfalls they might face if they were to follow the advice of women's magazines too closely. Being a v.g. consumer then, the texts imply, means being a bit more savvy than either Bridget or Becky are when making consumption decisions.

Chapter Three
# The Girls' Guide to Breaking *The Rules*

"When an emotionally painful event occurs, and we tell ourselves that it is our fault, we are actually saying that we have control of it: if we change, the pain will stop. This dynamic is behind much of the self-blame in women who love too much."

—Robin Norwood, *Women Who Love Too Much: When You Keep Wishing and Hoping He'll Change* (1985)

Ellen Fein and Sherrie Schneider, two married, American women, were catapulted into the public eye in 1996. Within the span of a year, they were featured in publications ranging from the *New York Times* and *People Weekly* magazine, and they appeared on such television programs as *Dateline* and *The Oprah Winfrey Show*.[1] *Saturday Night Live* even spoofed the duo on their popular late night comedy program ("*The Rules* Backlash"). What was responsible for this media saturation and Fein and Schneider's newfound celebrity status? A little dating, self-help book called *The Rules: Time-tested Secrets for Capturing the Heart of Mr. Right*.[2]

Fein and Schneider's self-help book, published "Three decades after Helen Gurley Brown's [editor of *Cosmopolitan* magazine, 1965–1996] classic *Sex and the Single Girl*" (Gleick 58), operated in opposition to Brown's declaration "that men are 'cheaper emotionally and a lot more fun by the dozen'" (Gleick 58). Rather, it implied that "all that solo flying seems to be less than thrilling" (Gleick 58) and provided its single readers with thirty-five rules to follow when dating that promised "if you continue to do *The Rules* at every opportunity and pray for patience, you will eventually meet and marry the man of your dreams" (Fein and Schneider 21). From its onset, Fein and Schneider's book was read, debated, disputed, sometimes followed, and sometimes rejected by women and men all across America. Some women believed that rules such as "Be a 'Creature Unlike

Any Other'" (22) and "Be Honest But Mysterious" were empowering tenets for women, forcing them to focus on themselves as opposed to the men in their lives (99). Other women scoffed at the publication, finding such rules as "Don't Accept a Saturday Night Date after Wednesday" (51) or "Stop Dating Him if He Doesn't Buy You a Romantic Gift for Your Birthday or Valentine's Day" to be arbitrary and ridiculous (70). Die-hard fans claimed that following *The Rules* had enabled them to become married within the year while the opposition argued that game playing would never result in lasting relationships.[3]

Critics were equally divided. Writing for *America*, Catherine Walsh argued, "The rules encourage women to take responsibility for their lives and not be victims in romantic relationships" (9). Cristina Nehring of the *Atlantic Monthly* disagreed, "In fact, the assumption in all this literature is that its audience is not pleasure-seeking but desperate; not confident, adventuresome, and looking for tips on how to have a good time, but frightened and looking for hints on how to avoid disaster—how to avoid further time as a single girl" (142). *The Rules* had become a cultural phenomenon; Elizabeth Gleick, a writer for *Time*, stated, "*The Rules* is not just a book; it's a movement" (58). Around the country, *Rules* seminars began emerging, and Fein and Schneider even offered phone consultations for readers looking for additional advice not covered in their book.[4]

The mixed reviews by both readers and critics that greeted *The Rules* were not an uncommon reaction for self-help books, particularly relationship manuals. Editorial reviews from Amazon.com of John Gray's self-help book, *Men Are From Mars, Women Are From Venus: A Practical Guide for Improving Communication and Getting What You Want in Your Relationships* (1992) range from the *Library's Journal* assessment that "Gray addresses the topic of male-female relationships with humor, insight and understanding" to *Publishers Weekly's* assertion, "While graphically illustrative, the hyperbolic, overextended comparisons, particularly in the chapters that refer to men as rubber bands and women as waves, significantly detract from Gray's realistic insights." In *Women and Self-Help Culture: Reading Between the Lines*, Wendy Simonds discusses the critical reception of self-help books implicitly about gender, tying the critics' responses to our societal assumptions about women's reading practices.[5] Her sociological study of female, self-help readers points to the disparity between critics' expectations about the harmful effects of these texts and women's actual critical reading strategies. Simonds details the critical discussion concerning the merits of self-help books that took place in the late 1980s and early 1990s:

> Commentary on self-help books addressed to women has made its way into editorial columns, feature stories, and even comic strips . . . experts have been cited in feature stories, voicing the various charges that are often leveled against current self-help books: In a *New York Times* feature article on self-help for women, Susan Reverby explains that "women read these books because they are having genuine difficulty in relationships . . . But what they get are simple psychobabble answers" (Lawson 1986) . . . *Vogue* writer Susan Bolotin exhorts, "It's time that women said no to the majority of self-help books . . . It's time they said no to feeling responsible for everybody's happiness . . ."(1987: 254) . . . At best, critics doubt the promised effect of self-help books on readers and see them as a waste of time. At worst, they label them as politically backward, narrow, and even potentially damaging to more gullible readers. (172–74)

Simonds's observation is that, generally speaking, critics see the genre negatively—"At best . . . a waste of time . . . at worst politically backward, narrow, and . . . damaging" (174). But Simonds goes on to say that her "readers do not necessarily turn to self-help books because they expect the books to deliver all they promise. Readers read because they hope to find some comfort, some insight, some information in self-help literature" (174). In other words, Simonds argues that her readers are more discerning than critics often give them credit for; these women, Simonds observes, are capable of critical reading, applying what they find useful, and discarding that which they find essentially unhelpful.

Chick lit authors, as we saw in the proceeding chapter, often present the readers of their texts with critiques of women's manuals. Fielding and Kinsella both satirize female, consumer behavior in their novels in order to question the consumer ideologies being offered by women's magazines. Like Fielding and Kinsella, authors Melissa Bank (*The Girls' Guide to Hunting and Fishing*, 1999) and Laura Zigman (*Animal Husbandry*, 1998) assess another popularly consumed advice manual—the self-help book. In their works, which incidentally were published a few years after *The Rules* reached their height of popularity, Bank and Zigman write female, main characters searching for explanations about the way love works and hoping to make sense of their past relationships, much like the real-life readers of self-help books.[6] Instead of mocking their characters' reading practices, however, Bank and Zigman present their real-life readers with discriminating, fictional self-help readers. Bank's depiction of her main character Jane

Rosenal and Zigman's depiction of her main character Jane Goodall reverse the readers' expectations of the passive, female consumer of self-help texts by presenting women readers who actively reject the advice offered by these manuals. In doing so, Bank and Zigman address the limitations that self-help books have for readers and offer their readers an alternative "reading model" or "model reader." As a result, these chick lit authors create fictional self-help books for real-life readers that stand in opposition to already existent self-help texts.

Though self-help books are widely read and distributed (from bookstores to supermarkets), little scholarship has been written about the genre.[7] In one of the earliest critical studies, *Psychobabble: Fast Talk and Quick Cure in the Era of Feeling* (1977), R.D. Rosen puzzles over what he sees as a trend in the late 1960s and early 1970s in which Americans became increasingly cognizant of their emotions and searched for a vocabulary that would enable them to express such feelings. Though Rosen's book begins by examining self-help books by David Viscott, he also devotes time to trends in counseling such as co-counseling, rebirthing, and primal therapy. Like Rosen, Kenneth C. Davis's book *Two-Bit Culture: The Paperbacking of America* (1984) addresses much more than the self-help publishing industry. Davis's book examines the impact that mass market paperback books had on the general, American reading public, and he contributes much of that impact to Pocket Books, a publishing company launched in 1939 that distributed paperback books to "drugstores, chain stores, bus stations, and airport terminals" (xii). As author Wendy Simonds notes in *Women and Self-Help Culture: Reading Between the Lines* (1992): "Before Pocket Books appeared on the scene, hardcover books were quite difficult to find and expensive to own, and earlier schemes to market paperbacks had never been successful on a large scale" (98). Pocket Books' impact on the market, then, was profound, and even today, the company continues to be one of the major producers of self-help books.

Steven Starker's 1989 *Oracle at the Supermarket: The American Preoccupation with Self-Help Books* presents the most comprehensive analysis of self-help books as a whole, tracing their origins back to "the traditions and values of Protestant New England" (13). Starker's book historicizes the genre from pre-eighteenth century England up until the early 1980s; he details the major movements and identifies the key texts during each era. Starker explains that the self-help movement as we know it today has its roots in the 1920s where "psychology and psychiatry [began] moving into a central place in American healing and popular culture" (59). From there, the genre took off in the 1930s, in part because of the development of Pocket Books.

The 1940s saw the publication of some of the first blockbuster books such as Rabbi Liebman's *Peace of Mind* (1946) and Dr. Benjamin Spock's *The Common Sense Book of Baby and Child Care* (1946). Self-help books like Spock's present their readers with "expertise on medical, psychological, spiritual, [and] financial" matters, and books that address these issues continued to be published throughout the 1950s and 1960s (Starker 1).

While all types of self-help books continued to be produced in the 1970s, books emphasizing sexuality, love, and marriage began to really take off during that decade. As Starker explains, this phenomenon: "transformed [sex] into one aspect of enhancing the 'self'" (91). Thus, books that dealt with sex and, in turn, relationship maintenance became wildly successful, and in the 1980s, scores of self-help, relationship manuals were produced. Among them were such titles as Connell Cowan and Melvyn Kinder's *Smart Women, Foolish Choices: Finding the Right Men, Avoiding the Wrong Ones* (1985) and *Women Men Love, Women Men Leave* (1987); Robin Norwood's *Women Who Love Too Much: When You Keep Wishing and Hoping He'll Change* (1985), Susan Forward and Joan Torres's *Men Who Hate Women and the Women Who Love Them: When Loving Hurts and You Don't Know Why* (1986), and Steven Carter and Julia Sokol's *Men Who Can't Love: When a Man's Fear Makes Him Run From Commitment (and What a Smart Woman Can Do About It)* (1987).

Though the self-help industry did not start as a "gendered" industry, beginning in the 1970s, self-help publishers began targeting predominantly female readers, and the popular perception was that the genre existed primarily for women. In fact, in a 1987 interview for *Vogue*, then vice president and editorial director of Bantam Books, Stephen Rubin, commented, "'Men don't buy these kinds of books'" (Bolotin 254). In 1992, Wendy Simonds's *Women and Self-Help Culture: Reading Between the Lines* revealed that the real-life readers of these self-help texts recognized that they were the genre's target audience:

> Self-help literature is a genre that participants recognize as existing specifically for women. This is true even for self-help books that are not overtly marketed toward a female audience (books that do not have the word 'women' in their titles and that do not have obviously 'feminine' covers). Participants see women as either uniquely equipped with positive abilities that enable us to use this kind of book, or as uniquely disadvantaged or incompetent in a society that discriminates against women, and thus induces us to turn to self-help books as a crutch for guidance. (34)

Simonds's sociological study was one of the first critical studies that examined the gendered nature of self-help texts.[8] Published on the heels of the 1980s boom in relationship manuals, Simonds's book examines why self-help literature has been heavily criticized, why it has been relegated to low culture, and whether this relegation has anything to do with the fact that it has been marked female. In interviewing real readers of self-help texts, Simonds explores the connections between self-help reading, gender identity, women's reading practices, and their consumption behaviors.

While *Women and Self-Help Culture* chronicles the real-life reading habits of self-help readers, Simonds's book also gives insight into who the constructed reader of these relationship manuals are. Though the basis of Simond's chapter "Making It Readable: Editors and Authors of Self-Help Books" consists of interviews with editors and authors of self-help books, what emerges from these interviews is a better sense of the intended audience of these texts. For instance, one editor comments, "'... I think, as a rule, women are more introspective than men. We have been trained ... to be more sensitive, more nurturing, more aware of others' feelings'" (114). This comment reveals some of the assumptions that this editor has of her target audience; not only are women biologically "'more introspective,'" but they have been socially conditioned to be "'more sensitive, more nurturing, more aware of others' feelings'" (114). These qualities, according to this editor, are some of the reasons why self-help books have resonated with women. And, it is these qualities that might be considered when a target audience is imagined for a particular manuscript.

Reviewers of self-help books written in the 1980s characterized this intended audience even further, reading the self-help texts themselves to determine how those manuals characterized their women readers. In her article for the *New York Times*, Carol Lawson determined that "As a group they paint a picture of contemporary women that is not flattering" and that "in a great many cases" they depicted women who "will cling to a thoroughly destructive relationship rather than be alone and without a man" (C26). Susan Bolotin, in writing for *Vogue*, and Ann Landi, of *Mademoiselle*, found self-help books to be equally dangerous. Both writers felt that the texts put undue pressure on women to fix the existent problems in their relationships. Bolotin felt that the books contained "an antifeminist message: women should feel responsible for their failure to change their attitudes established by millennia of experience" (246) while Landi asserted "The bottom line in all these books is the implication that women are in charge of relationships, it's our responsibility to a) find a man and then b) fix him or leave him if he's not satisfactory" (247).

In "Shrinking Violets and Caspar Milquetoasts: Shyness and Heterosexuality From the Roles of the Fifties to *The Rules* of the Nineties," Patricia McDaniel echoes Bolotin's and Landi's observations. McDaniel's article examines the "dramatic shift in the representation of white middle-class women's shyness, contrasting it with representations of white middle-class men's shyness . . . focusing on the ideological implications for heterosexual power dynamics" (547). Though the self-help books, etiquette manuals, and advice books that she uses to back up her claims all represent male and female shyness differently throughout the 1950s until the 1990s, McDaniel argues that what remains consistent is the fact that women were, and still are, as Bolotin and Landi have observed, responsible for the "'emotional labor'" involved in maintaining these relationships (552). This cultural belief, then, has contributed to self-help books being targeted at women—the demographic who "needed" them the most. The titles of the self-help books from the 1980s support McDaniel's observation. Steven Carter and Julia Sokol's book *Men Who Can't Love: When A Man's Fear Makes Him Run from Commitment (and What a Smart Woman Can Do About It)* implies that though it is the men who cannot love and cannot commit, it is the "smart woman" who can and should do something about it. Likewise, such titles as Connell Cowan and Melvyn Kinder's *Smart Women, Foolish Choices: Finding the Right Men, Avoiding the Wrong Ones* and Norwood's *Women Who Love Too Much: When You Keep Wishing and Hoping He'll Change* indicate that even though men may be responsible for problems that might occur, women are the ones who should read the book and strive to correct those problems.

Fein and Schneider's book *The Rules: Time-tested Secrets for Capturing the Heart of Mr. Right*, though published in 1995, is written in much the same spirit as the books from the 1980s that preceded it. Like these other self-help texts, Fein and Schneider's book emphasizes that it is a woman's responsibility to find the perfect man and maintain a relationship with him; she is the one who can capture Mr. Right if, and only if, she does *The Rules* correctly.[9] Fein and Schneider establish pre-existing male behavior and, in doing so, imply that men are exempt from making adjustments. For instance, Fein and Schneider make such declarations as "Men like women. Don't act like a man, even if you are head of your own company. Let him open the door. Be feminine" (19) and "Men love a challenge—that's why they play sports, fight wars, and raid corporations" (36). Yet, they never once suggest that men can change this behavior. In fact, Rule 18 advises, "Don't Expect a Man to Change or Try to Change Him." Rather, women are responsible for making modifications to their behavior. Even if you are the type of woman who likes to share your feelings with your boyfriend, Fein and Schneider advise against opening up too fast in Rule 19. Like the self-help books of the 1980s, *The Rules* asserts that women perform the emotional labor necessary to begin and sustain a lasting, long-term relationship.

While Fein and Schneider were dictating to women readers proper dating etiquette, chick lit authors were questioning just how realistic, and effective, this advice actually was by depicting characters who question, and often act in opposition, to these relationship handbooks. Writing in the first person, Helen Fielding and Sophie Kinsella created passive consumers who ingested the advice offered to them without interrogating how fitting, or ill-fitting, it might be to their lives. Chick lit authors such as Carol Wolper (*The Cigarette Girl*, 1999), Melissa Bank (*The Girls' Guide to Hunting and Fishing*), and Laura Zigman (*Animal Husbandry*) use first person narration, however, in a decidedly different way. Rather than creating characters that exhibit exaggerated consumer behavior, these authors depict sympathetic heroines struggling to make sense of the advice manuals that surround them. In writing characters that narrate their day-to-day struggles to live by their own, rather than prescribed, standards, these chick lit authors present their readers with alternative model readers—readers who are capable of successfully navigating the advice offered to them by these self-help books.

When Carol Wolper's book, *The Cigarette Girl*, first came out in 1999, *Entertainment Weekly* deemed it, "Snappy . . . truly engaging . . . for everyone who thought . . . *The Rules* the handbook of the devil" while Bret Easton Ellis alluded to both John Gray's relationship manual *Men Are From Mars, Women Are From Venus* and Fein and Schneider's handbook when he commented: "Carol Wolper is from Mars, not Venus. Her novel is at once a cool insider's look at modern romance and a shrewd take on the movie business in L.A. There's no whimsy here, no apologies, no rules."[10] Their comments immediately characterized Wolper's text as reactionary—speaking out against the dating manuals that had recently proliferated the market.

Though Wolper's text primarily critiques the movie industry, Wolper also evaluates the trend of self-help books through her discerning character Elizabeth West who, at one point in the novel, notes that she finds the advice offered by these books to be both ridiculous and at odds with how she herself plans on living her life:

> I think I should stop right here and say I know this is not what I'm supposed to do. I'm not supposed to be so aggressive with men. How many books out there advise women that the way to a man's heart is through withholding? (21)[11]

In this passage, Elizabeth notes the way in which her own behavior differs from the behaviors encouraged by self-help books. In fact, she finds her inability to identify with these texts is so great that she finds the term "self-help" to be a mislabeling; discovering none of her "self" in these texts.

The label that Elizabeth wishes to adopt instead, that of the "withholding section," is very telling of the genre as a whole but particularly relevant to Fein and Schneider's book. *The Rules*, in particular, encourages women to help themselves by "withholding" from their partners. As Fein explained to Oprah Winfrey when she appeared on her October 11, 1996 show:

> It's is like a job interview. You don't open yourself up on a job interview and say, "Well, you know, actually, I'm on unemployment right now; I haven't had a job in six years, but I'd really like to work for you." You're a little mysterious, and that's how it is on a date. ("Dating Rules" 7)

Fein and Schneider not only encourage their readers to withhold emotionally, but they also advise withholding sexually. Though, in "Rule 15: Don't Rush into Sex and Other Rules for Intimacy," they do acknowledge that one might be inclined to have sex with her date—"Now you might argue that you don't mind having sex with him on the first or second date and taking your chances, that it's okay with you if he doesn't call again because you're both grown-ups and you can take your lumps" (81)—they quickly follow with the assertion, "We know from experience, of course, that most girls who say this are lying to themselves. Deep down inside it's not okay with a woman if she sleeps with a man and he doesn't call" (81). They go on to stress the advantages of playing it safe and encourage woman, once in bed, to "stay emotionally cool no matter how hot the sex gets" and to also "wait a good amount of time before you begin holding lengthy seminars about your needs during sex," tenets which seems to deny women of the pleasure they might get from the physical act (82). Their book, then, stresses both the emotional and physical ways that a woman might "withhold" from her date in order, ironically, to further a connection between herself and a man.

Wolper responds to texts like *The Rules* by constructing a character who recognizes the limits of emotionally "withholding" and who acts out against this advice by being sexually aggressive toward men. In doing so, Wolper writes a character whose behavior stands in direct opposition to the feminine behaviors encouraged in self-help books like Fein and Schneider's. Rather than depicting Elizabeth performing the emotional labor in her relationships, Wolper chooses, instead, to have her focus on developing a sexual relationship with men—an emphasis that self-help authors like Fein and Schneider rarely address in their relationship manuals. At one point in the novel, Wolper has Elizabeth reflect:

> Sometimes I wonder. Did I do a Rip Van Winkle in reverse? Did I awake after decades of sleeping to find we've drifted back to the fifties? Let me go on record right here and say that I never have been and never will be a *Rules* girl. Zone or no zone, I refuse to turn my love life into a strategic arms agreement. If their advice is don't fuck him for the first four dates, my advice is don't fuck him for the first four hours. (22)

In her closing sentence, Wolper underscores the unrealistic nature of manuals such as *The Rules* through Elizabeth's inability to relate to them. First, her use of the word "fuck" and her declaration that she doesn't "fuck him for the first four hours" is in direct odds with the sexual ideologies of the 1950s—ideologies stressed in Fein and Schneider's manual. In choosing to stress Elizabeth's sexual assertiveness, Wolper characterizes Elizabeth as a woman at odds with Fein and Schneider's sexual advice—advice which boldly declares "But what if you like sex a lot too . . . You will just have to exercise a bit of self-restraint . . . Why risk him having him call you easy (and think of you that way) when he's talking to his buddies in the locker room the next day?" (81). Wolper responds to these recommendations, then, by having her character directly mock their advice and develop her own set of rules—in this case sexual rules—which are in direct opposition to theirs. In constructing Elizabeth in this way, then, Wolper exposes the limitations that these self-help books have for real-life readers who identify with Elizabeth.

Melissa Bank's *The Girls' Guide to Hunting and Fishing* presents a character similar to Elizabeth West in that Jane Rosenal also rejects the tenets offered by *The Rules* in the short story entitled "The Girls' Guide to Hunting and Fishing" that concludes Bank's collection. Jane, unlike Elizabeth, is much more conflicted when it comes to determining the usefulness of manuals like Fein and Schneider's. Bank's collection of short stories, then, becomes a chronicle of Jane's attempts to decipher such manuals as a means of finding the perfect "guide" for her life. And, in having Jane work out her own feelings about such self-help texts, Bank constructs a fictional self-help manual for her female readers. With *The Girls' Guide to Hunting and Fishing*, Bank offers her readers an alternative "reading model" as well as a decidedly different "model reader." Instead of depicting the female reader of self-help books as a passive consumer who mindlessly ingests the advice offered to her, Bank constructs a more discerning reader of these manuals in order to challenge our perceptions of the constructed reader created by the writers of these self-help texts.

Bank's work of fiction consists of seven short stories, five of which center directly on the character of Jane Rosenal.[12] The text begins with the story entitled "Advanced Beginners" which details in the first person the introduction of Jane's brother Henry's first serious girlfriend to both Jane and her family; the collection concludes with the title story "The Girls' Guide to Hunting and Fishing" where an adult Jane encounters the potential for a lasting relationship with a dog lover named Robert. Advice takes all forms and plays an integral part in Bank's text. Jane's friends and family consistently offer her advice concerning how to live her life. Additionally, Bank begins each section of her novel with a quotation from a variety of advice manuals, some of which are clearly self-help books. In addition to *The Rules*, Bank quotes from D.D. *Lessenberry's 20th Century Typewriting*, Amy Vanderbilt's *Book of Etiquette*, *The Sailor's Handbook*, edited by Halsey C. Herreshoff, and the *Junior Girl Scout Handbook*. Additionally, she quotes from Betty Friedan's *The Feminine Mystique*, J's *The Sensuous Woman*, and Benjamin Spock's *The Common Sense Book of Baby and Child Care*, and Ellen Fein and Sherrie Schneider's *The Rules*, all books labeled self-help by various cultural critics.[13]

Bank's text begins with the poem "One Art" by Elizabeth Bishop, which appears even before Bank's table of contents. The poem details the "art of losing" and concludes with the stanza: "—Even losing you (the joking voice, a gesture/I love) I shan't have lied. It's evident/the art of losing's not too hard to master/though it may look like (*Write* it!) like disaster." Critics of Bishop's concentrate mainly upon the form of the poem, noting how the villanelle, an intensely structured form, is in direct odds with the subject matter of the poem—overwhelmingly and oftentimes uncontrollable emotion that accompanies loss.[14] The poet attempts to create a speaker who can manage this emotion through carefully controlled writing; the result is a feeling of tension for the subject is at odds with the form of the poem. The closing of the poem presents a speaker so besieged by "disaster" that she has to command herself ("*Write* it!") to articulate it. Bishop's speaker is not unlike Bank's protagonist Jane, who suffers many losses throughout the book—the loss of her brother to his new girlfriend, the loss of her boyfriend Jamie and then her boyfriend Archie, the death of her aunt Rita and subsequently her father, and the loss of Jane's own expectations about the way her life will turn out in exchange for the way her life actually is.

Like the speaker of Bishop's poem, Jane desperately struggles for control, often glibly responding to tragedy in the hopes of not having to confront her real emotion. For instance, when Jane quits her job as an editor after the death of her father, Archie, a man twenty-eight years her senior whom she has moved in with, insists that she comes to work for him. Her response "'I could bring you up on charges for that . . . Work harassment in the sexual place'" is a typical glib response that masks all of the undercurrents of pain contained beneath Jane's surface (196). One of Jane's chief struggles with her relationship with Archie is that he expects her to live up to his expectations rather than allowing her to follow her own dreams. So, his insistence on her coming to work for him is another way that he attempts to control her life. Bank, however, does not portray Jane as one who reflects on these facts; rather, she responds flippantly as a means of masking her pain. Like Bishop's writing style, Bank's style is carefully controlled, revealing minimal detail. Each short story is broken up into small, tight sections, lasting no more than a page or two at the most. Bank relates mostly action as opposed to feeling. When Jane's father dies, Bank simply writes, "My father died later that night" without any further direct reflection on what that fact means to Jane (185). Bank's crafting of Jane as a speaker who relates exceedingly painful events in a straightforward manner mimics Bishop's writing style, and Bank draws that initial connection for her readers by beginning her text with Bishop's poem. Like the cover lines on women's magazines or the italicized sections of *Bridget Jones's Diary*, Bishop's poem clues the reader into the major themes of Bank's novel and helps in characterizing Bank's narrator.

Bank not only draws upon the writing style of Elizabeth Bishop, but as mentioned earlier, her text is heavily influenced by advice manuals, including but not limited to self-help books. Not only do Bank's epigrams come from popular advice manuals, but certain characters that Jane comes in contact with also use the "distinctive linguistic devices" of etiquette manuals (Foster 3). As Gwendolyn Audrey Foster explains in *Troping the Body: Gender, Etiquette, and Performance*, the etiquette writer uses such devices and "speaks to the reader in sweeping declarative statements" in order to "console, validate, or chasten the reader, assuming a personal relationship not unlike that of an older, and presumably wiser, family member" (3). Jane's aunt Rita addresses her in such a way, advising Jane to "'Look up when you walk'" (77) and "'When you're out . . . try to appear captivated'" (79). Her mother encourages her to call home if found alone with a boy who is out of control, and her gym teacher tells her to "*Go down on all fours and eat grass*" in order to avoid rape (63). Jane uses this advice much in the same way that a reader might use a self-help book. When given advice, like that from Aunt Rita, Jane honestly attempts to abide by it, hoping that it will make her a better person. And, when Jane actively seeks advice from others, she follows it. For instance, when her friend Donna suggests that she start reading a self-help book entitled *How to Meet and Marry Mr. Right*, Jane goes to the bookstore to purchase the book and obediently follows the rules. In nearly every story, Bank depicts Jane being offered, and soliciting, suggestions for her own self-improvement.

Bank's character, however, soon discovers that she has trouble following the advice that others give her, though it is ostensibly simple and straightforward. For instance, in fifth grade when Jane asks her mother for suggestions on how to make a boy like you, Jane's mother advises, "'Just be yourself'" (242). Though Jane's mother matter-of-factly tells her what to do, her advice confuses an adolescent Jane who isn't exactly sure what it means to be yourself. At other times, Jane feels that the advice she encounters is at odds with what she herself believes. For instance, when trying to follow the rules of *How To Meet and Marry Mr. Right*, Jane often finds herself feeling uncomfortable, almost as if she is performing expected behaviors rather than just being herself as her mother had earlier advised. Bank writes a tension into Jane's character that arises from the conflict that Jane often sees between the advice offered to her by her family and friends, the books that she reads, and what Jane herself thinks.

Like Wolper, Bank uses her main character's sexuality as a vehicle for critiquing the self-help texts referenced in her collection. Bank's character consistently encounters advice that encourages her to deny and/or suppress her sexuality, just as Fein and Schneider's text does. For instance, as mentioned earlier, Jane's mother offers a sixteen-year-old Jane advice for dealing with "boys out of control," stating "*Call us and we'll come get you*" (63). Though her mother wishes to be helpful, her comment reveals her own gendered assumptions about sex. By implying that it is only the boys whose hormones will rage out of control, Jane's mother, much like Fein and Schneider's self-help book, completely negates female sexuality. While boys' sexual desire is so intense that it requires calling upon an outside force to control it, girls' sexual desire is completely absent. Additionally, Jane's mother's advice also presents Jane with the idea that sex is potentially frightening; desire, if not controlled, can produce a dangerous situation. Her gym teacher reinforces this sentiment with his earlier warning about how to avoid rape. Bank also makes this direct equation between danger and sexuality when she has a sixteen-year-old Jane express her apprehension about her increasing breast size:

> . . . all of the sudden it seemed, there my breasts were, and my mother and I kept having to go to Lord & Taylor for bigger bras. Boys gave me more attention now, and it made me nervous. My breasts seemed to say

something about me that I didn't want said. My Achilles' heel, they put me in constant danger of humiliation. (21)

Instead of being pleased or flattered as a result of this newfound attention from boys, Jane is nervous. Bank further emphasizes this connection by crafting her following sentence so that it actually contains the phrase "put me in constant danger." In this instance, Bank chooses to make the danger even more specific to Jane; now, instead of "boys out of control" or rapists as the actor, Bank presents Jane internalizing that female sexuality can be responsible for producing a potentially problematic situation, and she shows the way in which she wishes to suppress it, pushing it down so as to avoid humiliation. In the passage that follows this observation, Bank reveals the connection that Jane sees between her body, sex, and love. Jane observes:

> My theory was that if you had breasts, boys wanted to have sex with you . . . Whereas if you had a beautiful face, like Julia [her brother's girlfriend], boys fell in love with you . . . The sex that you had would be about love. (21)

Here, Bank once again underscores Jane's dissatisfaction with her developing body—a dissatisfaction that implies Jane's belief that there is a "good" and "bad" body for women to have. Bank writes that Jane's "breasts seemed to say something about [her] that [she] didn't want said," and Jane's reflection implies that what she didn't want said had something to do with her sexuality (21). She feels that her blossoming body signifies that she is a sexual creature, not a woman to love but rather a woman who men only want to have sex with.

Jane's anxiety about not being loved is a continuing theme throughout the book. At the onset of the book, Jane comments on the fate of her neighbor, noting: "Oliver Biddle, who was middle-aged, yet lived with his parents" was "my own personal cautionary tale walking a miniature schnauzer" (17–18). She elaborates, claiming, "Oliver Biddle was who you became if you couldn't find anyone to love except your parents" (18). Bank evokes Jane's childhood observations and language in her next short story "The Floating House." Jane and her boyfriend Jamie have been asked to spend some time with Jamie's gorgeous, ex-girlfriend Bella. When Jane confesses her insecurities to her brother Henry, he notes that even "the best man . . . will be attracted to other women" (60). Jane's response, "I hear this as another fact I am too old not to know. More proof of how unprepared I am to love anyone," recalls her earlier comment concerning Oliver Biddle's fate (60). Jane fears that her inability to accept the possibility that Jamie can be attracted to Bella without acting on it means that she is unprepared for love and the inevitable result, she fears, is that she will be left on her own.

This fear is compounded as her perceptions about love are continually challenged. Though Jane observes that Julia is the type of woman that men fall in love with, her brother eventually breaks it off with her. His reason, that there was too much of an age gap, sounds like a poor excuse to Jane and leaves her puzzled. At the end of the chapter, she reflects, "I didn't know what happened between him and Julia. It scared me to think that my brother had failed at loving someone. I had no idea myself how to do it" (43). From the onset of the book, Bank sets up the expectation that Jane is puzzled about how love works, and as readers, we see that the remainder of the book revolves around Jane's attempts to forge lasting relationships with men.

Bank illuminates Jane's confusion through her choice of quotations; the quotes that begin each chapter are often at odds with what actually happens to Jane in the story. For instance, Bank begins the story "My Old Man" with two quotes that are in direct odds with the way that Jane actually conducts herself. Bank chooses a quote from Betty Friedan's *The Feminine Mystique* that reads, "The only way for a woman, as for a man, to know herself as a person, is by creative work of her own" and a quote from *The Sensuous Woman* which reads:

> Pin up on your bed, your mirror, your wall, a sign lady, until you know it in every part of your being: *We were destined to delight, excite and satisfy the male of the species.*
> Real women know this. (75)

The story that follows recounts Jane's meeting of Archie Knox, the infamous New York editor and a man twenty-eight years Jane's senior. Bank reveals in this story that Archie and Jane are involved in a very paternal relationship in which Archie consistently criticizes Jane's choices. Archie warns Jane that her relationship with her boyfriend Jamie is damaging, and he encourages her to break up with him. Archie also feels that Jane should strive to be more successful in her career, moving beyond her role as an editorial assistant.

Not only is Jane unable to find "creative work of her own," but she is also, as we have seen from earlier analysis of Jane's body image issues, unable to "delight, excite and satisfy." In this story, Bank's unfolding of Jane and Archie's courtship reveals that Jane's perception of herself is in direct conflict with J's advice. Interestingly enough, what initially attracts Jane to Archie is not his looks or personality but his date—the type of woman Jane admires and hopes, on some level, to be. After thinking that an older woman and her husband are staring at her, admiring her beauty, Jane realizes that, in actuality, they are looking directly behind her, and she turns around to see:

> You noticed her limbs first, long and tanned, and then her eyes and cheekbones and lips, perfect, like in magazines. She had on a hot-pink minidress with straps as thin as string . . . He was teasing her, and she said something like, *Okay*, and she flexed her arm. He squeezed her biceps, and I saw, and faintly heard, him whistle. She laughed and he kept his hand there, around her beautiful arm. (78–79)

Though Archie is admittedly handsome, Jane remembers and is most impressed by the woman's looks and her "beautiful arm." Jane's admiration in this moment mirrors the envy that Bridget Jones shows for the models in magazines; while Bridget aspires to be thinner, more like her ideal, Jane covets the look that Archie's date possesses. Knowing Jane's dissatisfaction with her own appearance, then, as readers we are left to wonder if part of Jane's motivation for dating Archie lies in the fact that she feels she can become this woman through him. Just as women follow the advice of women's magazines, hoping to achieve the ideal promised within its pages, Jane's plan for improving her self-image is to date the man who dates the models. Perhaps she reasons that she must be "good enough" if Archie wants her after having been with such an extraordinarily good-looking woman. Bank's depiction of Jane, here, reveals that she is less than a "real" woman in J's terms since she is consistently unable to recognize the way in which she herself might "delight, excite and satisfy." This inability to appreciate what she has to offer is compounded by the fact that Archie is impotent; his inability to perform sexually once again deprives Jane of having any positive feelings about her own sexuality.

Bank concludes her collection of short stories with the title story "The Girls' Guide to Hunting and Fishing." In this story, Bank presents her reader with a decidedly single Jane who lives with her dog Jezebel, a detail that calls to mind Jane's fear of eventually becoming Oliver Biddle. And, Bank's parallel between Jane and Oliver Biddle emphasizes the perceived severity of Jane's situation. As a way of potentially rectifying her single state, Jane decides to take drastic measures—consulting a *Rules* type self-help book called *How to Meet and Marry Mr. Right*, a title that brings to mind *The Rules* subtitle, "Time-tested Secrets for Capturing the Heart of Mr. Right." Bank furthers the parallel between Jane's self-help book and *The Rules* by setting her story up with a quotation from Fein and Schneider's dating manual:

> ... [W]hen you're with a man you like, be quiet and mysterious, act ladylike, cross your legs and smile. Don't talk so much. Wear black sheer pantyhose and hike up your skirt to entice the opposite sex! You might feel offended by these suggestions and argue this will suppress your intelligence or vivacious personality. You may feel that you won't be able to be yourself, but men will love it. (225)

Bank's choice of quotes highlights the manipulative nature of Fein and Schneider's suggestions so when Donna, Jane's friend who introduces her to *How to Meet and Marry Mr. Right,* describes the book as "'a guide to manipulation,'" as readers the parallel between the actual and the fictional is further cemented (229). Bank's story, then, centers on Jane's relationship to this ill-fitting text and around her attempts to find relationship advice that is more suited to her character.

At this point in Bank's collection, Jane has endured several difficult relationships, perhaps the most difficult with Archie whose alcoholism and sexual dysfunction has made for a tumultuous affair. Because of her romantic history, Jane has a fairly bleak outlook on love. Though she has met and connected with Robert at her friend's wedding, she comments, "... What if [Robert] does call? I'll just mess it up. The only relationships I haven't wrecked right away were the ones that wrecked me later" (240). Her insecurity about relationships prompts her to go to the bookstore where she forgoes fiction in exchange for self-help. There, she finds the book that her friend Donna told her about, and once home, she begins to read it, imagining the authors:

> There isn't a photograph of the authors, Faith Kurtz-Abromowitz and Bonnie Merrill, but after a few pages, I see them perfectly ... I have known them my entire life: in gym class, playing volleyball, they were the ones clapping their hands and shouting, 'Side out and rotate—our team is really great!' In college, Bonnie was my Secret Santa. In personnel offices, when I joked about my application phobia, Faith was the one who said, "Just do the best you can." (240)

The women that Jane envisions are the women that she has always strived to be, versions of the managed woman on Archie's arm. Jane not only imagines what the two authors might look like, but she also breathes them into being. As she makes decisions about how to conduct herself in her relationship with Robert, she imagines that Faith and Bonnie follow her around, offering suggestions as to how to conduct her affair. They tell her to "'be the one who gets off the phone first'" and to "'Make him long for you'" (246). Though Jane expresses concern about turning to these women for advice, she also acknowledges that their book promises its reader the ultimate prize—"'the man of your dreams!'" (240). And, since Jane has not had what she considers a successful relationship, she feels she has nothing to lose by reading and following the rules offered.

In having Jane go so far as to imagine what Faith and Bonnie look like, Bank illuminates some of the larger issues that are at work in self-help books in general and, more particularly, in Fein and Schneider's dating manual. Just as Jane is able to construct the characters of Faith and Bonnie based on the text that she is reading, readers of *The Rules* are able to construct an ideal woman that Fein and Schneider encourage their readers to become. While self-help texts in general encourage particular, feminine behaviors such as performing the emotional labor necessary for cultivating a successful relationship, Fein and Schneider's manual, in particular, presents its readers with an even more clearly defined ideal woman. In skimming over the table of contents to *The Rules*, a reader can conjecture that a "successful" woman is the type of woman who is timid (Rule 2—Don't Talk to a Man First), aloof (Rule 5—Don't Call Him and Rarely Return His Calls) and guarded (Rule 19—Don't Open Up Too Fast). Fein and Schneider draft specific rules that when followed produce the type of woman who will capture the heart of Mr. Right. Jane's ability to imagine the type of women that Faith and Bonnie are, then, points to the way in which self-help manuals often create pointed images for their female readers to follow. In this sense, then, self-help books are not unlike women's magazines; both mediums revolve around an image of an ideal woman that they have constructed prior to production.

Jane attempts to abide by the rules that Faith and Bonnie lay out for her, but she finds it increasing difficult. At one point on her date with Robert, Jane, in an attempt to rid her mind of Faith and Bonnie, tells them that she doesn't need their help. Though their rules are "guaranteed" and "time-tested," Jane's following them seems to push Robert further and further away; in fact, he explains to her that she seemed to be turning into a woman very different from the one he initially met. Jane's reflection on the relevance of reading self-help books as a way to fix her love life is not unlike Bridget Jones's own considerations. At one point in her novel, Fielding depicts Bridget contemplating her mother's ease establishing relationships: "Maybe their generation is just better at getting on with relationships? Maybe they don't mooch about being all paranoid and diffident. Maybe it helps if you've never read a self-help book in your life" (60). Fielding draws a direct connection between Bridget's difficulty with relationships and self-help books, implying that these texts can be problematic for women readers. Bank, too, notes this difficulty, more subtly though, as we see Jane's relationship with Robert slowly disintegrate. As readers, we recognize that Robert is not a man who will be drawn to a woman who follows relationship rules; he's a cartoonist who says things like, "'I want to mate with you and die'" (256).[15] But Jane, believing in the text that she has read and the promises that it offers, is slower to understand. As readers, we see Robert slip away, and we recognize that Jane's blind devotion to this book has only produced more, rather than less, problems for her.

Despite the bleak moments in Bank's text, Bank provides her readers with a happy ending. The romantic fulfillment experienced by Jane at the end of *The Girls' Guide to Hunting and Fishing*, however, is incidental to the more important realization that Jane has about the manuals that have been preoccupying her. Recognizing that, like the mayfly, her time with Robert is limited, Jane confesses, "'You get all these voices about what a woman is supposed to be like—you know, feminine . . . And I've spent my whole life trying not to hear them. But . . . I wanted to be with you so much that I listened'" (273). Her admission is a huge step in her character development; as readers, we have seen Jane struggle with those voices, and here is one of the first times that we see her actually reject those voices and verbally reject them at that. Bank's ending, then, is fitting in terms of the larger context of her novel. Not only does Jane abandon Faith and Bonnie, but she also has sex with Robert in the closing paragraph of Bank's work. Bank's choice to end in this manner is fitting in light of all the anxiety that Jane has had about her sexuality. With this closing, Bank responds to the ideologies regarding female sexuality contained in self-help texts like *The Rules* by having Jane experience sexual and emotional fulfillment with a man. In fact, it is only when Jane abandons the expectations forced upon her can she be sexually free and emotionally happy.

Not only does Bank critique self-help books through the growth of her character, but her narrative structure also underscores her dialogue with self-help texts. The ordering of Bank's collection is significant, for she interrupts the main narrative—the story of Archie and Jane—twice. "The Best Possible Light," the only story that does not deal with Jane, follows "My Old Man," the story in which Jane and Archie first meet, while "You Could Be Anyone" follows "The Worst Thing a Suburban Girl Could Imagine," the story that details Archie and Jane's breakup. In "You Could Be Anyone," Bank adopts the conventions of the self-help text in order to once again critique the cut-and-dry advice offered to readers searching for solutions to complicated, emotional issues. "You Could Be Anyone" details an inadequate and unhappy relationship between an unnamed man and woman. The story, which is written in the second person, can be read on two levels. On the one hand, in placing the story between two stories about Jane, it is easy for the reader to imagine that this story, too, is about Jane. Additionally, the scenario presented is not one unfamiliar to Jane. However, the use of the second person opens the story up. While the reader can imagine that the story is the story of Jane, Bank's use of the second person also enables the reader to put herself in the place of the main character and directly identify with the story. The "you" of the story can literally refer to any one reader who can identify with the story's contents. Bank furthers the reader's ability to identify with the main character by naming her character Jane. The name, most often associated with the Sally, Dick, and Jane "Curriculum Foundation Series, popular from 1940–1965, is often viewed as a generic, female moniker" ("Dick and Jane School Books: History and Information"). This fact, coupled with the authors' uses of direct address, helps to further the reader's potential identification with the main character. Not only do self-help texts frequently use "you" to address their readers, but identification is also a key, motivating factor for the purchase of self-help texts. Readers often purchase these books in order to address a specific problem that they have encountered, and these books are often peppered with case studies of individuals who may be experiencing problems similar to the real-life reader. In using these narrative techniques, Bank further associates her fiction with self-help texts.

But while "You Could Be Anyone" begins innocuously enough, relating the progression of a relationship that, from the start, does not seem quite right, the story becomes much more complicated than the stories related in self-help books. At first, it seems as though the story will be one fit for the pages of Connell Cowan and Melvyn Kinder's 1985 text *Smart Women, Foolish Choices: Finding the Right Men, Avoiding the Wrong Ones*. The woman of the story finds herself falling for a very attractive, well-bred, yet slightly dangerous man. However, Bank's story soon complicates the self-help genre. The woman of the story finds herself uneasy with the relationship—not because of the behavior of the man but for her own reasons. For instance, when the woman finds an engagement ring, she is not happy, as Fein and Schneider might suspect their reader to be; rather, she is "'crestfallen,'" unable to express fully what is bothering her (217). Bank complicates the story even further when the woman discovers a lump in her breast and faces dealing with cancer as well as the demise of her romantic relationship, despite the man's best intentions. The story, then, like many of the other stories included in Bank's collection, is more complex than the stories in *Smart Women, Foolish Choices*. Though "You Could Be Anyone" has important similarities to self-help books, Bank ultimately confuses the structure of these texts by crafting a story that is more involved than the ones included in self-help books. In doing so, Bank challenges self-help texts' premises that there are easy answers to complex problems. *The Girls' Guide to Hunting and Fishing*, then, through its direct narrative about Jane Rosenal and through the stories which interrupt that narrative, serves as strong commentary on both the way in which self-help manuals encourage women to live up to unrealistic and unachievable ideals as well as the way in which they offer readers simple solutions to complicated problems.

Like Melissa Bank's *The Girls' Guide to Hunting and Fishing*, Laura Zigman's *Animal Husbandry* directly engages with self-help books of the mid-1990s. Published in 1998, Zigman's book responds directly to self-help works like Ellen Fein and Sherrie Schneider's *The Rules*, which imply that biology is a key component to understanding male and female behavior in relationships. In her article, "Shrinking Violets and Caspar Milquetoasts: Shyness and Heterosexuality from the Roles of the Fifties to *The Rules* of the Nineties," Patricia McDaniel explains that self-help authors in the nineties attempted "to justify their advice through recourse to biology" (558). She cites moments in self-help books such as *The Rules* and John Gray's *Men Are From Mars, Women Are From Venus* where the authors link male and female behaviors to biology. For instance, McDaniel quotes Fein and Schneider, "'[i]n a relationship, the man must take charge. He must propose. We are not making this up—biologically, he's the aggressor'" (558). And, when discussing Gray's book, McDaniel notes that Gray implies the different communication styles between the two sexes are not necessarily learned behavior but a biological birthright (559). In her novel, Zigman challenges this trend in self-help writing; she depicts her main character Jane Goodall attempting to get over her failed relationship with Ray Brown by conceptualizing a biologically grounded theory that explains why men leave the women they profess to love.[16] In having Jane construct, and yet ultimately reject, her self-written, self-help text, Zigman challenges the ideologies of these advice manuals by exposing their inadequacies. Like Bank's novel, *Animal Husbandry* asserts that self-help books offer their readers rather limited solutions to complicated, emotional issues. Zigman's alternative is to construct a fictional, self-help manual for her readers, which refuses to offer a simple resolution for problems encountered in a relationship.

Zigman's book begins in the present with Jane previewing for the reader her relationship with Ray. From the first chapter, we glean that the affair was significant, that Jane was disconsolate when it was over, and that Jane attempted to get over the affair by collecting biologically grounded data that explained the mating behaviors of animals. Zigman's book, then, flashes back to Jane and Ray's first encounter, relating the progression of the relationship and its eventual demise which is complicated by the fact that Ray, having left his fiancé for Jane, has now found a completely different woman with whom he works with to take Jane's place. When Ray leaves Jane, Jane, in addition to dealing with the pain of her break-up, not only has to find a new apartment since she had recently given up her own to move in with Ray, but she also has to continue to go to work everyday where she runs into Ray, the executive producer of "*The Diane Roberts Show*, a serious late-night David-Susskind-esque talk show taped in New York" for which Jane works (24).[17] For weeks after the break-up, Jane wanders around aimlessly, eating lots of ice cream and drinking lots of whiskey with her new roommate Eddie, a chauvinistic, ladies' man who also works with her.

What saves Jane, however, is the Old-Cow-New-Cow theory that she develops from a newspaper article that discusses a study done on cows. Observing the mating patterns of cows, scientists revealed that bulls become easily bored with cows that they have already mated with. No matter what the scientists did to attempt to disguise the old cow (dress her up in clothing, smear new cow scent on her) the bull consistently sought out a new cow. After reading this article, Jane concludes that "the sad, sorry truth [is] that men leave women and never come back because all they really want is New Cow," and she begins to collect data from a variety of sources to back up her claim (3).

Zigman depicts Jane consulting a multitude of sources in order to formulate her relationship theory, and the texts Zigman refers to speak to popular expectations about women's reading practices and comment upon the hybrid form of self-help books. The data that Jane collects comes from a multitude of sources from scientific, scholarly journals to self-help books to television shows to magazines. At various points in the novel, Jane mentions the texts that she is reading. When she sneaks into Eddie's room in the hopes of learning more about him by perusing through his bookcase, she finds "between *The Federalist Papers* and *An American Tragedy* . . . a textbook on abnormal psychology and a few other nonacademic but pertinent titles" (174). On the shelf are such self-help books as Christopher Lasch's *The Culture of Narcissism* and *Men Who Can't Love: When a Man's Fear Makes Him Run from Commitment (And What a Smart Woman Can Do About It)* by Steven Carter and Julia Sokol. When Jane later records what expenses she has incurred as a result of her breakup with Ray, she notes that she bought ten self-help books. In addition to looking at these texts, Jane details other influences on her theory—Freud, Jung, Skinner, *Nova*, *Nature*, *Love Connection*,

*Natural History, Scientific American, GQ, Esquire,* and *Cosmopolitan*; these sources reveal Jane's wide-ranging influences.

Zigman not only constructs a character affected by diverse sources, but she also incorporates such disparate sources into the construction of novel. Zigman's novel contains twenty-nine epigrams from twenty-six different sources. Like the sources that Jane mentions directly, Zigman's epigrams consist of a variety of sources, ranging from psychology to biology.[18] Some of these books, like Otto Kernberg's *Borderline Conditions and Pathological Narcissism* are hard to classify; Kernberg's text grounds itself scientifically, yet critics like Steven Starker include it in their analyses of the self-help genre.

Zigman's abundant use of exceedingly diverse sources and her inclusion of "hard to label" books like Kernberg's calls to mind the line that self-help books often straddle in terms of genre. As mentioned earlier, many self-help books attempt to ground themselves in the scientific, turning to biology to explain the reasons for human behavior. At the same time, self-help books are largely dependent upon psychology. For instance, in her chapter "Self-Help Books about Gender," Wendy Simonds discusses the emphasis that self-help authors often place on the role of the mother, calling to mind Freud's Oedipus complex. Despite self-help authors' reliance on these two disciplines, oftentimes their books are neither biology nor psychology but rather a hybrid form of writing, one which attempts to ground itself in science but which is often the result of something else entirely—personal experience. For instance, Fein and Schneider might cite biological reasons for human behavior, and they might also refer to psychological jargon to back up their claims. On the October 11, 1996 edition of *The Oprah Winfrey Show* entitled "Dating Rules," a woman who identified herself as a therapist defended the rules by stating, "I'm a therapist and I run '*The Rules*' support group here in Chicago. And I see a lot of women who have been hurt, who have been taken advantage of. And they don't have the boundaries, so we are giving them guidelines in a way to have a life and . . . to make dating fun, to have fun with it, and not to be hurt" ("Dating Rules" 24–25). Her use of the term "boundaries" shows the way that Fein and Schneider's book can easily be interpreted through the language of psychology. However, the opening chapter of Fein and Schneider's book reveals that the rules came out of a discussion with a friend named Melanie who passed along the time-tested dating secrets of her grandmother. Zigman exploits this tendency of self-help books to blur disciplinary lines by referencing a variety of sources in her text. In fact, when Jane attempts to provide her theory with a label, she notes that it is a "psycho-scientific discovery," again emphasizing the slipperiness that comes with attempting to definitively categorize self-help (178). By having

Jane use science, psychology, self-help, magazines, and television to support her claims about male behavior, Zigman draws attention to the way in which self-help books are often an amalgamation of ideas and influences.

Zigman's extensive quotations also speak to expectations that we may have regarding women's reading practices. Instead of constructing a character who relies solely on the advice of self-help books and magazines to craft her own relationship theory, as the publishing industry might have us think, Zigman creates a character who consults a plethora of texts that become influential for her Old-Cow-New-Cow theory, revealing to her readers that a woman's reading habits can extend beyond what we might anticipate. While on one level, Zigman presents her readers with a female character confronting challenging, scientific texts, by including these texts, Zigman also reveals her own reading practices, for as readers we can assume that Zigman herself has read the texts included. Zigman's inclusion of these texts, then, serves as a multi-layered comment upon women's reading practices. In referencing these varied texts, Zigman not only creates a female character with a diverse reading background, but she also reveals her own assorted reading tastes. And, in doing so, she assumes that female readers, like her character and herself, are capable of reading outside the genre that is in front of them.

In general, Zigman's dialogue with the genre of self-help and her conversation regarding women's reading comes not from direct references to it or from character development but rather from her narrative structure. At the onset of the book, it is not entirely clear what purpose the epigrams will serve. When initially reading Zigman's book, the reader may assume that these quotes are in some way connected to the text that follows, perhaps previewing the narrative to come, as Bank's epigrams did. However, as the narrative progresses, it becomes quite clear that these quotes come from Jane's research and directly contribute to the formulation of her theory. In fact, the entire book seems to be Jane's production, her own self-help book, if you will, for surviving her break-up. Jane's first person narration reveals during the course of the novel that Jane has filled seven notebooks. Zigman describes:

> ... case files—which I filled with newspaper clippings, magazine articles, xeroxed pages from books, and anything else that helped to explain why Ray dumped me, why Eddie dumped everyone, why Jason would undoubtedly dump Joan—why everything seemed so impossibly, inexplicably fucked up. (185–86)

In reviewing the opening chapter in light of this knowledge, it becomes apparent that Zigman's story is the story that evolved from Jane's case files.

Zigman's opening chapter both introduces the Old-Cow-New-Cow theory and the main character/author of that text, but as readers have noted, the connection between the two may not be evident initially. As one reader-reviewer wrote on Amazon.com, "The first couple of chapters don't really make sense—the sentence structure is not there at all and the ideas that are thrown out don't connect" (Kelly). Her comment reveals the disconnected feel of Zigman's opening. Yet, upon completion of the novel, Zigman's purpose, in retrospect, becomes evident; from page one, her novel is modeled after the avidly consumed, relationship manuals of the 1990s. Like these texts, Zigman's novel opens with Jane's summary of the major events in her life that prompted her to write the book and a brief description of who she is and why she is qualified to relate this information to her readers. Just as self-help authors justify their reasons for writing such manuals, Jane explains to her readers why she is qualified to write this book. Jane's credentials, then, are not all that different from Fein and Schneider's. Though Jane is not a writer or psychologist proper, she is, as her friend Joan tells her, "'someone who's been in the trenches. Someone who gets it. Someone who can communicate that to the multitudes of women who don't'" (221).

Zigman further cements this association through the labeling of her chapters. Her opening chapter is entitled "Preface: The New Cow Theory." A preface is not normally a fully integrated part of a work of fiction; rather, it is usually set off from the main narrative, serving to introduce the material to come. In delineating her opening chapter as such, Zigman immediately associates her novel with the self-help industry, and she continues to do so throughout the book. At the start of each chapter, in addition to the quotes, Zigman includes chapter headings such as "Precopulatory Phase: Stage I The Myth of Male Shyness," "Precopulatory Phase: Stage III The Metamorphosis of Cow to New Cow and the Role of the Current-Cow Sob Story," and "Post-Copulatory Phase: Stage VI Diminished Bliss, The Dawning of the Age of Discontent, and the Mysterious Metamorphoses from New Cow to Old Cow." These chapter headings are tongue in cheek divisions that read like the chapter headings of a self-help book. Like Fielding, Zigman ironically comment on the self-help industry; her narrative structure mocks self-help books' structural conventions.

In having Jane reconstruct her relationship with Ray from hindsight, Zigman repositions Jane from reader of self-help books to author of relationship manuals. While Jane may read numerous self-help books for advice on how to deal with her failed relationship, like Elizabeth Bishop's speaker, the only way that Jane can actually heal is to write through her grief and construct a personal narrative that enables her to come to grips with her situation and move on with her life. Readers of Zigman's novel echo this observation. As Kelly, a reader from Seattle, Washington, observes, "it seems as though Ms. Zigman has had a personal experience with someone like Ray and writing _Animal Husbandry_ has been like a sort of writing therapy for her." Though in this comment Kelly confuses the character and author, she zeros in on an important theme of Zigman's work—the therapeutic qualities that writing can have.

Zigman's novel, however, becomes more than Jane's actualized self-help book; it also serves as a fictional self-help book for her readers, as evidenced by reader reaction to the text. In reading reviews on both Amazon.com and Amazon.co.uk, a common denominator in readers' reactions was the reader's ability to relate to the novel. The title of the review, "Absolutely fab—EVERY WOMEN HAS BEEN THERE!," written by ckelly@ed.ac.uk, a reader from Edinburgh, reveals not only who readers see as the intended audience for Zigman's book, but it also further defines the purpose of Zigman's book. Readers of *Animal Husbandry* seem to read her novel as a means of connecting with someone else who has been through a similar traumatic experience. A reader from Memphis, Tennessee comments, "I originally bought this book for a friend who has been dumped by a string of 'bovines' but I couldn't possibly give it to her until I'd screened it myself. I ended up just loaning her my copy because I couldn't bear to part with it!" She continues, "All single women (& friends of single women) who have ever been dumped will enjoy this book." UnamunoChk@aol.com, another reader reviewer, writes, "After reading the first chapter of this book on Amazon, I sent a link to 25 of my women friends, telling them that this was a must read . . . I thought the book pretty well described the emotional disembowelment of being dumped and its messy aftermath." In her review, ckelly@ed.ac.uk comments, "It's a book we can all identify with; being dumped by your truelove/soul mate." Readers seem to find comfort in this book in a way similar to that of self-help readers who often turn to self-help books, searching for answers, explanations, common experiences, and most of all advice.

Some critics of *Animal Husbandry* might assert that this type of reader-response indicates that Zigman merely reproduces the self-help genre. However, Zigman deploys the narrative strategies of self-help books to a very different end. Though Zigman's novel may function on a similar level as dating manuals, offering its readers comfort and advice, the focus of Zigman's novel is very different than the focus of self-help books like Fein and Schneider's. Zigman's book is all about Jane's attempt to better understand herself as a means of healing her self, not as a means of finding an appropriate man to date or marry. The emotional labor that Jane performs is for the betterment of herself/her self. Zigman underscores this fact by ending the novel with Jane still single. Though the closing of the book presents Eddie consoling Jane in what could seem to be a romantic overture, the next chapter begins with the statement: "Well, I'm sorry to say there is no surprise ending here. No fabulous night of luv with Eddie" (299). Though self-help texts provide readers with simple solutions to complex, emotional problems (i.e. follow Rules 1–35, marry within the year, and banish all feelings of loneliness), Zigman's story, like Bank's, is not prescriptive and presents a "messier" version of life. Rather than closing the novel nicely with Jane finding a man to replace Ray, Zigman chooses to have Jane still grieving yet simultaneously at peace—an ending much more realistic, and much less contrived, than the Hollywood ending supplied in the movie version of the novel, *Someone Like You* (2001). The film ends with Jane (Ashley Judd) falling for Eddie (Hugh Jackman) and closes with the two kissing. Additionally, the end of the novel is important because Zigman presents readers with Jane rejecting the self-help genre that she has actively participated in as both a reader and writer. The closing paragraph not only illustrates this rejection, but it also stays true to its focus on Jane and her healing:

> And every once in a while I still dream about him. But the dream is different now, and I'm different in it.
> In the dream I see him in a place that seems familiar but isn't: on a beach we never went to; across a crowded room of strangers; in a field as barren and devoid of features as a moonscape.
> Our eyes lock.
> And there, in the soundless, gravityless atmosphere of that place, the place where memory and experience and love and grief meet to form acceptance—the place where Old Cows and New Cows don't exist—I turn away and whisper words I thought would never come.
> *Moo who?* (301)

In asking "*Moo who?*" Jane nullifies the existence of old cows and news cows, the tenet upon which her self-help book is based. For her, they no longer exist, and more importantly, it is she herself who is responsible for banishing them.

Zigman both ends and begins *Animal Husbandry* with Jane's rejection of the genre. In the closing of the novel, Jane states, "I called Joan and told her that Dr. Marie Goodall had died peacefully in her sleep. It was time to get on with my life" (300). And, in the opening, Jane notes that she is "a recovering monkey scientist," a statement that has much more significance in retrospect (5). What Zigman has Jane reject then is not her own personal story of loss but her theory about why loss happens. Zigman not only depicts Jane rejecting the advice offered by self-help books, but she also exhibits her rejecting her role of relationship advisor when she concedes: "'Sometimes things just happen. They just are'" (211). This observation stands in direct opposition to the advice offered by such self-help authors as Fein and Schneider. Here, Zigman implies that ending the date first or letting the man take the lead will not fix certain romantic situations; rather, some situations "just are." Zigman depicts Jane relinquishing her tendency to find a clear-cut explanation for complex, human emotions, and in doing so, she complicates the concept of female, emotional labor by showing that, in Jane's situation, reading the "right" manual, or writing it for that matter, does not always work.

On October 11, 1996, Ellen Fein and Sherrie Schneider appeared on *The Oprah Winfrey Show* to discuss their recently published book. Winfrey's television program proved to be an interesting forum for the discussion particularly because the show is simultaneously connected to, yet at times critiques, the self-help industry. Self-help authors, like Fein and Schneider, are frequently guests on Oprah's program; in fact, one such author, Dr. Phil McGraw, saw such success on *Oprah* that he launched his own show in October 2002 (Peyser 50). Furthermore, Winfrey dispenses her own advice on her television show and in her magazine *O: The Oprah Magazine*, which first hit stands in 2001 ("The World According to Oprah" 43). On television, she recommends readings to her Oprah Book Club; she informs her audience of recent news events; and she covers popular culture phenomena. Her magazine includes sections on how to "Live Your Best Life," celebrity, reading recommendations, "The O List" (a list of Oprah's favorite products) as well as advice columns by Dr. Phil McGraw and financial advisor Suze Orman.[19]

While Oprah Winfrey may encourage the consumption of particular products, *The Oprah Winfrey* show often presents viewers with differing opinions about contemporary topics. The October 11, 1996 show was a case in point. Rather than reviewing Fein and Schneider's manual herself, Winfrey invited the authors, Regina Barreca, author of *The Penguin Book of Women's Humor*, and John Scalzi, an AOL relationship columnist to discuss *The Rules*. And she included voiceovers of real-life readers and encouraged her audience to comment on their experiences with it as well. This format is one that Winfrey frequently adopts. For instance, when reviewing the most recent book club selection, Winfrey invites the author and real-life readers to discuss the merits, and shortcomings, of the book, usually over a meal. Rather than having one, authoritative voice speak on the text, this format allows for multiple perspectives on a given topic. Fein and Schneider's book, as noted earlier, provoked a heated discussion amongst its participants, so much so, in fact, that Winfrey again returned to on her June 19, 1997 show entitled "*The Rules* Backlash." At one point in the discussion, Winfrey interrupted and asked, "Why can't they both be right? Why can't you be right, Rebecca be right and they be right?" ("Dating Rules" 19). She continued, "Why can't you look at the rules with a sense of humor . . . and a sense of—of balance . . . and you incorporate what works for you and . . . what doesn't work for you, you—you throw away?" (20). Winfrey's comment is an important one. First, she reacts in opposition to the essentializing nature of self-help texts, acknowledging that what women are not one unified, collective whole but a diverse group of individuals who may not all agree on what rules to follow. Secondly, she implies that women readers are more discerning than the panelists or audience members are giving them credit for being; women, she argues, can accept and reject Fein and Schneider's advice at will. In their novels, Bank and Zigman seem to be in agreement with Winfrey's observations, presenting protagonists capable of critically reading the texts presented to them, accepting and rejecting self-help advice when it is appropriate, and creating their own texts when the manuals they encounter fall desperately short.

Chapter Four

# Down with Marriage: The Search for Romantic Alternatives

> "Mention sex and the single girl will blush a lot.
> Though she wrecks every single guy with what she's got . . .
> Then a guy she can't ignore
> tells her what she's waited for
> and suddenly she's not single anymore."
>
> —"Sex and the Single Girl," performed by
> Fran Jeffries in *Sex and the Single Girl* (1964)

In 1962, Bernard Geis Associates published a self-help book entitled *Sex and the Single Girl* which, according to the inside book jacket:

> . . . tells the unmarried girl how to be irresistibly, irrepressibly, confidently, enviably single. There is not a coy, sanctimonious or condescending word in this entire book . . . only hundreds of practical, workable, specific suggestions written with sometimes shocking candor by a woman who was herself single for thirty-seven years.

The woman who writes with such "shocking candor" is Helen Gurley Brown, the infamous re-designer and editor of *Cosmopolitan* magazine.[1] Like her magazine, Brown's book offers young, single women guidelines for living their lives successfully. *Sex and the Single Girl* details everything from what to wear to the office to step-by-step instructions concerning how to conduct an affair. Brown decrees in her opening chapter that "There is a tidal wave of misinformation these days about . . . how tough is the plight of the single woman—spinster, widow, divorcée" (4) and blames the majority of women's magazines, in part, for dismissing the single girl as "a creature to be pitied and patronized" (5) rather than viewing her as she should be seen—"as the newest glamour girl of our times" (5).

Though Brown asserts that she wishes to correct America's misapprehensions about single women, her own book is not without its contradictions. As Betsy Israel remarks in *Bachelor Girl: The Secret History of Single Women in the Twentieth Century*, "even though [Brown's single] girl 'lived by her wits ... sharpened ... honed ... coping with people trying to marry her off,' she was still an elaborately decked-out slab of bait" (212). While Brown's book aims to correct misapprehensions about what the book jacket of the 1962 edition deems "the least understood and most maligned minority group of all times," the opening chapters of her book focus on finding a man. In fact, Brown begins her book not with an anecdote about a particularly enjoyable time she had while single but rather with the declaration that she "married for the first time at thirty-seven" (3). She then proceeds to tell her readers about her husband, "a motion picture producer, forty-four, brainy, charming and sexy," a man whom she could never have met if she had not cultivated herself during her single years (3). Brown then follows Chapter One with a chapter on how to adequately take advantage of the available men in your life and another chapter on where to meet more eligible men. The remainder of her book devotes itself to such topics as "How to Be Sexy," "The Care and Feeding of Everybody," and "The Shape You're In," chapters which detail the necessary skills that single girls should develop. Though ostensibly Brown's book is "not a study on how to get married but how to stay single—in superlative style," the specter of the eligible bachelor hovers in the book's background (11). In this respect, *Sex and the Single Girl* does not differ that much from *The Rules: Time-tested Secrets for Capturing the Heart of Mr. Right*, which like Brown's book, offers women suggestions for making themselves look more attractive to men. Though Brown clearly recognizes the biases held against single women, her book offers the ultimate conclusion that being single is only a temporary stop on the road to a girl's final destination—marriage.

In *New Millennial Sexstyles*, Carol Siegel discusses Helen Gurley Brown's text, comparing Brown's manual to *The Sensuous Woman* by J and noting the way in which the narrative structure of both these sex manuals rely heavily on romance literature conventions. She writes:

> The books begin with a situation in which an insecure but basically superior woman (a stand-in for the reader) meets a difficult, selfish, and hard-to-understand man and becomes fascinated with him. Both romance and advice genres develop narratives of romantic interaction in which the woman is always well-meaning, although she makes interesting mistakes, and the man is always elusive and deceptive. Often a

contrasting male figure comes on the scene. The woman makes the right choice and lives happily ever after. (42)

Siegel's description of *Sex and the Single Girl* and *The Sensuous Woman* reads much like the basic plotline of another popularly consumed, female medium—the Hollywood romantic comedy. Much like the self-help books that Siegel discusses and like romance novels, these films are structured around the interactions of a "well-meaning" heroine and an "elusive and deceptive" man who, after a series of mishaps, eventually discover their love for one another by the close of the film. Siegel notes that both romance novels and self-help books "valorize marriage as closure and as remedy for women's life problems, beginning with the premise that there is no real alternative" (42). This valorization of marriage is frequently present in romantic comedies as well. Usually, without fail, the hero and heroine of a romantic comedy overcome a series of obstacles and find themselves together in the end.

I open this chapter by comparing *Sex and the Single Girl*, the 1964 romantic comedy adapted from Brown's advice manual, and Roger Kumble's 2002 *The Sweetest Thing*, analyzing the way in which romantic comedies of the past and present posit a limiting view of female sexuality. By emphasizing a happily ever after ending, these films imply that women can only be completely fulfilled if they enter into a monogamous, heterosexual relationship. Finding this representation problematic, chick lit authors Candace Bushnell and Carol Wolper respond to this assumption in their books, *Sex and the City* (1998) and *The Cigarette Girl* (1999). Rather than depicting heroines primarily responsible for the emotional labor involved in cultivating a relationship, Bushnell and Wolper present heroines who revel in their sexuality and, in doing so, redefine the traditional, female heroine posited by these films. While romantic comedies encourage state-sanctioned marriage, Bushnell and Wolper construct sexually aggressive women questioning the ways these films encourage them to behave, exploring nontraditional sexual unions, and attempting to break the ideological chains that threaten to bind them.

In *Bound to Bond: Gender, Genre, and the Hollywood Romantic Comedy*, Mark D. Rubinfeld discusses this tendency of romantic comedies to close the formal narrative with "social regeneration through coupling" (112).[2] In addition to identifying this trend, he discusses the ideological implications of it. He observes:

> To state the obvious, the goal of these Hollywood romantic comedies is to romantically bring the hero and the heroine together and, more specifically, to bring them to the altar. But the coupling between the

> hero and the heroine, of course, symbolizes more than just coupling. First, and most obvious, because the coupling is between a hero and heroine, it represents heterosexual coupling and, through the absolute absence of any alternative types of coupling, rejects all alternative types of coupling. And, second, because the coupling is always officially sanctioned by either the church or state, the wedding ritual represents a social action that regenerates communal values. (112)

In his analysis, Rubinfeld both documents the tendency for romantic comedies to rely upon this convention and exposes societal prejudice embedded in the text against homosexuality and in favor of state-sanctioned marriage. Like cultural studies critics Roland Barthes and Stuart Hall whom he acknowledges in his introduction, Rubinfeld observes the power that popular culture mediums can have in shaping people's perceptions. Rubinfeld explains that just as Barthes exposed myths as "social constructions posing as natural truths" in *Mythologies*, he himself seeks to "cut through the natural truth of the Hollywood romantic comedy—to denaturalize its narrative assertion that *men and women are, without question, and without questioning their assigned roles in the familial economy, bound to bond*" (xix).

Making this observation is a first important step in enabling a connection between romantic comedies and advice manuals. Unlike women's magazines and self-help books, the purpose of romantic comedies is not to instruct, and unlike other advice manuals, these films do not rely on such narrative conventions as direct address to reach their audience in the same way that, for instance, self-help texts do. However, these films still contain myths/messages concerning acceptable and unacceptable behaviors, particularly relevant to female viewers. In stressing the importance of social regeneration through coupling, Rubinfeld indirectly reveals the ideological assumptions that these films contain regarding sex, love, and marriage for female viewers. In presenting marriage as the only, viable option for the heroine, romantic comedies posit that female sexuality, particularly outside of wedlock, is something that needs to be controlled and eventually concentrated upon one man. For instance, though the premise of the 1964 adaptation of Helen Gurley Brown's *Sex and the Single Girl* is that women can live a fulfilling life outside of wedlock, the ultimate conclusion of the film is that marriage is the only acceptable option for women. And, though one would hope that this message might have changed in years since, the 2002 film *The Sweetest Thing* offers a similar resolution. Though they may not explicitly intend to instruct their viewers, romantic comedies, then, often deploy specific and scripted gender ideologies.

Richard Quine's *Sex and the Single Girl* preoccupies itself with the policing of women's sexuality. The premise of the movie revolves around answering a simple question, "Does she or doesn't she?" Dr. Helen Brown (Natalie Wood) is a successful research psychologist who has just published the book *Sex and the Single Girl*; the movie opens with a shot of the city, followed by the first scene, which takes place in the boardroom of *Stop* magazine, the "filthy rag" that has recently run an exposé on Dr. Brown, implying that she is not the experienced, worldly woman she has pretended to be but rather a "23-year-old virgin." As a result of this article, Dr. Brown's patients, as revealed in the next scene, are canceling their appointments left and right, concerned that a "23-year-old virgin" has nothing to offer them in terms of sexual advice. The narrative proceeds as Bob Weston (Tony Curtis), a ruthless writer for *Stop* magazine, attempts to uncover whether Helen "is or isn't" for an upcoming article; in order to meet with Helen professionally, Bob impersonates his married friend Frank (Henry Fonda) and seeks counseling for his marriage that is falling apart. What happens instead, predictably, is that the incorrigible bachelor, Bob Weston, falls for the devout single girl, Helen Brown.

Adapting Helen Gurley Brown's text for the screen was admittedly a difficult task; the self-help book contains no formal plot and no characters. Director Richard Quine's decision, then, to concentrate on the question of "Did she or didn't she?" is an interesting choice for the adaptation, especially given the fact that Brown, in her book, makes it abundantly clear that she certainly isn't a virgin and that other women shouldn't be either. In fact, at one point in her book, Helen Gurley Brown discourages virginity, asking, "Is there anything particularly attractive about a thirty-four-year-old virgin?" (231). She also quotes, "one young women who remained chaste for many years" as having said "'I have yet to encounter a happy virgin. Quite the contrary, I feel she eventually finds social, religious and maternal approval quite inadequate compensation for not ever really belonging to anyone, and her state of purity becomes an almost embarrassing cross to bear'" (225). The movie, unlike Brown's book, is less upfront about sexuality and consistently avoids answering the question "Did she or didn't she?" directly. At times, when the viewer begins to feel that he/she might know the answer, the script undercuts and contradicts that belief. When Bob and Helen meet for the first time in Helen's office, Bob asks, "Have you ever lived with a man? Have you ever been married?" Helen replies, "No, I haven't been married. I've had lots of experiences." Though we may take Helen's reply to mean that she has had lots of sexual experiences, Natalie Wood's portrayal of Helen Brown undercuts this assumption. Though Wood's character is clearly committed to her work and her progressive ideas about female sexuality and though she presents a tough veneer to her colleagues, we see, at times, Helen's vulnerability. Wood plays Helen with a certain wide-eyed innocence, which makes the viewer doubt Helen's experiences. Helen frequently asks Bob imploringly, "Do you really think I'm pretty?" This question is asked with such need that we begin to wonder if any man has ever paid attention to Helen before Bob. And, when Helen realizes that she has fallen in love with Bob, whom she believes to be a married man, she calls her mother crying. Later, when she visits Sylvia, the real Frank's real wife, to confess that "Frank" has been coming to see her, Sylvia questions her motives. "Why are you doing all this?" she asks. Helen replies, "Because my mother told me to." Helen's character, in these moments, is at complete odds with the portrayal of single women in the text that she has written; a far cry from a sexually fulfilled, independent single woman, Helen acts in these moments like a child who can not fully realize her adult potential.

Perhaps even more interesting than Wood's character is the character of Gretchen, played by Fran Jeffries. Gretchen is Bob Weston's lover, and unlike Wood's character, it is abundantly clear that Gretchen isn't. We first encounter her in Bob's apartment where she is dressed in a midriff-revealing, two-piece outfit, singing a song entitled "Sex and the Single Girl." Later, we see Gretchen and Bob intensely kissing on Bob's couch. The sound of breaking glass interrupts their activities, and as viewers, we are to infer that if the interruption hadn't occurred Gretchen would not have put a stop to the activity. This scene stands in direct contrast to the scene in Helen's apartment where she and Bob begin kissing. Unlike Gretchen, however, Helen stops the action, demanding that Bob leave after he admits his love for her. Gretchen appears to be Bob's constant companion, though there is no intention on either person's part to make any kind of permanent commitment to one another. Gretchen makes it abundantly clear that her career as an actress and singer means much more to her than any traditional lifestyle. She says to Bob at one point, "Oh no, honey. I wouldn't give up my career for marriage, kids, or happiness." The phrasing of her response, "marriage, kids, or happiness," indicates that Gretchen has inadvertently chosen the "unhappy" path. Rather than choose a lifestyle that, according to the movie, would provide her with guaranteed happiness, Gretchen chooses to pursue the alternative. The alternative eventually leaves her in a very bad spot. Though as viewers we know from the start of the movie that Helen and Bob and Frank and Sylvia are destined to be together, we are less sure of where Gretchen's fate will lead her. And, in the end, we see her coupled off with Rudy (Mel Ferrer), the slimy, sexual predator who pursued Helen earlier in the film. Gretchen gets paired off by default and with the movie's least likeable character. And as if that fate isn't warning enough for young, single women, Jeffries is the only character of the six not to be billed in the promotional materials for the movie.[3] *Sex and the Single Girl*, then, serves as a sort of sexual etiquette manual, dictating to women the correct and incorrect ways to behave in order to snare a man. Helen, in remaining ambiguously chaste, has ended up with the movie's handsome hero while Gretchen, with her loose morals, has landed lecherous Rudy.

Admittedly, romantic comedies of the late twentieth century and early twenty-first century provide their readers with much more progressive messages about female sexuality. Or do they? While historically America has made attempts toward eradicating sexist practices, the messages imparted by recent romantic comedies still posit that women's sexuality is something that needs to be contained, controlled, and eventually concentrated upon only one man. The narrative resolutions of these films then suggest that a heterosexual, state sanctioned marriage is the only viable alternative for women. In fact, in *Bound to Bond: Gender, Genre, and the Hollywood Romantic Comedy*, Mark D. Rubinfeld notes that 124 of the top 155 movies from 1970–1999 offered the theme of social regeneration through coupling—an alarmingly high number. Even a more recent film like *The Sweetest Thing*, produced just after the initial onslaught of chick lit texts, was billed as depicting empowering portrayals of young, single, successful women yet still fell back on the old Hollywood conventions for a romantic comedy.[4] This film's ultimate message does not differ essentially from the message of *Sex and the Single Girl*; like Quine's film, *The Sweetest Thing* comes to the conclusion that women can only be completely fulfilled if, in the end, they enter into a monogamous, heterosexual relationship.

Like *Sex and the Single Girl*, Roger Kumble's 2002 film, *The Sweetest Thing*, focuses on the life of single, successful, city dwelling women. However, unlike Natalie Wood's character, Christina Walters (Cameron Diaz) and her two friends Courtney (Christina Applegate) and Jane (Selma Blair) are explicitly, sexually active, attempting to enjoy their own "sexual revolutions" free of commitment and without the fear of getting hurt.[5] According to the movie poster released upon the opening of the film, these women are "not looking for Mr. Right. They're looking for Mr. Right Now" ("*The Sweetest Thing*"). The women's views of relationships, however, become complicated when Christina meets a man named Peter at a local nightclub and, having felt a connection, attempts to track him down. Christina and Courtney's pursuit of Peter provides the major action in the movie while Jane's sexual exploits provide an entertaining and comic subplot for the film.

*The Sweetest Thing* opens with an indication that the gender stereotypes maintained by romantic comedies are going to be radically reversed. Before the opening credits even begin, we see the phrase "Tell Us About Christina Walters" in white on a black screen. What follows is a series of testimonials from five disgruntled men about their "relationships" with the film's heroine Christina Walters. The first man sets the tone for the interviews to follow, saying, "Do you know the kind of woman who can get any guy she wants? That's Christina Walters. We dated, briefly, but she's not the commitment type. She's a player. She just likes to have fun." The other men reinforce this perception of Christina; one man complains that he "lay down all that groundwork," buying her drinks, but she refused to give him what he wanted in return—sex. Another man talks confidently about how he waited the required three days before calling her; however, when he dials her "number," Mr. Movie Phone answers. And a fourth man obsessively laments Christina's failure to call him. These testimonials reinforce the fact that Christina Walters will not be the traditional romantic comedy heroine. In fact, from the onset of the movie, Christina is characterized as the proverbial "prick."[6] When it comes to the dating game, Christina Walters exhibits stereotypical, male qualities. She's a "player;" she never calls when she says she will; and she's the heartbreaker when it comes to playing the dating game.

An aerial, establishing shot of San Francisco immediately follows these testimonials, and the camera then zooms in on Christina Walters who is dancing up the steep San Francisco streets. Christina's dance is soon interrupted by the sound of her cell phone ringing; her friend Courtney calls to find out how her day went. The two discuss their days' successes before entering the apartment they share with Jane whom they find crying on the couch about her break-up with her boyfriend Kevin. In an attempt to console and counsel their friend, Christina and Courtney offer the following advice:

*Christina*: You know what . . . we're all guilty of it. You made yourself too available.

*Courtney*: Yep. It's a classic mistake, sweetheart.

*Jane*: Not according to this . . . [Holds up *True Love: The Ten Commandments*.] Commandment Number Four . . . Commandment Number Four: Thou shalt be open to love's possibilities. Boundaries are the enemy of love.

*Christina*: Sweetie, lookit. You know what, this book is relationship propaganda. Listen to me. Dating is all about boundaries.

*Courtney*: Honey, you have to protect yourself. All right. We've all had our heart stomped upon one too many times because we went and served it to them on a big ol' platter. A good defense is the best offense.

*Jane*: Ugh. I'm so tired of playing games.

*Christina*: This is not about playing games, okay? This is about self-preservation. Honey, you can't just throw yourself out there, all exposed and vulnerable every time. That is how you get smacked down. Do you understand? Don't go looking for Mr. Right. Look for Mr. Right Now. And, eventually, if he's worthy, then one day that "Now" part will just drop away, naturally, you know . . .

This scene has an interesting charge to it. First of all, Christina and Courtney's use of affectionate nicknames for Jane such as "Sweetie" and "Honey" as well as the way Diaz's and Applegate's heights are exaggerated in relation to Blair's imply that Christina and Courtney are to be viewed as Jane's parental figures.[7] However, the advice they offer is very different from parental advice and very different from the advice offered by the self-help book that Jane reads. Christina and Courtney emphasize protection and self-fulfillment. In addition, both imply that marriage and/or lifetime commitments are not worth looking for at all; they will only come about as result of engaging in immediate gratification.

Though the film indicates that these women hold nontraditional views of relationships, as viewers we may wonder on some level just how faithful Christina and Courtney can remain to their relationship advice. Our expectations for Hollywood romantic comedies may not allow us to fully entertain the assumption that Christina and Courtney will remain "loveless" throughout the film. Furthermore, as viewers, our expectations of the romantic comedy genre may lead us to infer that Christina and Courtney are not privy to the fate that awaits them, and we suspect that Christina's devotion to her Mr. Right Now philosophy might waver—perhaps she just hasn't met the right man as of yet. This scene is in some ways reminiscent of *Sex and the Single Girl*. At one point in the film, Helen argues with Rudy, emphasizing that she will not relinquish her state as a single girl:

Rudy stop it. You are such a prude. I am simply appalled by the double standard that you men keep trying to impose on us women. Well, I for one am simply not going to submit . . . Well, anyway, when I do get married, it's not going to be for love or sex or romance. I can get all of those things outside of marriage just as easily as you can . . . And I shall insist on the right to have as many love affairs as I please. I am certainly not going to sacrifice one iota of my dignity or freedom for any man.

Though Helen says she will not "sacrifice one iota of [her] dignity or freedom for any man," as viewers, we imagine otherwise. When the phone begins to ring in the middle of Helen's speech, we are privy to the fact that Bob is calling Helen, and before Helen herself even knows, we know that Bob's charms are irresistible to her. Likewise, we anticipate Christina's inability to stick to her resolution, in part, because we have been conditioned by Hollywood to expect a happily ever after ending. Christina's earlier acknowledgement that the "now" part of the equation might just fall away indicates that that ending might not be so unrealistic after all. Though the initial scenes of the movie seem to reverse the expected conventions of a Hollywood romantic comedy, cues within the movie still indicate that it relies heavily on the conventions of the Hollywood romantic comedy, although just how heavily the film relies on them is delayed until the film's closing.

Christina, Courtney, and Jane represent sexually liberated women who no longer hold onto the belief that love and marriage are the only answer. The film contains graphic sexual scenes. Jane, in particular, uses sex to recover from her broken relationship; she immediately has sex with a guy who is "So cute" yet "So stupid" as a means of curing her depression. Throughout the course of the film, we see her graphically French kiss her new man, emerge from her bedroom, asking for Advil and rubbing her sore vagina, engage in sex with him in the dressing room of the clothing store where she works, and literally get caught during the act of oral sex because of her new man's piercing. At the close of the film, there is no indication that Jane has pursued a more serious relationship with this man; rather, the film makes it quite clear that Jane has used this man for temporary pleasure. Likewise, at the same club that Jane met her man, we see Courtney approach and aggressively flirt with a man she's never met before. And, that same night, Christina explains her rationale for introducing her friend Jane to Peter; she explains, "I wasn't suggesting that the two of you get married. I just thought maybe you could get it on." All three women seem to enjoy liberal views of sexual relationships.

Though these scenes indicate that these characters are twenty-first century "New Women," the film, at times, undermines its initial challenge of stereotypical gender roles.[8] Though Jane engages in sex without the promise of commitment, she is still not free of the shame that has been associated with premarital sex. At one point in the film, Jane takes a semen stained dress to the cleaners, hoping to leave it there without explanation. However, while there, she not only gets interrogated by the friendly, elderly owner of the cleaners who knows her mother and grandmother, but she also runs into her priest and her elementary school teacher, who has brought her class on a field trip to learn about cleanliness. Jane's embarrassment in these moments is without question. She attempts to avoid questions about the stain from the owner of the shop; she shields her eyes at various points during this scene; and she hurriedly answers additional questions from her teacher and priest in an effort to escape the shop quickly. This scene directly equates Jane's sexual act with the feeling of shame; an equation which undermines the progressive view that the film initially posited about women's sexual freedom.

Furthermore, toward the end of the film, Christina and Courtney's serious relationship discussion is juxtaposed with Jane's humiliating oral sex scene—a move that further reinforces the warning that having sex like Christina, Courtney, and Jane do can result in embarrassing situations and lead to a ruined reputation. After Christina and Courtney discover that it is Peter and not his brother getting married, Christina chastises herself for getting emotionally attached to someone she hardly knows. She says, "I'm such an idiot . . . I meet a guy for two minutes, and I'm chasing after him like he's someone special." Courtney replies, "Well, maybe you want someone special for once. Maybe you were thinking that you were tired of the game." When Christina then asks Courtney if she is tired of the game, she replies, "Yep" without hesitation. The women conclude that there is more to life than what they initially thought and begin to realize that their lifestyle may not be the best decision. Immediately following, they return home to discover that Jane has gotten caught on her lover's penis piercing while giving him oral sex. Police officers, fire fighters, and emergency personnel invade the women's home and surround Jane. The number of unnecessary people present to help find a solution exaggerates the severity of the situation. Christina and Courtney's eventual solution to the problem (to have Jane sing to loosen her vocal chords) is comic, particularly when the whole crowd begins singing along to Aerosmith's "And I Don't Want to Miss a Thing." What is not exaggerated or comic, however, is Jane's humiliation; tears fill her eyes as the seriousness of her dilemma is articulated by those gathered. Her submissive posture (she is kneeling on the floor) and her public display of a private moment—her getting caught literally *and* figuratively in the act—again introduce the theme of shame into the plot. And, when juxtaposed with the proceeding discussion concerning how "the game" has gotten old, the scene reads as a warning for women intent on pursuing sexual pleasure without commitment.

The conclusion of the film initially holds promise for subverting traditional Hollywood romantic comedy themes, but ultimately, it falls back upon them with its second ending. The first ending of the film promises an alternative to social regeneration through coupling when the movie's closing key kiss, a standard Hollywood romantic comedy convention that signals the ending of the narrative, appears to be less than satisfying for Christina. After Peter tracks Christina down and falls asleep on her doorstep, waiting for her to appear, the two argue, and Peter runs away, thinking that Christina does not care for him. Christina goes inside her apartment to overcome her fear and, once she feels she's conquered it, she chases Peter down. The two kiss, signaling a satisfying close to the narrative, but then Christina says, "That was weak." They kiss again, and Christina walks away, saying, "I'll call you, okay?"

This ending obviously subverts the viewer's expectations and undermines the traditional romantic comedy; however, in the next scene, we see Peter on the couch relating his story of Christina Walters as the other men in the beginning of the film had. Behind him a hand makes a dog puppet mock him as he speaks, and he turns to grab Christina, who is the puppeteer, and pull her over the couch. Their friends appear, and the camera pans to their wedding photo—a typical Hollywood ending after all. This scene serves to again reinforce the fact that social recognition can only occur through coupling and that women ultimately must be tamed and validated by the male hero.[9] Christina's puppet is significant, too, for it is reminiscent of the dog that we see earlier in the film. While Christina and Courtney are at a rest stop during their road trip to Peter's wedding, they stop in to use the men's bathroom. Christina goes into the stall furthest from the door where she discovers a graffiti drawn yellow brick road. She follows it to a picture of a dog that has a hole for his mouth. She promptly receives a penis in her eye when she gets closer to the image; apparently, unbeknownst to her, she has stumbled upon a glory hole. To repeat this image in the closing of the film is an interesting choice, for it reminds us of Christina's humiliating experience and provides viewers with another way that Christina receives a symbolic "penis in the eye," by relinquishing her clearly defined, sexual sense of self.

Like *The Sweetest Thing*, romantic comedies of the chick lit boom frequently present viewers with an alternative female heroine while ultimately falling back upon traditional portrayals.[10] These films often rely on the age-old good girl/bad girl dichotomy, stereotypically depicting the women of these movies.[11] For instance, in *Bound to Bond: Gender, Genre, and the*

*Hollywood Romantic Comedy*, Mark D. Rubinfeld discusses the film *Jerry Maguire* (1996) in order to illustrate what Rubinfeld deems "the bitch foil plot." Rubinfeld deconstructs Kelly Preston's character Avery Bishop, Jerry's fiancé, as a means of showing how the only character who "[refuses] to co-star in a narrative, ending with marriage, that is all about satisfying someone else's needs" is one of the only characters in the movie whom the audience is actively encouraged to dislike (53). On an even more basic level, Avery Bishop not only represents the bitch, but she represents the classic bad girl; she serves as a foil to Renée Zellweger's classic, good girl character, Dorothy Boyd. As Rubinfeld notes, the viewer's first introduction to Preston occurs when we see her having sex with Jerry Maguire, played by Tom Cruise. She shouts, "Never stop fucking me!" and, after having an orgasm, she immediately declares that she would be happy to engage in a threesome if he wanted her to. She then jumps off Jerry and heads to the kitchen, looking for fruit. The first major scene of the film with Zellweger's character, by contrast, is much tamer. While seated in business class, Dorothy hears Jerry telling the story of his proposal to Avery. Fascinated, Dorothy leans forward, intently listening to every word. While Avery Bishop comes off cold and unapproachable, Zellweger, much like Natalie Wood, plays the character of Dorothy with air of innocence, sweetness, and loyalty. While Avery declares, "There is a sensitivity thing that some people have. I don't have it. I don't cry at movies. I don't gush over babies," Dorothy Boyd is the only person idealistic and loyal enough to respond to Jerry's speech after he is fired. Promising "something real and fun and inspiring in this God forsaken business," Jerry implores his co-workers to join him in his new business. While everyone else looks on, Dorothy, moved by the speech, jumps to follow. Zellweger's character presents a stark contrast to Preston's.

Romantic comedies consistently continue to exploit the good girl/bad girl paradigm, and they implicitly identify the good girl as the virgin and the bad girl as the whore. Rubinfeld notes this tendency for the Hollywood romantic comedy to revolve around "the threat of female sexuality" (55). In his chapter, "The Temptress Foil Plot," he explains that this plot "involves hiding its heroine early in the narrative while focusing attention, instead, on a more sexually desirable female (i.e., the temptress) as a foil" (56). Repeatedly, romantic comedies vilify women who are overtly sexual creatures while upholding and rewarding those women who keep their sexuality in check. For instance, one of the chief ways that Avery's character is vilified is through her detached approach to sex. The movie depicts Avery as a sexually aggressive woman; her initial declaration of "Never stop fucking me!" works to set her up as such. Zellweger's character, by contrast, is shown in her first scene catering to her son, Ray (Jonathan Lipnicki).[12] Furthermore, her interest in Jerry's engagement story shows that unlike Avery, Dorothy is fascinated by love and romance rather than sex. Another such example of this dynamic occurs in the 1998 remake of the Disney classic, *The Parent Trap*, another film mentioned in Rubinfeld's text. Meredith Blake, the buxom blond played by Elaine Hendrix, is clearly the villain of this particular film, attempting to seduce Nicholas Parker (Dennis Quaid). She eventually discovers, however, that she cannot compete with Parker's first wife, Elizabeth James (Natasha Richardson), the demure and proper British mother of the twins. Though there is clearly sexual chemistry between Nicholas and Elizabeth, Elizabeth does not overtly exploit her sexuality as Meredith does.

Both *Jerry Maguire* and *The Parent Trap* punish its sexual transgressors. In *The Parent Trap*, the twins consistently torture Meredith. In Meredith's final scenes, she is tricked into accompanying the twins and their father on a camping trip where she is subjected to a variety of atrocities; the twins put rocks in her backpack and a lizard in her hair. In the end, Meredith winds up humiliated and alone. While she is sleeping, the twins push her air mattress out onto the lake, and Meredith wakes up in the middle. She stomps back to shore and declares to the twins' father that she is shipping the twins off to boarding school as soon as the two are married. She declares, "It's me or them. Take your pick." Nick picks the twins, and that is the last we see of Meredith. Likewise, after Jerry Maguire dumps Avery, we see her only once more in the film. She enters the press box where Jerry is and gives him the "L" sign for "loser." The closing shot of the film shows Jerry, Dorothy, and Ray walking past a baseball field; as viewers, we are left to wonder over Avery's fate. There is no traditional, happily ever after ending for her. Just as Natalie Wood ends up with Tony Curtis, Zellweger ends up with Tom Cruise in the end. Being the bad girl seldom pays off in the movies.

Yet, interestingly enough, romantic comedies experienced profound success despite their often times sexist portrayals in the later half of the twentieth century:

> Excluding all Hollywood romantic comedies that bombed so badly at the box office that they were in and out of the movie theaters faster than their coming attractions, the five years from 1995–1999 were a time of record new releases and ticket sales for the genre. They were, in the parlance of Hollywood, blockbuster years. In 1999 alone, there were fifteen Hollywood romantic comedies that sold more than 3.398 million tickets at the box office. These fifteen movies easily broke the old record number of ten Hollywood romantics comedies released in a

single year, first set in 1987 and then tied in 1998. As a matter of fact, there were more new Hollywood romantic comedies released in the five-year period from 1995–1999 than there were in the entire fourteen year period from 1970–1983. (Rubinfeld xiii–xiv)

Coincidentally, the success of romantic comedies at the box office occurred at the same time that chick lit writers were first publishing their books. And, many of these chick lit texts directly respond to the limiting views of female sexuality offered by these films. Candace Bushnell's *Sex and the City*, for instance, de-emphasizes the romantic promises of romantic comedies and concentrates instead on the sexual habits of her characters. Those characters who might normally be villainized in a romantic comedy become the heroines of Bushnell's book. Yet, her text does more than simply reverse the good/bad paradigm. Her narrative consistently undermines the happily ever after ending that readers of her text might expect, and, in doing so, she critiques the reductive nature of romantic comedies, particularly in regard to female sexuality.

Before it was the wildly successful television series for HBO, *Sex and the City* began in November 1994 as a series of columns written by Candace Bushnell for "the New York Observer [sic]—a salmon-colored weekly paper doted on by Manhattan's media elite" (Bellafante 66).[13] *Publishers Weekly* has accurately described Bushnell's book with its disconnected narrative about people who live lives in a crowded city nearly devoid of any real emotional contact as offering "a brash, radically unromantic perspective" (244). Bushnell's opening chapter, entitled "My Unsentimental Education: Love in Manhattan? I Don't Think So . . .," sets up the expectation that Bushnell's book will not reiterate classic romantic ideologies but rather expose the way in which those expectations are unrealistic in the twentieth century. This initial chapter explores the lack of love in New York City, noting that "Cupid has flown the co-op" and stressing that New Yorkers have come to a point where they must search for alternatives to the classic fairytale ending (2).[14] Bushnell writes:

> Welcome to the Age of Un-Innocence. The glittering lights of Manhattan that served as backdrop for Edith Wharton's bodice-heaving trysts are still glowing—but the stage is empty. No one has breakfast at Tiffany's and no one has affairs to remember—instead, we have breakfast at seven A.M. and affairs we try to forget as quickly as possible. (2)

Her characterization of the age in which Manhattanites currently live immediately situates the book within the literary tradition that preceded her. Like

Edith Wharton, Bushnell chronicles the New York City elite. And, in this paragraph, she also links *Sex and the City* with an additional, textual medium—film—by referencing such classic Hollywood romances as *Breakfast at Tiffany's* (1961) and *An Affair to Remember* (1957). Yet again, this paragraph also serves to stress the unromantic state of affairs that New Yorkers have found themselves in. Here, Bushnell emphasizes the way in which these films no longer connect with their audiences with her absolute statement "*No one* has breakfast at Tiffany's and *no one* has affairs to remember" (my emphasis). And, she further stresses New Yorkers' disconnection from these films when she asks:

> And what turned out to be the hot non-Tim Allen Christmas movie? *Disclosure*—for which ten or fifteen million moviegoers went to see unwanted, unaffectionate sex between corporate erotomaniacs—hardly the stuff we like to think about when we think about love but very much the stuff of the modern Manhattan relationship. (2)

The 1994 film starring Michael Douglas and Demi Moore, as Bushnell notes, is a far cry from the Hepburn and Kerr classics, and like Bushnell's text, it offers an entirely different view on relationships to its viewers.[15] Immediately, Bushnell wishes to distance her text from romantic comedies, preferring instead to articulate a more jaded view of relationships.

What Bushnell offers her readers is a radically unconventional portrayal of heterosexual relationships. She explores such topics as couples-only sex clubs and the ménage à trios. More importantly, Bushnell's book contains a cast of female characters, many of whom exude sexuality and whom experiment sexually. One woman, Ray, talks loudly about her boyfriend's penis at a local restaurant and then feigns having an orgasm to the surprise of the other customers, a scene reminiscent of the 1989 romantic comedy *When Harry Met Sally*. Yet Ray's delivery is remarkably different from Meg Ryan's; as Bushnell notes, "something seemed to be happening to her. It was like the high beams were on, but no one was driving" (56). Miranda, a recurring character, has sex with a man in a closet at a friend's party, and Carrie, arguably the protagonist of Bushnell's text, nearly has a lesbian encounter while her boyfriend, Mr. Big, is away on business. Unlike *The Sweetest Thing*, in which Jane is demoralized for her sexual experimentation and Christina relinquishes her clearly defined, sexual sense of self for Peter, *Sex and the City* reveres women like Samantha Jones, sexually active women who make no apologies for their lifestyle choices and who remain committed to their views on sex. Bushnell writes of Samantha: "We all admired Sam. First of all, it's not that easy to get twenty-five-year-old guys when you're in your early forties. Second, Sam is a New York inspiration. Because if you're a successful single woman in this city, you have two choices. You can beat your head against the wall trying to find a relationship, or you can say 'screw it' and just go out and have sex like a man. Thus: Sam" (40). Bushnell provokes readers to reexamine the good girl/bad girl, virgin/whore paradigm by frequently flip-flopping the two roles. In *Sex and the City*, those women who adopt more traditional lifestyles are villainized while sexually aggressive women are revered. Jolie Bernard, a former rock and roll agent who has given up Manhattan single life to get married and move to the suburbs, is presented as a pathetic woman who has lost all the former trappings that made her interesting. Bushnell's strategy still relies on the dichotomy, yet her reversal prompts readers to reexamine the sexual roles to which they have grown accustomed. For Bushnell, a "whore" like Samantha Jones isn't just a "whore;" rather, she can also be heroine.

Though the beginning of Bushnell's book posits the narrator as the main character, about halfway through the text it becomes apparent that the central story being told is the story of Carrie and Mr. Big. Bushnell's characterization of Carrie is fraught with contradictions. And, just as simplified, self-help texts could not address the complex, emotional trauma that both Jane Rosenal and Jane Goodall underwent, Bushnell seems to suggest that Carrie's search for love is much more complicated than romantic comedies might expect her to think. Like a romantic comedy heroine, Carrie appears, at times, naïve and optimistic about what life has to offer her. When the group of women goes to visit Jolie Bernard in Greenwich, Carrie says, "'Look. Grass. Trees. Breathe in the aroma of freshly mown grass,'" and as a result, Carrie "mysteriously beg[ins] to feel better. Everyone looked at her suspiciously" (81). Though she sometimes possesses a sort of hopeful optimism, Carrie is also very cynical when it comes to the possibility of love, romance, and a happily ever after ending. The Greenwich scenery calms her, but she later wonders while looking at Jolie's collection of photographs: "What was it like to be Jolie? How did it happen? How did you find someone who fell in love with you and gave you all this? She was thirty-four and she'd never even come close, and there was a good chance she never would" (85). Rather than hold on to dreamy fantasies of Prince Charming, Carrie acknowledges that there is a "good chance" that fairytale will not come true for her. Bushnell's depicts Carrie as doubting the inevitability that these romantic comedies promise women.

Another way in which Bushnell complicates her characters' relationships to romantic comedies is that she shows them questioning whether, if presented with the happily ever after ending, they would accept it. After her visit to Greenwich, Carrie calls Mr. Big to discuss her experiences that day:

> "It was awful," she giggled. "You know how much I hate those kinds of things. All they talked about was babies and private schools and how this friend of theirs got blackballed from the country club and how one of their nannies crashed a new Mercedes."
> She could hear Mr. Big puffing away on his cigar. "Don't worry, kid. You'll get used to it," he said.
> "I don't think so," she said.
> She turned and looked back to their table. Miranda had shanghaied two guys from another table, one of whom was already in deep conversation with Sarah.
> "Gimme shelter—in Bowery Bar," she said, and hung up. (87)

Their conversation reveals Carrie's reluctance to accept the type of lifestyle for which Jolie has settled. Carrie fears that she cannot forsake the Bowery Bar, a site that symbolizes a successful, single existence; in fact, she seeks "shelter" in it—shelter from a choice with which she does not feel entirely comfortable. Though the idea of love and commitment appeals to Carrie, at the same time, she does not wish to sacrifice a lifestyle that has proven so far to make her happy. Unlike the romantic comedy heroine who unquestioningly falls for the leading man, Bushnell depicts Carrie as satisfied with her current life and wondering if she is willing to change it.

Consistently, Bushnell shows how Carrie has internalized the binaries posited by romantic comedies through her views about her life. Carrie frequently feels that she has only two choices—either remaining single or developing a committed relationship. And, implicit in this decision is the fate of her sexuality, for Carrie has, on some level, bought into the sexual ideologies put forth by romantic comedies. Marriage, to Carrie, signifies a loss of sexual identity. While single, Carrie does not need to control her sexuality or concentrate it upon one man while, when married, she feels that she would. As a result, Bushnell depicts Carrie acting out against the loss of her sexual self. Soon after her negative experience in Greenwich and directly after a conversation about the marital problems of her friend Belle, Carrie enacts her unwillingness to accept a traditional lifestyle by engaging in a non-traditional, sexually charged act—topless dancing. Her act is symbolic on two levels. First, for Carrie, dancing topless serves to reaffirm her sexual self—a self that she fears might be stifled if she accepts the role that Jolie Bernard has. Secondly, her act reaffirms her independence. Not only is Mr. Big not present when she dances, but she also does not plan on telling him what she did. He finds out only because one of his friends mentions it to him. Her act serves to create some emotional distance between the two of them and to enable her to retain a sexual sense of self that she fears might dissipate if she involves herself in a serious, monogamous relationship.

Bushnell's text, however, is not suggesting that this dichotomy be perpetuated by merely exchanging the good for the bad. Rather, her characters are more complicated than that. Very often, there is a palpable sadness surrounding characters like Carrie. Though readers may like and identify with her as they would with the heroine of a romantic comedy, they are also forced to see how Carrie oftentimes feels conflicted because of how she is affected by romantic ideologies. For example, though Carrie feels liberated by her striptease at the Baby Doll lounge, she reconsiders her decision after speaking with Mr. Big. The reader senses that, on some level, Carrie regrets making Mr. Big upset, and Bushnell depicts her thinking about a way to signify how she really feels about him: "She wanted to take the pictures [of him smoking his cigar] and glue them to a piece of construction paper and write 'Portrait of Mr. Big with His Cigar,' across the top and then, 'I miss you,' with lots of kisses at the bottom" (95). Though she wants to express her feelings for him, Carrie's ultimate conclusion is that "She stared at the pictures for a long time. And then she did nothing" (95). There is a sense of sadness that infuses Bushnell's text in these moments. Carrie feels trapped by the expectations that surround her, and she is unable to choose any path, whether it is one of the two that society presents her with or another path entirely. Rather, she remains inert. Writing this inertia into Carrie's character is one of the ways that Bushnell articulates the crippling effects that romantic ideologies can have upon women.

Bushnell's text is fraught with ambiguities. Frequently, she constructs the endings of the Carrie and Mr. Big chapters in such a way that they undermine any happily ever after ending that the reader might anticipate. Bushnell's ending to Chapter 18 serves as an example. When Mr. Big asks Carrie what she is writing about in her column, she tells him, "'Remember how we said that someday we'd move to Colorado and raise horses and shit? That's what I'm writing about" (156). Carrie's use of the word "shit" belittles the plans that the two of them have made together while Mr. Big's reply, "It's a beautiful story," underscores the sentiment that their idea to move to Colorado is nothing more than a fantasy (156). The plans that the two made together, according to Mr. Big, are nothing more than a story—a fictional idea that will never be actualized. The chapter's title, "How to Marry a Man in Manhattan—My Way," adds to the contradictions within this chapter, for Carrie and Mr. Big cannot even acknowledge the possibility of their future plans let alone make legally binding their commitment.

The final ending of Carrie and Mr. Big's story is equally discouraging for a reader searching for the classic Hollywood ending.[16] In the closing chapter, Carrie and Mr. Big are continually fighting, profoundly disagreeing and bickering about nearly everything. Carrie, in this chapter, ends up feeling hopeless. Her hopelessness stems from two contradictory impulses: 1) she seems unsure of where the relationship is headed, discouraged by the stagnant nature of their relationship and 2) the next logical step, state sanctioned marriage, is equally unattractive to her. Her angst becomes magnified when she hears from her friend Amalita who calls her broke and with a small child, after the dissolution of yet another relationship. Amalita's story is a frightening one, and her experience signals what can happen to women who rely too heavily on men both financially and emotionally. During Carrie's visit, Amalita encourages her to hang onto Mr. Big, but like Carrie, we may wonder how Carrie's decision to do so would make her any different from Amalita or, in fact, what the likelihood is that Carrie's ending would be different from Amalita's ending. Ironically, Amalita is encouraging Carrie to pursue a path in life that has just left her empty handed.

When Carrie returns to Mr. Big, the two have the following exchange:

> She lit candles, and they sat in the dining room. Carrie sat up very straight in her chair. Mr. Big talked on and on about some deal he was in the middle of doing, and Carrie stared at him and nodded and made encouraging noises. But she wasn't really paying attention.
> When he was finished talking, she said, "I'm so excited. The amaryllis finally bloomed. It has four flowers."
> "Four flowers," Mr. Big said. And then: "I'm so happy that you've taken an interest in plants."
> "Yes. Isn't it nice?" Carrie said. "It's amazing the way they grow if you just pay a bit of attention." (226)

Though Carrie remarks on the way things can grow if you just pay a little attention, attention is just what is lacking from Carrie and Mr. Big's relationship at this point in time. Carrie is in no way interested in Mr. Big's discussion of his business deal, and in turn, Mr. Big is equally uninterested in what Carrie has to say about her flowers. As readers, then, we are left to wonder just how much their relationship can grow without this much needed attention.

The nature of this narrative structure works in such a way as to leave the reader unable to predict the direction that Bushnell's narrative may take. Unlike with romantic comedies, where the viewer can frequently predict the trajectory of the narrative, *Sex and the City* leaves the reader off balance. For instance, just when the reader may have lost all hope for Carrie and Mr. Big, she reads in the text's epilogue, "Carrie and Mr. Big are still together" (228). While one might argue that with this line Bushnell provides her readers with the classic Hollywood, romantic ending, the back and forth, up and down narrative structure of her entire text subverts this ending. Even though we may want to believe that Carrie and Mr. Big are still together, the disturbing scene with Amalita and the disconnected way that we have seen Carrie and Mr. Big relate to one another cannot be erased. It becomes hard, then, to read the closing as a hopeful, happy ending; instead, the reader is left with a feeling of discomfort. This narrative approach, then, speaks in response to the general reductiveness of romantic comedies. Through *Sex and the City*, Bushnell asserts that, like self-help books, romantic comedies often over simplify the complex choices that women must make about their sexual *and* romantic lives.[17]

Like *Sex and the City*, Carol Wolper's 1999 novel *The Cigarette Girl* works to challenge readers' traditional notions of romance. The cover design of the paperback edition of the book, which mimics the design of a cigarette box, comes complete with a warning label that reads: "Warning: May be hazardous to conventional romantic fantasies. Read at your own risk." Though we might immediately assume the romantic fantasies in question are those promised by romance novels, the novel's summary on the back cover evokes another association. The summary informs the reader that the novel takes place in Los Angeles and that its main character, Elizabeth West, is a screenwriter of action films. The novel's connection to the film industry, then, calls to mind a powerful medium for communicating romantic ideologies—the romantic comedy.

Wolper's heroine, Elizabeth West, is an action film screenwriter who, at age twenty-eight, finds herself trapped in "the zone," "the seven-year period between the ages of twenty-eight and thirty-five when women feel the pressure to resolve the marriage and baby issues" (3).[18] Surrounded by friends who are coupling off and influenced by a mother who works for an upscale home furnishings store that is a favorite of soon-to-be-brides, Elizabeth begins to feel the pressure to resolve these life issues and searches around her for her very own Mr. Maybe—a man who possesses the potential to become something much more.[19] What Elizabeth discovers, however, throughout the course of the novel, is that everyone else's expectations for her life are not necessarily her own, and sometimes men who seem to be a sure bet actually fall a distant second to the man who seems grossly inadequate.

The novel opens with a quote from Carrie Fisher in the 1990 film *Postcards from the Edge*. Fisher asks, "Why don't you fuck the bimbo and have the cigarette with me?" The epigraph of Wolper's novel serves three purposes. First, it immediately characterizes the heroine of the novel; second, it introduces the novel's major issue—sex; and third, it implies that movies will play an important part in the text. This quote, which comes from a movie, again reinforces the film industry's representations of women; the implication here is that there are two types of women—bimbos you can "fuck" and "cigarette girls" who provide the preferable post-coital talk. Since the title of Wolper's text is, after all, *The Cigarette Girl*, we immediately begin to associate Elizabeth with the second type of woman. Elizabeth certainly is no bimbo. The novel, which is told in the first person, gives us a glimpse into Elizabeth's psyche, and her story is peppered with clever quips, theories on relationships, and insight into her philosophies.

Elizabeth's intelligence, however, does not preclude her from enjoying a liberal sex life much like the characters of Bushnell's text. Elizabeth and her friends frequently gather to discuss their sex lives, and like the graphic language used in the book's epigraph, they, too, talk explicitly about sex. Elizabeth's friend "Julie declare[s] that a woman of the nineties makes good money and gives great blow jobs" (41), her friend Mimi upbraids Elizabeth's lover David for "'not calling . . . right away after the first fuck'" (158), and Elizabeth herself asserts, "'I would crawl across cut glass to suck his dick'" (264). The three women frequently gather for shopping sprees, lunches, and expensive Los Angeles dinners to share the details of their sex lives. Unlike Natalie Wood's character, however, Elizabeth's talk is not merely speculation without experience; Elizabeth recounts her own sexual exploits at various points in the novel, and we see her have sex with David on their first date. She explains, "he proved to be a great fuck. The night was part fairy tale, part porno movie" (27). Wolper's characterization of Elizabeth and her description of Elizabeth and David's first sexual encounter blur the carefully delineated lines established by romantic comedies. Rather than portraying Elizabeth as *either* the cigarette girl *or* the great fuck, Elizabeth has the potential to be both. Wolper ascribes Elizabeth with the characteristics of both the good and bad girl of romantic comedies. And, her description of the night spent with David further reveals Wolper's attempts to break down romantic comedies' binaries. Though Elizabeth observes directly that romantic comedies present viewers with storylines that end in a "'loving but never lustful embrace,'" Wolper's description of Elizabeth's encounter with David reacts against this tendency (116). Again, rather than characterize their night by referencing *either* romantic comedies *or* porno movies, Wolper shows the way in which Elizabeth's experience can be both romantic and sexual.

Though she participates in sex liberally, part of Elizabeth is still intrigued by the fairy tale that she has been promised by her mother, society, and, more particularly, by the romantic comedies that she loathes. After one of her lunches with Mimi and Julie, Elizabeth and her friends run into two happily married friends in the elevator. Elizabeth comments, " "In a flash, we'd gone from happily single to miserably single. All because we had the misfortune of seeing two people whose actions suggested that they were experiencing everything we were brought up to believe we should have, didn't yet have, and might never get" (43). The key phrase of this observation is "everything we were brought up to *believe* we should have;" though admittedly, Elizabeth's good mood deteriorates upon seeing these two people, her discomfort stems, in part, from the fact that she has been taught to believe in the promise of a happily coupled existence yet cannot seem to fit her life into that prescribed mold. Elizabeth's mother is unable to accept her conflicted feelings about this path. Each time Elizabeth visits her mother in her home goods store, frequented by newly engaged couples, her mother, much to Elizabeth's chagrin, fills her in on all the latest trends in bridal registry. These visits frustrate Elizabeth who reflects that she "didn't grow up dreaming about my wedding day;" rather, she "grew up dreaming about [her] wedding night" (83). Though Elizabeth's comment focuses on her sexual identity, a part of her is still feels bothered by the fact that she is unable to envision for herself the life that is expected of her.

In addition to her mother's pressure, Elizabeth is equally troubled by romantic comedies, the manuals that she feels most directly contradict the path that she has chosen for herself. She comments to her therapist, " 'Actually, I despise romantic comedies. A cute couple—destined to live happily ever after—endures a series of cute misadventures before falling into each other's arms in a loving but never lustful embrace . . . The last time I experienced anything close to that sweet, sappy scenario, I was in the fifth grade' " (116). For Elizabeth, the ideologies imparted by these texts are outdated, inappropriate, and at odds with the life that she has chosen to lead. On one level, Elizabeth wholeheartedly rejects these texts by choosing an active, "lustful" sex life, but more significantly, Elizabeth's career path, writing for action films, further cements her rejection of "Estrogen movies . . . All emotion, no edge. Not my thing" (7). The scripts of these films do not fit the lifestyle that she feels compelled to lead.

Wolper depicts Elizabeth using both romantic comedy and action film scripts as a model for the script that she sees as her life. Frequently, she contextualizes the events that occur as fitting either mode. While at the house of Jake, her boss and hopeless crush, their romantic, sexually suggestive exchange, worthy of a Hollywood, romantic comedy, becomes interrupted by the sound of gunshots coming from a neighbor's house, a scene more akin to the action films that Elizabeth writes. The effect of movies on Elizabeth's life is so pervasive that Wolper frequently relays significant moments of dialogue in the form of a movie script. This narrative move further cements the connection between her text and the film industry.

Frequently, though, Elizabeth finds that her life does not fit neatly into one of the precisely scripted genres; rather, her life often defies carefully constructed genres. The extent to which these scripts do not fit her life is revealed toward the end of the novel. While at Mimi's bachelorette party, Elizabeth encounters a legendary producer named Max, and she pauses before relaying further action to discuss the significance of the scene to come:

> Okay, I have to stop here. Stop the way I always like to do toward the end of the second act of one of my action scripts. I love putting the action on hold for a moment and taking a couple of pages to introduce a character who has nothing to do with the plot but comes into a character's life and says some interesting and helpful stuff and then goes on his way. Always, without exception, the studio cuts this scene from the script. "It doesn't advance the story," is the usual reason given. My argument is, it advances the story if part of the story has to do with how these characters think and feel, but I always, without exception, lose this argument. (194)

Her reflection reveals that even though she writes action-film screenplays she consistently deviates from the formula, attempting to allow for character development in a way that action-films traditionally deny. Though she is committed to this genre for her career, she finds the formula lacking when drafting the script of her life. When Elizabeth encounters David's other girlfriend at the premiere party, she again discovers that the formulaic plots of action-films cannot encapsulate her life. Upset, she reflects, "David wasn't the bad guy here. That was the problem. I didn't know who the bad guy was. Action movies are so much easier. Eventually, you always can distinguish the good guys from the bad. Here I was in what felt like Act Three and I still had no clue" (252). Elizabeth's observations reveal her inability to give her life a genre label, and subsequently she is left confused. More importantly, after she tearfully flees the premiere party, her life further spins out of control; a stalker nearly attacks her before Jake comes to her rescue. Again, Wolper resists including elements of only one genre in her novel. She instead mixes multiple genres together to draw attention to the way in which romantic comedies can present viewers with limited scripts to follow.

Wolper's ending further reinforces Elizabeth's failure to connect her life to one of these models, which makes it necessary for her to abandon the model scripts entirely and develop a new script of her very own. Doing so requires her to write her own ending—an ending that is without action in the action-film sense and which completely defies the traditional ending of a Hollywood romantic comedy. Throughout the novel, the reader gets the impression that Jake, Elizabeth's boss, is the man with whom Elizabeth would most like to be—a situation that may call to mind Bridget Jones's interest in her boss, Daniel Cleaver. She reflects:

> I was madly in love with Jake. This was not a good thing. If I were twenty, twenty-two, twenty-six, okay fine. But I was twenty-eight. It was time to have a relationship. It was not time to be in love with a guy I couldn't have a life with. It was time to leave. Time to go home. Time to move on. Time to grow up.
> I didn't leave. (75)

Jake, with his attraction for bimbos named Barri and Blaze, is the antithesis of what Elizabeth feels she should be searching for at this point in her life. He will not provide her with stability or any sense of a concrete future; in other words, he is not the type of man that can complete her fairy tale ending. Despite this fact, Elizabeth feels strangely drawn to him, and when he pulls up to rescue her from the stalker she encounters at the end of the novel, Elizabeth goes with him to his hotel room, and the two have sex. The following morning, Jake reveals that his girlfriend Blaze is pregnant and that he is going to try to make things work with her. Having abandoned one child early in his life, he decides that he needs to try to see things through with Blaze and their soon-to-be child.

Elizabeth's reaction to this news reveals the transformation that she has undergone throughout the novel, and it further reveals just how completely she has decided to reject the romantic ideals that have been controlling her life. While sitting on the porch the next day reflecting about what just happened, she acknowledges that the scenario seems, to outsiders, hopeless: "If this were a movie, someone might sum up the plotline like this: Girl in the zone falls in love with a man who is seriously involved with another woman who at any minute could become his wife and in seven more months will definitely be the mother of his child" (268). Wolper's inclusion of the qualifier, "If this were a movie," is what is important here; if it were a movie, this might be the scenario. Elizabeth continues, noting that the situation, while "true," is not "the whole story" (268). She goes on to say that she's happy being "'just friends'" with Jake and that she's also satisfied with having him call her "'just for sex,'" noting that a close friendship and a great sex life are two really important factors in her own happiness (269). Though this realization surprises her, she also notes that "This was the first time in months that I felt free of the zone—which is another way of saying happy" (269). Interestingly enough, Wolper has Elizabeth discover that what she expects will make her happy, to find a secure, stable, traditional relationship, has been the problem all along, and the non-traditional choice that she would have never expected to fulfill her is the one that actually does.

Elizabeth's decision to be with Jake is actually a move toward rejecting proscribed happiness; she says:

> "I'm supposed to think happiness is about a guy, a baby, a family. But what if happiness can also be about a guy and no kids? Or a baby without a guy? Or a guy and someone else's kids? Or no guy? Or lots of guys? Or a friend and a kid? Or friends-plus and no kids? Why are all my girlfriends and I in a frenzy thinking there's only one way to live this life? Who wrote this fucking rule book?" (271).

Again, Elizabeth notes that she is aware of what she is *supposed* to believe, but the rule book—in this case romantic comedies—falls grossly short for her. Elizabeth's happily ever after ending differs dramatically from the one prescribed by romantic comedies.

Wolper's ending, in which Elizabeth decides that living as Jake's mistress will make her happy, does not only directly conflict with the traditional endings of romantic comedies, but it also potentially conflicts with the reader's expectations for Wolper's novel. While Wolper's novel contains critiques of the film industry, she also relies heavily on the conventions of films at times. As mentioned earlier, she includes dialogue in the form of a script. And, her novel is heavily laden with stereotypes much like the ones that viewers encounter in films. Blaze acts as Elizabeth's foil; Elizabeth discovers her initial romantic interest is wrong for her; and there is a dramatic rescue scene toward the novel's conclusion. Wolper's inclusion of these conventions, however, helps to make the novel's ending even more surprising thus subverting the romantic comedy industry even more strongly. Just when the reader may feel that she has a handle on where the narrative is headed, Wolper includes an unsuspecting turn of events. The second explosion, then, really is the one that the audience wasn't expecting, and Wolper's surprise payoff for her readers is that she has crafted an ending which concludes unexpectedly *and* happily.

The 1999 paperback edition of Carol Wolper's text has an arresting image on the front cover. The photograph, taken by Guy Aroch, a New York fashion photographer, depicts a woman who looks remarkably like Marilyn Monroe, posed in a typical pin-up stance. Her arms are raised above her head, her lips are pursed, and her legs are positioned at an alluring angle. The figure represents the epitome of female sexuality; she exudes sex appeal, and her resemblance to Marilyn Monroe, a sexual icon of the past, strengthens that association. What complicates the photograph, however, is the fact that the woman's stomach and legs are bound together by 1950s-style bras. The bras restrict her range of motion, freezing her in this position. Aroch's photograph captures the tension that follows in Wolper's text; though this woman clearly revels in and exploits her own sexuality, consumer culture simultaneously traps and restricts her by it. In terms of Aroch's photograph, a product marketed to and consumed by women inhibits her sexual liberation; in the case of Wolper's novel, romantic comedies discourage Elizabeth from fully embracing her sexuality. Though consumer culture mediums might encourage certain acceptable views of female sexuality, as represented by the allusion to America's pin-up tradition, at the same time, they strive to contain others, as represented by the bras that bind this woman. Wolper's and Bushnell's texts explore these mixed messages about female sexuality and present readers with heroines who are questioning the ideologies offered by a powerful consumer culture medium. Both writers construct women who attempt to navigate these ideologies, searching for a path that more adequately fits their own lifestyle and struggling to break the chains that bind them. And, in doing so, Bushnell and Wolper critique a visual, advice manual that instructs women to contain, control, and concentrate their sexuality upon one man.

Chapter Five
# Living the Life of a Domestic Goddess: "It's a Good Thing"

> "A recent study of high school home economics courses in the United States found an alarming 23 percent drop in performance over the past five years . . . Spot inspections by my staff of suburban homes around the nation revealed store bought poultry and eggs, unstenciled walls and floors, ungilded things, and under some beds dustballs the size of Volvos."
>
> —Tom Connor and Jim Downey, *Martha Stuart's Better Than You at Entertaining* (1996)

"It is never good to have things rotting about the place," advises Bridget Jones, Helen Fielding's fictional creation, on the opening page of *Bridget Jones's Guide to Life*. Published in 2001, the text is a hybrid women's manual—part women's magazine (with a chapter entitled "How to Lose Weight"), part self-help book ("The Road to Healing Your Life"), and part etiquette manual ("Social and Sexual Etiquette"). Fielding's guide also mimics such publications as Martha Stewart's *Living* magazine, complete with sections on "The Fragrant Home" and "Cooking." However, while Martha Stewart claims readers can "master culinary faux bois with our 'Woodland Sweets'" (Stewart, "A Letter From Martha" 8), Fielding's Bridget Jones instructs readers that when receiving guests one should "find glasses and mugs in all areas of flat and put in dishwasher" and ensures them that cheese, though moldy, can be eaten if the mold is cut off (3). Like *Living*, *Bridget Jones's Guide to Life* comes complete with photographs to illustrate the step-by-step process being described, though instead of showing readers how to create marshmallow snowflakes, Fielding's text illustrates the best way to order pizza, complete with pictures of Bridget dialing for Domino's and opening the pizza box.[1]

Fielding's instructional manual, like her novel, is satirical. By presenting readers with outrageously funny instructions that stand in opposition to those instructions included in popular domestic-advice manuals, *Bridget Jones's Guide to Life* mocks the excessive domestication exhibited by publications such as Stewart's and the implied promises these publications offer readers.[2] For instance, while Bridget tells readers a "well stocked" cupboard should consist of such ingredients as Silk Cut, four bottles of white wine, and matches, Martha Stewart's instructions for stocking a cupboard are much more extensive. Sugar alone receives a paragraph long description.[3] The text pokes fun at Stewart's excessive domestication as well as the implied promise of upward mobility denoted by such phrases as "faux bois."[4] In a day and age where women, like Bridget, are rushing from work to dinner out with friends, who has time for marshmallow snowflakes, Fielding seems to ask. Rather than make pink cucumber soup, Fielding answers, women like Bridget are more likely to call for delivery.[5] And, just as other chick lit texts have called into question the validity of women's manuals, *Bridget Jones's Guide to Life* interrogates the relevance that domestic-advice manuals have to young women's lives.

*Bridget Jones's Guide to Life* is one of many chick lit texts to engage with the ideologies offered by domestic-advice manuals such as Stewart's. Though their characters are single women seemingly far removed from occupying a "traditional" domestic space, chick lit authors, from Helen Fielding to Candace Bushnell to Anna Maxted, often preoccupy their characters with household tasks and the home. In *Animal Husbandry*, after finding the ideal New York City apartment to share with her boyfriend Ray, Jane Goodall extensively lists the household items she will need to acquire to complete her home; Helen Fielding's main character attempts to cook a meal as instructed by British chef and cookbook author Marco Pierre White; and though the premise of Anna Maxted's novel *Getting Over It* (2000) is her main character Helen Bradshaw's coping with her father's death, an equally important plotline deals with her search for the ideal home. This preoccupation with the home is thus informed by the characters', and ultimately their authors', familiarity with domestic-advice manuals that, like women's magazines, present their readers with an "idealized mirror image" of what their home *should* contain and what their given behaviors within that private sphere *should* be (McCracken 13).

But just as a grey cardigan is more than just a grey cardigan to Becky Bloomwood, purchasing new sheets and/or mastering a recipe signifies something larger to these chick lit characters. Like Becky, these women think that acquiring particular household goods and domestic behaviors will produce what Kathleen Anne McHugh in *American Domesticity: From How-To Manual to Hollywood Melodrama* deems the "sentiments" associated with domesticity (6). For McHugh, and other cultural critics, the domestic refers to "more than housekeeping tasks and the physical structure of the home" (Walker, *Shaping Our Mothers' Worlds: American Women's Magazines* viii). Rather, it refers "to home, family, maternity, warmth, hearth, to the creation of a private place where we can be who we really are, to a set of experiences, possessions, and sentiments that are highly symbolically valued in our culture" (McHugh 6).[6] In other words, the pull these women feel to buy a pasta maker or a Calphalon pot goes beyond the desire for new appliances. Rather, these women seek to gain the "home, family, maternity, warmth, hearth" associated with domesticity by acquiring consumer goods and socially *expected* behaviors.

What these women find, however, is that attaining the props associated with "proper" domesticity and performing its behaviors do not give them the sense of fulfillment that they anticipated feeling. Domestic-advice manuals, with their depictions of perfectly ordered households and savory meals, become representations of what Jessamyn Neuhaus, writer of "The Way to a Man's Heart: Gender Roles, Domestic Ideology, and Cookbooks in the 1950s," deems "expressions of desires and fears" (546). Neuhaus addresses popular culture representations of domestic women in the 1950s when she writes, "The woman who baked, basted, glazed, and decorated throughout postwar cookbooks were figments of the postwar American imagination. They were expressions of desires and fears in a nation strained by war and baffled by the unstoppable social changes that shaped the 1950s" (546).

Neuhaus's observation is specific to postwar America, yet her phrase "expressions of desires and fears" captures the sentiments expressed by chick lit characters toward the domestic-advice manuals they encounter. Chick lit authors depict their protagonists as having ambivalent relationships toward these manuals. While their protagonists are often drawn to the goods and skills marketed to them by these domestic publications, they also exhibit great anxiety about what these goods and skills represent. For instance, as we saw in the previous chapter, Carrie of *Sex and the City* immediately begins to feel better when she enters Greenwich; however, Bushnell complicates Carrie's feelings for suburbia by having her react against them upon her return to New York City. Likewise, in *The Cigarette Girl*, Carol Wolper's Elizabeth West finds herself trapped in the zone, yet simultaneously Wolper depicts her main character making life choices that will not result in a traditional marriage. While these characters are drawn to "home, family, maternity, warmth, hearth," they are also skeptical about how fitting this model is to their lives.

This chapter articulates the varied ways that chick lit authors critique domestic-advice manuals. In the same way that chick lit authors respond to women's magazines, chick lit novelists take issue with the promises offered by these domestic-advice publications. While these novels depict characters like Bridget Jones, Jane Goodall, and Carrie Bradshaw purchasing household goods and acquiring domestic behaviors in order to achieve the domestic sentiments that they currently lack, these books also portray the characters' anxieties about what these goods and skills represent. One of the chief anxieties explored by these novelists is the question of whether or not it is possible to attain the sentiments associated with domesticity if one chooses untraditional life choices and creates a home devoid of husband and family. While this chapter will discuss Fielding's, Zigman's, Bushnell's, and Wolper's critiques of domestic publications, British novelist Anna Maxted's *Getting Over It* will serve as the keystone of this chapter. Following the death of her father, Maxted's main character, Helen Bradshaw, is forced to redefine what family, and in turn home, means to her, and as a result of this renegotiation, she struggles to understand who she is and how to make a home space for herself. In Maxted's novel, "moving on" has dual significance, for Maxted consistently realizes Helen's emotional recovery through her attempts to find and buy a flat. Displaced from her apartment and then from her mother's house, Helen finally "gets over" her intense grief when she purchases, furnishes, and finally inhabits her new flat alone. Like other chick lit authors, Maxted depicts her protagonist as struggling with the ideologies of domestic-advice manuals, which offer particular constructions of family and home, yet she ultimately writes a heroine who finds an alternative that more adequately fits her lifestyle.

The twenty-first century domestic-advice manuals that writers like Maxted critique in their novels emerged from a larger tradition of household management books and magazines.[7] In both America and England, books like Catharine Esther Beecher's *A Treatise on Domestic Economy* (1841) and Isabella Mary Beeton's *The Book of Household Management* (1869) were extremely popular.[8] Beecher's book "outlined a woman's duties as including not only the care of husband and children—including moral instruction of the latter—but also the supervision of servants, maintaining a proper social life, and duties to the larger community" (Walker, *Shaping Our Mothers' Worlds: American Women's Magazines* 55). In the preface to her book, "Mrs. Beeton," as she was more widely known, informed readers as to the purpose of her book, noting:

> What moved me, in the first instance, to attempt a work like this, was the discomfort and suffering which I had seen brought upon men and women by household mismanagement. I have always thought that there

is no more fruitful source of family discontent than a housewife's badly cooked dinners and untidy ways. (ix)

Mrs. Beeton feared that since men were being "so well served out of doors—at their clubs, well-ordered taverns and dining-houses" that they would no longer value the services provided by their wives (ix). To combat this problem, she asserted, "a mistress must be thoroughly acquainted with the theory and practice of cookery as well as be perfectly conversant with all the other arts of making and keeping a comfortable home" (ix). Her book of household management did just that, including not only recipes for the homemaker but also chapters of advice for the mistress of the house.

Household instruction guides did not only reach the public in the form of books. In the nineteenth century, there was also a proliferation of women's magazines that focused on cooking, the home, and gardening. One of the earliest manuals was produced by Samuel Beeton, Mrs. Beeton's husband. As Cynthia White notes in her book *Women's Magazines 1693–1968*, the *Englishwoman's Domestic Magazine*, which began in 1852, was "the first women's periodical to deal systematically with the subject of domestic management" (46). The magazine, which was distributed monthly for twopence an issue, made household management manuals more accessible to a broader public and "achieved a greater popularity than even Beeton himself had anticipated" (46). White acknowledges that in England "The last twenty years of the nineteenth century witnessed the arrival of, among others, the *Housewife* (1886), *The Mother's Companion* (1887), *The Ladies' Home Journal* (1890), *Woman at Home* (1893), *Home Notes* (1894), *Home Chat* (1895), and the *Home Companion* (1897)" (74–75). In America, such magazines were greeted with equal enthusiasm. In *The Magazine in America 1741–1990*, John Tebbel and Mary Ellen Zuckerman note "In the last three decades of the [nineteenth] century, the *Ladies' Home Journal* [1883], *McCall's* [1897], *Delineator* [1873], and *Pictorial Review* [1899] appeared for the first time" (93).[9]

These magazines serve an important role in the history of domestic-advice manuals. As mentioned above, because of their affordability, the inception of household magazines made domestic advice available to more individuals. And, though the audience base broadened, the content of and approach taken in domestic-advice manuals was often reproduced in the magazines. Introducing domestic advice into magazines, however, also contributed to the blurring of the genre line. Some magazines existed solely for the dissemination of domestic advice while other magazines contained more varied content—a trend that continues today. While Martha Stewart's *Living* devotes itself to the care and keeping of one's home, a publication like *McCall's* more broadly interprets what constitutes the domestic; it may include tips for effectively cleaning one's oven alongside an article about improving one's marriage. Thus, the definition of what constitutes a "domestic magazine" and a "women's magazine" became complicated as domestic advice was incorporated in a variety of forms within magazines. As a result, the association of the feminine and the domestic became even further linked.

At the close of the nineteenth century, the domestic science movement began, which would fundamentally alter women's relationships to the home.[10] As Laura Shapiro notes in *Perfection Salad: Women and Cooking at the Turn of the Century*, this "major domestic reform movement" (4), was pioneered by such women as chemist Ellen Swallow Richards who hoped to further women's participation in the sciences by applying "scientifically based ways to understand[ing] [the] home" (Leavitt 41). Shapiro asserts that this movement was led by "an inquisitive circle of ambitious cooks, teachers, writers, and housekeepers" (4). She continues:

> Traditional methods of housekeeping began to look disturbingly haphazard to [these women], once they gained an impressionistic understanding of the principles of nutrition and the danger of germs. Moreover, the very way women approached the day's work seemed irrational and unprofessional compared with the way a well-regulated office or factory could be run. (4)

As a result, domestic science became incorporated into girls' and women's education; courses were taught in primary and secondary schools as well as colleges and universities. Women's magazines contributed to the advancement of the movement as well. In 1912, the *Ladies' Home Journal* produced a series of articles in which writer Christine Frederick began to "promote the full managerial revolution of the home" (Ehrenreich and English 146). Publications of this time period and "homemaking experts" aimed "to elevate their area of expertise beyond the stage of recipes and household hints and onto the higher ground of scientific professionalism" (Ehrenreich and English 136).

In the twentieth century, the domestic science movement had so infiltrated women's consciousness that "There was no need for crusading writers and lecturers to set the standards and dictate the tasks of homemaking" (Ehrenreich and English 160–161). Rather, "the principles of 'right living'— had been, for a growing proportion of women, built into the material organization of daily life" (Ehrenreich and English 161). What women were experiencing after World War II, however, was a reconnection to their homes, which many had been forced to abandon in order to help out with the war effort. After the war's resolution, traditional family structures were re-instituted, and the predominant role encouraged of women during that time was that of ideal homemaker, epitomized by such popular culture icons as June Cleaver and Donna Reed. As historians have noted, during this time period, domesticity was marketed in ways that it had not been before through the development of household appliances and packaged and semi-prepared foods. However, as cultural critics from Betty Friedan to Laura Shapiro to Stephanie Coontz have noted, the 1950s were also a period in which women began to question their relationships to their homes.[11] Housewives, historians of this time period have noted, were beginning to feel unrest, wondering what other opportunities might exist for them. This cultural climate produced the women's movement of the 1960s in which the emphasis on the home was replaced by social activism. In the years following, feminists urged women to combat "'the housewife's syndrome'" through creative work of their own (Friedan 20).[12] Additionally, women were encouraged to re-envision their relationship to their homes; writers like Alix Shulman, author of "A Marriage Agreement," urged women to fight for the equal division of household labor. More and more women were encouraged to abandon their close association with the home and the prescriptive gender roles of the 1950s.

The alienation that women felt from their homes in the 1960s and 1970s continued into the next two decades as more and more women opted for employment outside the home. The media, as Susan Faludi documents in *Backlash: The Undeclared War Against American Women*, had a less than favorable response to these economic gains for which the feminists of the 1970s had fought so hard. She notes that a 1986 special report aired on ABC and focused on the question, "'What has happened to American women?'" (77). According to the program, American women were suffering from "'The emotional fallout of feminism'" (77–78). These women, the show argued, were victims of what has become known as "having it all syndrome" or "superwoman syndrome," the phenomenon that plagues Wendy Wasserstein's protagonist in *The Heidi Chronicles*.[13] Women of this era were characterized by the media as either incapable of juggling the demands of a career and home life or unable to achieve a satisfying home life because of their demanding career and the severe "man shortage" (3).[14]

This cultural climate produced fertile ground for Martha Stewart's empire to take root. Capitalizing on the idea that women were becoming further alienated from their homes, Martha Stewart encouraged women of the late 1980s and 1990s to reclaim their home space.[15] Initial reception to Stewart's catering business, which started in 1976, and her first book

*Entertaining* in 1982 resulted in the rapid growth of her empire ("The Martha Yearbook" 35). Taking advantage of this feeling of estrangement from the home and the materialism that accompanied the 1980s, Martha Stewart realized that "Domesticity had lost its structure" and pushed for "Activities like crafts, cooking, decoration, and entertaining [to retain] their commodity status" (Magnolia 28). As Tiffany Magnolia records in "Martha and the Many Loaves: The Savior of Domesticity at the End of the Twentieth Century," Martha Stewart was responsible for producing:

> . . . a magazine, started in 1990; a TV show, started in 1993; a K-Mart line, started in 1995; a syndicated newspaper column, started in 1995; a website, started in 1997; and a radio show, started in 1997. Unlike Julia Child who defined cooking with PBS shows and cookbooks, Martha exists in all four primary media: print, television, radio, and electronic. (29)

Benefiting from technological advances, Stewart was able to transform Mrs. Beeton's approach to household management into a multi-media experience and enlarge our definition of domestic-advice manuals to include not only books and magazines but also cooking and home decorating television shows as well as a morning talk show and "how-to improve your home" webpages.[16] Today, then, the term domestic-advice manual can be broadened to apply to magazines, cookbooks, catalogs, cooking shows, and home decorating shows—those mediums that place a primary emphasis on the home.[17]

Though Stewart profits from these twentieth century advances, her magazine relies heavily on precedents set earlier in the magazine industry. *Living* differs dramatically from women's magazines like *Cosmopolitan* in terms of its content and target audience, but its basic principles are remarkably similar. Like women's magazines, *Living* encourages its readers to purchase products by using both overt and covert advertising strategies. Editions of *Living* contain advertisements for such products as Pfaltzgraff, Kenmore, and the Nautica Home Collection while articles included in the magazine, such as the one by Amy Conway on footstools in the September 1997 edition of the magazine, often mention particular home furnishing establishments.[18] For instance, Conway's article quotes both the owner of Rooms and Gardens, an antique store in New York City, and Aero, a home furnishing store in New York City, a subtle way to encourage business at both establishments (166). Martha Stewart herself is not one to shy away from promoting products. In "The Art of Showing Off; What Makes Martha Stewart Cook?" Laura Shapiro observes, "Stewart's willingness to endorse products is controversial, although she's not the only cook to take advantage of commercial opportunities. Currently, she's at work on a cookbook sponsored by Crabtree & Evelyn ... and she's also associated with Perrier Jouet Champagne, Sterling Vineyards and Aga stoves" (67). And, more recently, Stewart formed a commercial association with Kmart (Pollack 83) and Michaels, the arts and crafts store.

Additionally, *Living* encourages its readers to perform particular behaviors. While *Cosmopolitan* might suggest readers book a waxing appointment before swimsuit season, *Living* might encourage readers to make paper lanterns as in order to create "magic" in their backyards (Hamilton 105). Sometimes, *Living* links the two ideas, encouraging readers to buy particular products in order to complete a project. For instance, Stewart's publication *Good Things: A Collection of Household Goods and Projects* (1997) instructs readers on how to make "dish-towel curtains" by purchasing dish towels, cup hooks, and café clips. Instructions are provided concerning how-to assemble the curtains, and the end result is illustrated with a photograph to the left of the instructions. Like women's magazines, Stewart's publications encourage her readers to acquire "props" and perform particular behaviors.

Readers of *Living* may wonder what purpose these home improvement projects serve. In terms of the dish-towel curtain project, Stewart's primary purpose is not to market a particular product; Stewart does not have any particular investment in what type of dish towels or café clips the reader buys. Likewise, the project that she has proposed is not one of necessity. While it may be advantageous to have the windows of your home covered by curtains, it is not vital for those curtains to be made from dishtowels. Rather, the emphasis of the project is placed on its underlying implications. As we have seen, women's magazines often encourage readers to purchase goods and manage their bodies in order to capture the attention of men; thus, women are able to achieve a goal by obtaining those particular props and behaviors advocated by magazines. The aim of Stewart's publications is similar; though ostensibly these publications advise readers on various do-it-yourself projects, their understated claim is that readers can actualize the sentiments of domesticity by constructing a carefully ordered, managed, and elegant home.

Stewart herself has articulated this idea, noting that her photographs play an integral part in conveying what she deems "'the lifestyle,'" as noted by Laura Shapiro in her article "The Art of Showing Off: What Makes Martha Stewart Cook?" (Shapiro).[19] In this article, Shapiro explains "the lifestyle:"

> Laden with sumptuous photographs, her books invariably showcase Stewart herself starring in what she calls "the lifestyle": peering into a

wok in the kitchen of her 1805 farmhouse, filling an antique basket with fresh strawberries, serving scrambled eggs in miniature tart shells arranged on a breadboard or setting a table with the amethyst goblets and pink Depression glass that have become as familiar to her fans as their own stainless. (66)

Here, Shapiro defines by example. "The lifestyle" includes order (miniature tart shells contain potentially unruly scrambled eggs), elegance (amethyst goblets rather than plastic cups), and nostalgia (an 1805 farmhouse, an antique basket, Depression glass). Her examples conjure up images of carefully prepared meals with only the best ingredients and dining room tables stylishly set for a family gathering, denoting not only "'the lifestyle'" but also invoking McHugh's domestic sentiments (Shapiro, "The Art of Showing Off" 66).

Scenes such as the ones mentioned by Shapiro are carefully illustrated in Stewart's books and magazines. The photographs in Stewart's publications are constructed to encourage readers/viewers to participate in "the lifestyle." As Cynthia Duquette Smith observes in "Discipline—It's a 'Good Thing': Rhetorical Constitution and Martha Stewart Living Omnimedia," Stewart's publications "create elaborate settings for action, without showing much of the action itself" (359). She refers to the way in which people are often absent from the photographs included in Stewart's books and magazine. Her observation is on point. For instance, in the October 1999 edition of *Living*, Stewart includes a spread on Halloween celebrations by Amy Conway entitled "A Pumpkin Carving Party." Though some of the photographs do contain people participating in such activities as pumpkin carving, others, such as the photograph of caramel apples on page 206, simply present the food on a platter, as if waiting to be consumed. This photograph engages the audience directly; the stems of the candy apples, which are tree branches, seemingly pop off the page, toward the reader, as if encouraging the viewer to grab one. Additionally, in Stewart's 1997 home decorating book *Good Things: A Collection of Inspired Household Ideas and Projects*, there are photographs such as the one of a vintage shutter door on page 105. In the photograph, the door has been left ajar to highlight the pine tree cut out at the top; this photograph constructs a scene in which the viewer is encouraged to imagine the action that led to the scene. It is almost as if Stewart has intentionally allowed for the reader/viewer to imagine herself in that particular setting, promoting the consumption of both foods and goods marketed on the pages of her publications while simultaneously encouraging the reader's active participation in cultivating the skills needed to create a carefully ordered household. Again, like women's magazines, Stewart's publications encourage readers to acquire the "props" and perform the behaviors necessary to achieve "the lifestyle."

Though not the target audience for publications like *Living*, chick lit characters are conscious of domestic-advice manuals' ideologies and often influenced by them. For instance, Laura Zigman portrays her protagonist purchasing household goods just as Helen Fielding and Sophie Kinsella depicted their heroines compulsively purchasing clothing. In *Animal Husbandry*, Jane Goodall lists the items needed to complete her new apartment—a bed, sheets, pillowcases, Calphalon. And, when Helen Bradshaw finally purchases her own flat, her mother helps her to acquire the items she will need (solid oak chairs, faux steel kitchen units, a shiny new kettle) to complete it. Likewise, these characters often preoccupy themselves with performing suitable domestic behaviors. Fielding's novel contains two cooking scenes while Sophie Kinsella's novel depicts Becky Bloomwood, in an effort to save money, attempting to cook her own curry at home. Though these single, career women may seem far removed from "traditional" domesticity, their creators often show them purchasing household goods and performing domestic behaviors.

It is interesting to note that though chick lit authors consistently refer to other consumer culture mediums (from *Cosmopolitan* magazine to *The Rules*) by name there is limited mention of domestic-advice manuals.[20] This omission is partially due to the fact that domestic-advice manuals like Stewart's were such a large part of cultural consciousness in the 1990s that any reference to them, no matter how subtle, would be recognizable to the contemporary reader. Domestic-advice manuals in all forms flooded the market in the 1990s. This was the time when, as Tiffany Magnolia notes in "Martha and the Many Loaves: The Savior of Domesticity at the End of the Twentieth Century," Martha Stewart's empire really began to take off—her magazine *Living* in 1990, her television show in 1993, and a K-Mart line in 1995. Then in 1999, Martha Stewart Living Omnimedia (MSLO) went public ("The Martha Yearbook" 35). In "Martha Stewart's Intimate Invitations to e-commerce," Susan Brown Zahn explains the many facets of MSLO:

> MSLO is comprised of *Martha Stewart Living*, a monthly magazine; *Martha Stewart Living*, a syndicated television show; www.marthastewart.com, a Web site; askMartha, a daily syndicated radio show; "askMartha," a syndicated newspaper column; "From Martha's Kitchen," a Food Network cable television show; "Martha by Mail," a mail-order catalog company; and the Martha Stewart books. (55)

As Zahn observes, Stewart's publications and products proliferated the market in a variety of forms.[21] Additionally, as Pauline Adema notes in "Vicarious Consumption: Food, Television and the Ambiguity of Modernity," food television began to grow in the United States in the late 1990s with the success of the Food Network (113). Both American and British chefs, like Emeril Lagasse and Jamie Oliver, began to experience even greater success, and their individual cooking shows and appearances on morning shows, talk shows, and late night shows contributed to a celebrity status rarely enjoyed by chefs. Even without the exposure of television, other chefs, like Marco Pierre White, a British chef and restaurateur, were catapulted into the public eye. As Luke Jennings notes in "Bad Boy in the Kitchen," "The name Marco Pierre White was first bought to the attention of the metropolitan beau monde in January of 1987, when Harvey's opened on Wandsworth Common, South London" (136). White's cooking became famous, earning him Michelin stars, and his antics made for "Marco stories . . . in the press almost weekly" (Jennings 138). The 1990s, then, saw a return to both American and British kitchens as consumer culture became inundated with domesticity in a variety of forms (home decorating, cooking, etc.) conveyed through an array of mediums (magazines, books, television, etc.).

Helen Fielding responds to this market saturation in *Bridget Jones's Diary*. In constructing Bridget's New Year's resolution list, she has Bridget assert, "I WILL NOT . . . Waste money on: pasta makers, ice-cream machines or other culinary devices" (2). Just as Fielding depicts Bridget as the ideal reader of magazine, she also portrays Bridget as the ideal follower of domestic-advice manuals. Though we rarely see Bridget use any type of household appliance throughout the novel, Fielding makes it clear in her opening list that Bridget purchases the latest household goods no matter how impractical they may be for her lifestyle. Later in the novel, Fielding depicts Bridget daydreaming about marrying a doctor for whom she will "cook . . . little goat cheese soufflés" (49). Fielding does not mention Martha Stewart, Emeril Lagasse, or Marco Pierre White in this passage, but their presence is palpable. Though Bridget's diet up until this point has consisted of mini-pizzas and chocolate croissants, Bridget now imagines cooking a rather complicated meal. In these instances, Fielding satirizes the saturation of domestic-advice culture in the 1990s by gently mocking individuals like Bridget who blindly follow consumer trends.

Chick lit authors' refusal to mention domestic-advice manuals by name underscores the fact that though these publications serve as the medium through which information about goods and skills are conveyed it is the sentiments associated with domesticity that are more important for readers/

viewers of these texts to recognize and eventually acquire. In having Bridget daydreaming about cooking goat cheese soufflés but not mentioning whose recipe she will be following, Fielding emphasizes the feelings that accompany Bridget's potential cooking act. What becomes important to Bridget is not the final cooking act but the love and admiration of her doctor-husband that she imagines will accompany that act. Similarly, as readers, we never see Jane Goodall of *Animal Husbandry* leafing through a Williams-Sonoma catalog, but Laura Zigman does depict her carefully itemizing all the goods needed to complete the new apartment that she will share with her boyfriend Ray. In having her protagonist construct a list of household items to purchase, Zigman shows how, for Jane, listing becomes the first step in constructing a happy home. These women, then, are not necessarily concerned with the acts (of cooking, of organizing) themselves but the sentiments that accompany those acts. Just as "the lifestyle" becomes the most recognizable, and desirable, aspect of Martha Stewart's publications, the feelings invoked by a carefully ordered household or an elaborately prepared meal are what these women desire.

As Fielding's narrative progresses, it becomes apparent that, for Bridget, household goods symbolize those sentiments that Bridget associates with married life—order, security, and everlasting love. Bridget often idealizes her married friend Magda's life and frequently compares their experiences. While Magda lives in an ordered house with "crisp sheets and many storage jars full of different kinds of pasta," chaos reigns in Bridget's household (39). We see this chaos as Bridget prepares her own birthday dinner:

> Cannot go on. Have just stepped in a pan of mashed potato in new kitten-heel black suede shoes from Pied à Terre . . . forgetting that the kitchen floor and surfaces were covered in pans of mince and mashed potato . . . Oh my God—suddenly remembered tube of contraceptive jelly might be on side of washbasin. Must also hide storage jars with embarrassing un-hip squirrel design. . . . (82–83)

Bridget's household, with its "mince and mashed potato" covered floors, contraceptive jelly, and "un-hip" storage jars present a stark contrast to Magda's home, a haven of order. As noted earlier, Bridget desperately wants to order her life, her obsessive listing reveals that compulsion, and she sees Magda as having achieved that order as a married woman. The two women's lives contrast in terms of finances as well; Bridget observes, "I struggle to make ends meet and am ridiculed as an unmarried freak whereas Magda lives in a big house with eight different kinds of pasta in jars, and gets to go shopping all day" (132). The "eight different kinds of pasta in jars" symbolize the financial security that comes from being married. Not only does Magda have time and money to afford to shop all day, but Magda has the means to afford *eight* different kinds of pasta, complete with individual containers. This moment in Fielding text also points to the absurdity of excessive domestication; in reading about Magda's eight different kinds of pasta and jars, we may be reminded of Martha Stewart's suggestion to keep twelve different kinds of sugar on hand, each in their individual, mason jar. In having Bridget see Magda's life as ideal merely because of her eight different pasta jars, Fielding mocks Bridget's conviction that a properly equipped and maintained household will produce the domestic sentiments for which Bridget longs.[22]

Fielding further articulates the difference between Bridget and married people like Magda when she writes of Bridget's and her friends' reaction to an article in the newspaper entitled "The Joy of Single Life." Written by a "Smug-Married journalist," the article characterizes single people as "'Lonely style-obsessed individuals [who] seek consolation in packeted comfort food of the kind their mother might have made'" (244). Here, Fielding characterizes Singletons by the food that they eat; though they prefer the taste of mom's home cooking, they are forced to eat packaged foods due to their presumed lack of culinary skills. Fielding's characterization again reinforces the domestic anxiety that permeates her novel. Here, Fielding directly equates packaged food with the state of being single and, in turn, being alone. Fielding depicts Bridget as internalizing this equation, and throughout the novel, we see Bridget attempting to overcome this stereotype of single people and the feelings of solitude that accompany that state through the preparation of home cooked meals. For her birthday, she decides to invite nineteen friends over for a home cooked meal. Though she panics about the task that she has undertaken, she concludes before the event:

> Our culture is too obsessed with outward appearance, age and status. Love is what matters. These nineteen people are my friends; they want to be welcomed into my home to celebrate with affection and simply homely fare—not to judge. Am going to cook shepherd's pie for them all—British Home Cooking. (82)

Bridget's comment here is ironic, for while she claims that society is "too obsessed with outward appearance," she often undertakes meal preparation with the hope that she will impress her friends. Later in the novel, when planning a dinner for a smaller group of friends, she reflects:

> Will be marvelous. Will become known as brilliant but apparently effortless cook.
>
> People will flock to my dinner parties, enthusing, "It's really great going to Bridget's for dinner, one gets Michelin star-style food in a bohemian setting." Mark Darcy will be v. impressed and will realize I am not common or incompetent. (256)

Fielding reveals here the extent to which other people's opinions really do matter to Bridget and how much Bridget wants others to value her. First, Fielding exposes the class consciousness at play in these domestic-advice manuals. Not only do these manuals imply that one can achieve the sentiments associated with domesticity, but they also promise upward mobility. By carefully following the given instructions, "readers and viewers 'perform' a white, middle-class gentility through the careful arrangements of the commodities—the props, sets, and costumes—essential to the performance," as noted by Jay Mechling in "Martha Stewart and Taste Cultures" (68). Here, Fielding shows the consumer buying into this promise; Bridget hopes that cooking a sophisticated meal on par with Marco Pierre White will make her seem less "common" to Mark Darcy, a wealthy and highly educated man. Secondly, in Bridget's mind, providing a well-cooked meal will lead to "adoring glances and endless approbation," as Nigella Lawson hopes in the preface to her cookbook *How To Be A Domestic Goddess: Baking and the Art of Comfort Cooking* (vii). Lawson's text, though not a critical study, echoes the assertions of Kathleen Anne McHugh in *American Domesticity: From How-To Manual to Hollywood Melodrama*; Lawson consistently presents the preparation of food as the catalyst for these sentiments. Fielding establishes here the close correlation that exists in Bridget's mind between meal preparation, or "British *Home* Cooking" (my emphasis), and the larger associations connected with a home cooked meal. Bridget longs to attain "adoring glances," love, and companionship, not just shepherd's pie or grilled tuna, by carefully following the recipes provided.

As discussed in the previous chapter, Candace Bushnell illustrates a similar longing for love in *Sex and the City*. In her chapter "Downtown Babes Meet Old Greenwich Gals," Bushnell addresses the shortcomings of romantic comedies by showing Carrie's doubts about finding the happily ever after ending that she feels Jolie Bernard has found. This chapter, however, also critiques the domestic-advice manuals that were flooding the consumer market in the 1990s. Bushnell directly equates love and marriage with settling down, and she envisions that settling to happen in a home straight out of a Martha

Stewart magazine. Though there is no mention of Martha in the chapter, Jolie Bernard's house is "white, Colonial-style" with "a pointy slate roof and balconies" (81). As Sarah A. Leavitt notes in "It Was Always a Good Thing: Historical Precedents for Martha Stewart," "Though Martha Stewart explores other American cultures—such as midwest farms and Texas ranches—she, too, holds a special fascination for colonial America" (129). By characterizing Jolie's house as "white Colonial," then, Bushnell makes a subtle connection to Stewart. Not only does Bushnell construct a home that would live up to Stewart's standards, but she stresses the landscaping outside the home and the entertaining that happens within the home. She writes, "The lawn was very, green, and the trees that dotted the yard had borders of pink flowers around their bases" (81); inside, there were "cucumber sandwiches" and "quesadillas with salsa" (82). The neighborhood women inside, representative of the target audience for *Living*, also call to mind Stewart.

Though the four women resist attending the shower and complain about going all the way out to Connecticut on a beautiful Saturday afternoon, upon arriving, a hung-over Carrie changes her attitude. Miranda complains: "'They better not have any trendy gardening tools lying around . . . If I see gardening tools, I'm going to scream'" (81). Sarah responds, "'If I see kids, I'm going to scream'" (81). But Carrie counters their negativity, "'Look. Grass. Trees. Breathe in the aroma of freshly mown grass,' said Carrie, who had mysteriously begun to feel better (81). Her good mood prevails at the shower itself. At one point, she excuses herself to go to the bathroom, and Bushnell chronicles her trip:

> Carrie did not go to the bathroom. Nor was she as drunk as she appeared to be. Instead, she tiptoed up the stairs, carpeted with an oriental runner, and thought that if she were Jolie, she would probably know what kind of oriental rug it was because that was the kind of stuff you were supposed to know if you were married to a rich banker and making him a home in the suburbs. (85)

Carrie seems in awe of her surroundings. She comments on the oriental rug as well as the "thick white carpet" on the floor of Jolie's bedroom, a voyeur to a life with which she is unfamiliar. What impresses Carrie even more than the rugs are the feelings that she associates with this setting. While looking at Jolie's photographs on the wall, Carrie wonders, "What was it like to be Jolie? How did it happen? How did you find someone who fell in love with you and gave you all this? She was thirty-four and she'd never even come close, and there was a good chance she never would" (85). For a moment, in

Jolie's house, Carrie longs for the sentiments associated with the white Colonial. The real focus in this scene is on all the non-material "things" that Jolie seems to have been given, but Bushnell prompts Carrie's consideration of these feelings by first conveying how impressed Carrie is with Jolie's exquisite home decorating.

Though Bushnell depicts Carrie's desire for the sentiments associated with domesticity, she also questions the legitimacy of Jolie's lifestyle. First, Bushnell undercuts the idyllic, suburban home by adding insidious details. After describing Jolie's house and garden, she writes a golden retriever into the scene to complete it. However, Bushnell immediately complicates the scene: "a golden retriever raced barking across the lawn. But as the dog reached the edge of the yard, it was suddenly jerked back, as if yanked by an invisible rope" (81). Bushnell's narrative style, as previously shown, consistently undercuts itself, and here again, she adds this horrific detail to undermine an ostensibly ideal American scene. Doing so questions this suburban ideal held up to women.

Another way in which Bushnell questions this American standard is through Carrie's interpretation of Jolie's lifestyle. As noted earlier, Carrie reflects, "What was it like to be Jolie? How did it happen? How did you find someone who fell in love with you and gave you all this?" (85). Here, Carrie's observations about Jolie seem to directly contrast with Martha Stewart's how-to philosophy. Bushnell stresses that Jolie was given her home rather than having made it herself, as Stewart might advise. Yet, Bushnell's wording reveals a potentially dangerous interpretation of Stewart's publications. While Stewart actively encourages readers to purchase household goods and perform particular behaviors, she rarely addresses the means through which women should do this. As a result, a reader like Jolie may assume that the chief way to acquire means is to marry a man who will provide. In stressing that Jolie has been given her home, Bushnell exposes this possible interpretation of Stewart's text and critiques the passivity exhibited by women like Jolie.

Laura Zigman's character Jane Goodall expresses sentiments similar to Bridget and Carrie in *Animal Husbandry*. For Jane, household goods symbolize the level of commitment between her and her boyfriend, Ray. These goods are not merely objects unto themselves, as Bridget indicates, but for Jane, they are loaded with meaning, signifying the direction her relationship with Ray is headed and the depth of his love for her. After only two weeks, Ray tells Jane that he loves her and also suggests that they move in together. Two months after this proposal, the couple begins apartment hunting. Jane reflects on her excitement at the prospect: "I had been starring in the movie of my perfect New-Cow fantasy life for a while now, ever since he had said practically in the same breath, that he loved me and wanted to move in with me" (90). When depicting her main character thinking about sharing an apartment with Ray, Zigman does not have Jane articulate her happiness by continuing to talk about her emotions associated with this next step in their relationship. Rather, she has Jane list the household goods that they will acquire upon co-habitation:

> *The bedroom.*
> *The bed.*
> *The sheets and the pillowcases.*
> *The kitchen.*
> *The Calphalon.* (91)

With this list, Zigman calls to mind a bridal registry; she has Jane list the rooms in her new apartment (the bedroom, the kitchen) and itemize the objects needed to complete that room. In making this association, Zigman shows the way in which Jane attempts to concretize her relationship with Ray by actualizing a shared home. Yet Jane's preoccupation with furnishing her apartment prevents her from noticing the obvious flaws in her relationship with Ray. Zigman's characterization of Jane, then, critiques a cultural tendency to emphasize domestic goods over actual emotion. In this passage, Zigman reveals the unspoken pressure that Jane, and women like her, feels to achieve a domestic ideal, and she exposes the way in which domestic performance, in this case the making a home, becomes more important than the health of her actual relationship.

Fielding, Bushnell, and Zigman consistently infuse household items with meanings as constructed by the domestic-advice manuals that encourage consumption. These characters often desire these goods because they want to achieve the lifestyle and sentiments associated with an ordered household. Yet, while chick lit characters often feel a pull toward this lifestyle, they are simultaneously filled with anxiety about its appropriateness. For Bridget, this anxiety manifests itself in the form of a nightmare that causes her to wake up "in floods of tears" (165). Bridget dreams that she's in her A-level French course about to hand in a paper that she has not done any revisions on when she suddenly realizes that she is wearing nothing except her domestic science apron. She and Daniel argue about what the dream means; she thinks it reveals that she has not "'fulfilled [her] potential intellectually'" (166) while Daniel jokes, "'It means that the vain pursuit of an intellectual life is getting in the way of your true purpose . . . to cook all my meals for me . . . And walk around my flat with no pants on'" (166–67). His flippant comment unknowingly exposes the true tension of the dream—the pull that Bridget feels between her current lifestyle as a singleton and the one that she thinks she desires as a married.

This tension is not only a major theme in Fielding's novel, but it also preoccupies other chick lit novels as well. Chick lit authors depict their heroines dealing with this anxiety in various ways. They may question how fitting domestic ideologies are to their current lifestyle; they may wonder about their own ability to live up to the standard presented by these manuals; or, they may question their ability to achieve those sentiments associated with domesticity without all the pieces needed (i.e. husband, family, house). Again, a major theme of these novels becomes the heroines' (in)abilities to navigate their own paths in the face of these ever-present consumer ideologies.

Laura Zigman depicts her heroine questioning her relationship only a few lines after she shows Jane fantasizing about her perfect home life with Ray. Though Ray has asked Jane to move in with her, there still remains one big problem—his fiancée Mia. Thoughts of Mia interrupt Jane's daydreams of domestic bliss. When she tries to bring it up with Ray, however, he interrupts her, pretending that she is asking about the apartment. Jane persists, " 'Actually, I was talking about . . . you know' " (91). Though Jane can clearly imagine her new home complete with its household items, she cannot bring herself to say the name of the woman who could potentially disrupt her happy home life and to imagine what might happen if Ray does not actually leave Mia as he said he would. Instead, she chooses to process this possibility by visualizing the additional household items that will be needed if Mia becomes the couple's third roommate:

> Ray released my hands and went back to fondling his abs, albeit more distractedly than he had before. He sighed heavily and shook his head against the pillow. "I guess I have to tell her don't I?"
> I rolled my eyes. "Well, I would *think* so. Unless, of course, you want us *all* to move in together."
> *The extra pillow.*
> *The extra place setting.*
> *The extra toothbrush.*
> *The extra name on the mailbox.*
> *All those macrobiotic cookbooks and packages of miso and fluffy clouds of tofu floating in the watery.* . . . (91)

Throughout the beginning of the narrative, Zigman depicts Jane as feeling uneasy about her relationship with Ray. Though Jane wants to believe it will work out, she is also acutely aware of the problems with their relationship. Here, Jane expresses this unease by envisioning Mia's encroachment upon her home space. Since a well-ordered household signifies a bliss-filled relationship, this invasion of her physical space signifies unease with her relationship. In this scene, Zigman deconstructs both Jane's fantasy of acquiring the ideal domestic space by purchasing Calphalon and the consumer ideology that encourages product purchasing in order to achieve a particular lifestyle. Zigman's narrative further questions these notions when Ray, the perfect "J.Crew boyfriend," does in fact leave Jane for another woman—a woman who is not even Mia (33).

In the *The Cigarette Girl*, Carol Wolper presents readers with a strong-willed character who struggles to resist the domestic ideologies that constantly bombard her. As noted earlier, Elizabeth feels unspoken pressure from her mother to settle down. Not only would Elizabeth's mother like to see her commit to one man, but she would also like to see her settle in a nicely furnished home, preferably one with "only the best linens, china, and assorted home-decorating items" like those sold in the store that she manages (82). Like Bridget whose anxiety manifests itself in a dream, Elizabeth sometimes feels that she is living a nightmare: "Sometimes life around my mother can feel like a B-movie thriller. Call it *The Wedding Conspiracy*. Picture me as the protagonist, trapped and panicking" (85). She reacts against this conspiracy by deeming herself "'domestaphobic,'" but as she explains to her mother, she's still able to satisfy a man's appetite, just not in the kitchen (85).

Wolper depicts Elizabeth struggling resist the traditional role of wife and mother encouraged of her by society; she chooses a career in a male dominated field and an active sex life with multiple partners. Yet, despite these acts of rebellion against her mother, and more importantly what her mother stands for, Elizabeth still sometimes feels anxious about her life decisions. Though she asserts she is more interested in her wedding night, she follows this assertion with the comment that "this is still not the kind of conversation that a mother should ever have with a daughter struggling in the zone" (83). Interestingly enough, Wolper sets this conversation between Elizabeth and her mother in her mother's home, at the kitchen table, "a virtual Williams-Sonoma catalog come to life" (83). As readers, we are made to imagine Elizabeth asserting her independent identity in the face of "Every conceivable kitchen aid . . . blender, mixer, espresso machine, coffee-bean roaster, citrus juicer, all-purpose juicer, and a Calphalon pot in every size hanging from an overhead rack" (83). Household items literally encroach upon Elizabeth's space, signifying to readers how consumers can feel bombarded by household products and how women in "the zone" can feel pressured to fulfill the ideal offered by these publications.

Perhaps even more revealing of Elizabeth's struggle is her response to her mother's question, "'I can't believe you're my daughter. Where do you come from?'" (86). Elizabeth responds, "'Mars, not Venus,'" an allusion to John Gray's 1992 self-help manual *Men Are From Mars, Women Are From Venus* where Gray aligns male behavior with Mars and female behavior with Venus (86). Elizabeth's comment is significant because throughout the novel Wolper depicts her heroine as trying to overcome the feeling that she is just one of the boys. Elizabeth consistently struggles to maintain her feminine identity in the face of what she perceives as her masculine tendencies. Her choice to self-identify as male here reveals that she sees no room to reconcile what she perceives as her "female" yearnings for home, husband, and family with her "male" yearnings for a career and active sex life.

Again, though her protagonist fights against domestication at times, Wolper still expresses Elizabeth's a strong desire for the sentiments associated with marriage. After the wedding of her best friend Mimi, Elizabeth notices Mimi and her husband Evan off by themselves. She comments: "That's what it's about, I realized. That moment, played out in a thousand movie scenes, is what we want to find in real life. This is what makes all the other stuff bearable. And though I've never been able to understand spending thousands and thousands of dollars on a wedding, to have that moment I'd spend a million" (231). In this scene, Wolper reveals a tension between the pull Elizabeth feels to conform to society's expectations of her and her own desires to forge her own life path.

Like Elizabeth, Bridget's inability to fit into the domestic models is equally apparent—so much so, in fact, that the novel contains two episodes of failed attempts at domesticity. The first attempt comes when Bridget decides to host a birthday dinner in her flat; as mentioned above, though Bridget intends to serve a delicious meal, complete with shepherd's pie, Char-Grilled Belgium Endive Salad, Roquefort Lardons and Frizzled Chorizo, and Grand Marnier soufflés, it ends in disaster with the mashed potatoes all over the floor and Bridget, hair wet, in her bra and panties when the guests arrive. Later in the novel, she undergoes a similar challenge, inviting a small group of friends over for a dinner party. She consults a new cookbook by Marco Pierre White and decides to make "Velouté of Celery . . . Char-grilled Tuna on Velouté of Cherry Tomatoes Coulis with Confit of Garlic and Fondant Potatoes," "Confit of Oranges," and "Grand Marnier Crème Anglaise" (256). This attempt, too, ends in disaster. Instead of a "*concentration* of taste" (255), Bridget opens the pan to reveal "burnt chicken carcasses coated in jelly" (267). Additionally, her soup turns bright blue; her potatoes are hard as rocks; and her cherry tomato purée is "foaming and three times its original volume" (271). What started out as a carefully prepared meal ends with blue soup, omelettes, and marmalade. Fielding further underscores Bridget's domestic capabilities by interrupting both Bridget's planning of the meal and her execution of the meal with two outrageous and traumatic events. Bridget's entry detailing her invite list for the party and her conversation about the evening with Mark Darcy is followed by an entry that begins "Tom has disappeared" (260). Additionally, the dinner party itself is interrupted when Bridget's dad calls to declare: "'Your mother and Julio are wanted by the police'" (272).

Fielding deploys narrative interruptions to critique the advice offered by these domestic manuals. In making Bridget unable to complete a Marco Pierre White recipe, Fielding satirizes White's cookbook, exposing the unrealistic expectations in his text. White's elaborate recipes and his "*concentration* of taste" that requires having fish and chicken stock frozen and on hand, Fielding implies, are somewhat ridiculous, especially in the context of Bridget's chaotic life (255). In these two scenes, Fielding also further satirizes the domestic behaviors encouraged by such publications. As mentioned earlier, Fielding depicts Bridget struggling to make such complicated meals because she wishes to be valued by her guests—loved, admired, and not seen as common. Implicit in domestic-advice manuals like White's and Stewart's is the promise of these domestic sentiments and upward mobility. For instance, the spread entitled "Three-Generation Birthday Party" by Carol Prisant in the September 1997 edition of *Living* provides instructions for hosting a successful birthday bash, complete with gossamer tenting, rosé-wine punch, and a chocolate-truffle cake. The text describes the day as one in which "friends and family meet beneath willow trees" while the photographs depict members of the family hugging, a small boy atop his father's shoulders (174). The purpose of the spread is to impart detailed instructions on how to create a similar party, but it also implicitly emphasizes the sentiments associated with the day. Likewise, the menu planned emphasizes class and elegance. Rather than serve hot dogs, grilled tenderloin au poivre will be prepared. Marco Pierre White employs a similar tactic in regard to transcending class boundaries. According to Fielding, his text uses words like "Confit" which adds a certain sophistication to a food commonly known as marmalade, and the text's construction implies that serving such a food will allow the entertainer to achieve a certain elegance. Fielding's scene of failed cooking and entertaining points to this false pretense offered by domestic-advice manuals and satirizes consumers' beliefs that they can achieve both the sentiments offered by domesticity as well as upward mobility solely because of the household items they buy or the domestic behaviors they perform. Merely making velouté of celery will not help Bridget to achieve a happy marriage.

Chick lit authors often depict their characters as questioning and conflicted because the domestic models that surround them fail to meet the standards they encounter in domestic-advice manuals. Though both Elizabeth's and Bridget's mothers were raised in an era that encouraged women to fulfill their role as homemakers, both women convey to their daughters that they have been failed by that standard held up to them. In Elizabeth's mother's case, the ideal was never fully achieved. Elizabeth explains: "My mother grew up in Portland and came to L.A. when she was twenty-one. It was 1970, and the first guy she dated her, my father, she married" (82). The two divorced when Elizabeth was eleven, and in the years that followed, Elizabeth's dad remarried a woman much younger than himself and had two children with her. When Elizabeth visits her mother on her birthday and asks her what her plans for the evening are, her mother explains that she's going on a first date with a man she just met. Elizabeth's tone in conveying this information is sad; she laments the fact that her mother is alone, spending her birthday with some stranger. And, though Wolper never directly expresses it, as readers, we sense that some of Elizabeth's desire to disassociate herself from traditional relationships rests with the fact that her mother and father's marriage ended with her father happily married, substituting his old domestic arrangement with a new one, and Elizabeth's mother alone, working in a upscale bridal shop to satiate her need for romance. As mentioned earlier, though Elizabeth's mother's kitchen is filled with household appliances, the space lacks the necessary players to complete the fantasy—a husband and family.

Bridget's mother falls equally short of the ideal domestic role model. Unlike Elizabeth's mother, however, who lost her husband early on to divorce, Mrs. Jones discovers late in life that her marital situation is less than desirable. In February, Bridget discovers that her parents are having what her dad calls "problems," and that her mother is dissatisfied with her role as housewife. Her mother, Bridget soon finds out, suffers from what Betty Friedan in *The Feminine Mystique* calls "the problem that has no name." Unfulfilled with her life as a homemaker, Bridget's mother has a late in life feminist awakening; upon returning from her trip to Albufeira with Una Alconbury and Audrey Coles, she begins to demand payment for doing the housework and claims that " 'she'd wasted her life being [a] slave' " (42). Like Elizabeth, Bridget reflects on her mother's unhappiness, wondering if her own desire to meet a man and get married will actually make her as frustrated as her mother appears to be. After counseling her mother, Bridget notes with satisfaction that she enjoys her new role as "wise counselor" (43). She contemplates a new career path:

> I am having fantasies about becoming a Samaritan or Sunday school teacher, making soup for the homeless (or, as my friend Tom suggested, darling mini-bruschettas with pesto sauce), or even retraining as a doctor. Maybe going out with a doctor would be better still, both sexually and spiritually fulfilling. I even begin to wonder about putting an ad in the lonely hearts column of the *Lancet*. I could take his messages, tell patients wanting night visits to bugger off, cook him little goat cheese soufflés. . . . (43)

Her daydreaming ends, however, with the realization that such a life could force her to "end up in a foul mood with him when I am sixty, like Mum" (43). In this moment, Bridget sees her mother's marital dissatisfaction as stemming directly from her having performed the expected behaviors of her gender. Bridget's view of married life is further distorted when she discovers that Magda's husband Jeremy is cheating on her. These failed models cause Bridget to question whether the domestic bliss she perceived is actually a reality.

Helen Bradshaw, the protagonist of Anna Maxted's *Getting Over It*, also struggles with a failed domestic model. Like other chick lit texts, Maxted's novel begins with heroine Helen Bradshaw, a features writer for *GirlTime* magazine, declaring in her diary "*I am dumping Jasper, tomorrow*" (1).[23] The reader of Maxted's text might expect a light-hearted tale of failed romance and found romance, but instead, at the close of the initial chapter, Helen receives a call to notify her that her father has died of a heart attack. Maxted's novel centers on Helen's loss and the comical way in which she deals with her father's passing. Central to this storyline is Helen's relationship with her mother and the way in which they restructure their family unit and their home life upon his death. Like other chick lit characters, Helen wonders if she can achieve a successful domestic model in the absence of a male presence, whether that male presence is her father or a husband.

Anna Maxted uses the death of Helen Bradshaw's father as a way to critique the role that the home and homemaking plays in women's lives. When Helen's father passes, Helen and her mother switch roles, a reversal that causes Helen's perceptions of family—a key component of domestic space—to be upset. At the start of Maxted's novel, Helen does not anticipate being affected by her father's passing since the two were never close. However, what she finds throughout the course of the novel is that his death has upset her greatly and that the repercussions of his death, mainly her mother's intense and very public grief, have proven more difficult to manage than she thought. Though Helen would like to mourn her father's death, her mother prevents that from happening. From the minute her father dies, Helen is forced to take a leading role in dealing with everything that accompanies his death. She explains what it is about her mother that makes her unable to do so:

> At home, my mother reverts to a fairy tale of her own. She is a northwest London princess, with a handsome prince called Maurice to look after her. You'd never guess she was an intelligent, educated woman. She flaps if she has to program the VCR. She is famed for not returning phone calls from Nana Flo or anyone else who is emotionally taxing. She follows the thick ostrich school of thought—if you ignore your demanding friends and relatives they'll go away—instead of getting angry and offended. She wants everything to be nice and if it isn't, she stamps her feet until it is. (19)

Her mother's personality prevents her from handling either the emotional or practical implications of her husband's death; she refuses to view his body; she refuses to deal with the funeral arrangements; she refuses to pick up the death certificate. However, she wants to be the center of attention when it comes to mourning, crying very loudly and demanding that people treat her with the respect that she feels a widow deserves. At the funeral, she makes a scene when she realizes that her husband will be buried with his wedding ring on. And, when she feels that people have forgotten her grief, she fakes a suicide attempt, superficially wounding her wrists. In characterizing Helen's mother in this way, Maxted depicts the two women as having reversed mother/daughter roles and establishes the basis for her protagonist to reexamine her perception of what constitutes the home.

Maxted characterizes this unrest through Helen's complex relationship with the notion of home. In the opening chapters, Maxted includes brief references to the home in order to foreshadow the key role that home will play in the novel. When Helen calls the funeral home to make arrangements, she reflects, "*home!* are they kidding?" (22). And, when she is at her father's bedside in the hospital, Helen offhandedly remarks that her father wanted her to buy a flat of her own. These moments, no matter how brief or seemingly insignificant, serve as important function; they center the narrative on the theme of defining the home space.

Helen's father's death leaves Helen with an ambivalent view of the home, particularly because Helen envisions the proper home as having a mother *and* father. While staying at her mother's house, her friend Lizzy calls to say that she is sure Helen was a wonderful daughter. Upset, Helen responds by banging about her mother's house, declaring it is "'pitch dark and freezing cold'" (21). She turns on radiators and lights, feeling "chilly" but "calmer" (21). This moment is significant. Maxted depicts Helen responding to her emotional unrest by trying to recapture the warmth that has gone out of her home with her father's passing. Helen tries to evoke these sentiments by performing domestic behaviors as well. When Helen feels at a loss as to what to do for her mother, she decides to cook her meals. She states:

> I started off by cooking for my mother. I made vegetable risotto from the recipe on the back of the risotto rice pack (on the fifth attempt I stopped writing off saucepans and burning the rice), Tina's coriander chicken recipe (chop and fry onion and garlic in olive oil, chop and add chicken, then coriander, white wine, and half-fat crème fraîche—in deference to my father), and—because I can—potato wedges. (105–106)

Helen's mother responds to this act of kindness by throwing her plate against the wall in anger, after having eaten potato wedges one too many times. The pair's new ritual then becomes cooking lessons every Monday and Wednesday night. Again, it is as though Helen and her mother are trying to recapture the feelings associated with the home before her father died by performing everyday domestic tasks. Though Helen does not find these nights of "spoiling the broth and being shouted at" enjoyable, she does becomes upset when her mother tells her that her grandmother will be moving in and that Helen will no longer need to spend as much time at her parents' home (106). It is almost as if both Helen and her mother need this domestic security in the face of their family's rupture.

One of the chief ways that Maxted represents Helen's struggle to define the home is through Helen's search for a home. The beginning of Maxted's novel chronicles Helen's unhappy home situations. Helen's first home is one filled with stress and negativity after Helen sleeps with one of her flat mates, Marcus, who then ignores her. As a result, Helen lashes out at him by becoming increasingly volatile in his presence, and eventually, Marcus kicks her out. Helen then moves back with her mother and grandmother, an equally problematic situation, which leaves her feeling defeated: "I now live with my mother and grandmother . . . I'm too feeble to live on my own" (231). In characterizing Helen as feeling displaced (she is unsatisfied living with Marcus and living with her mother and grandmother), Maxted signifies Helen's changing identity. No longer her father's daughter, Helen is not quite sure who she is.

Maxted depicts Helen's attempts to resolve this dilemma realistically. She resists tying up the novel neatly; instead, her progression toward narrative resolution comes in slow steps, as evidenced by her four-hundred page novel. Maxted further "lengthens" her narrative by starting and stopping the main action. Nearly every chapter ends with a note of suspense, yet nearly every chapter begins retroactively, often with Helen recalling a significant moment from her past. This narrative technique makes the reader feel as though she is taking one step forward and two steps back. More importantly, this technique adequately represents Helen's emotional state. She has trouble moving on because she is literally trapped in the past. Furthermore, Maxted refuses to have Helen's love interest Tom, a kind veterinarian whom she "accidentally" meets before her father's funeral, swoop in to save the day.[24] Likewise, Helen herself does not experience an epiphany in which she resolves her problems—another common, narrative convention. Instead Helen's awakening happens slowly, in steps.

Two of the most significant moments occur midway through Maxted's narrative. After having a particularly bad morning (which includes bad clothes and flat hair), Helen gets a call from Cliff, her mother's psychiatric nurse. The two discuss her feelings about her father and her relationship with her mother, though Helen resists opening up about her feelings. Cliff encourages her to change the dynamic with her mother, to stop enabling her, and to "'move on,'" as he phrases it (235). He lectures, "'Helen . . . When someone dies, a door opens in a room where there's grief. There may be more rooms. If you have the courage, you can look further. Some people shut the door again'" (236). Here, Maxted metaphorically links Helen's emotional recovery to the home. While earlier we saw the way in which Helen attempted to emotionally heal her mother and herself through cooking, here we see Cliff asking Helen to concretize her grief by envisioning it as a physical structure. Cliff's choice of the words "move on" resonates with Helen who, at this point in the novel, is struggling to emotionally "get over" her father's death while simultaneously searching for a suitable home space. Though at this point in the novel, Helen cannot quite seem to "move on" emotionally Maxted enables her to interpret Cliff's message literally. After speaking with him, Helen hangs up the phone and dials the estate agents.

Helen's hesitancy to find a flat of her own goes hand in hand with her resistance to being alone. Though Helen dislikes her flat mates, she remains in the flat, and though living with her mother drives her crazy, she stays there for a significant amount of time, refusing to believe that buying a flat of her own is realistic. Furthermore, the major fight that Helen and Tom have results when Helen becomes enraged that Tom does not ask her to move in with him. Helen's friends recognize Helen's fear of living alone as well. Helen and Lizzy, a co-worker and close friend, have a conversation addressing this fear:

> Lizzy purses her lips and says, "Maybe it'll be good for you to be on your own a bit."
> I tut loudly and say in a bored tone, "Why?"
> Lizzy dabs her mouth with her napkin . . . and like an archbishop delivering the punchline to a sermon declares, "You've got to be happy alone before you can be happy with someone."
> I sit back, fold my arms, and try to look agnostic. "Liz," I say, "did you read that in *GirlTime*?"
> "I might have done," says Lizzy airily. "So?"
> I reply sternly, "I wrote it." (245–46)

Maxted's passage not only reveals Helen's fear of being alone, but it also shows the significant role that advice culture plays in Helen's life. Like other chick lit authors, Maxted reveals the multi-faceted ways in which this advice culture, from women's magazines to domestic-advice manuals, can affect female consumers. And, in ending the chapter with these lines, Maxted gives added weight to their significance. Though Maxted shows that Helen intellectually understands the importance of being happy with oneself, she also reveals that Helen cannot internalize that belief just yet. Even in this passage, Helen resists the belief that becoming comfortable living alone might benefit her psychologically and further her emotional development.

Helen's fear of being alone is one of the chief reasons why she dreads the first Christmas after her father's death. Helen's mother decides to forgo both joy and Christmas, but Helen feels that, personally, it is important to experience the holiday with some semblance of normality. In an attempt to prevent Helen and her mother from being lonely, Vivienne, her mother's friend, invites the two over for Christmas. Helen reflects, "On the morning of December 24, my mother and I receive a last minute invitation to Christmas Day lunch from Vivienne. I reject it because I don't feel like being around a complete family. I'd feel like a spare part" (280). The absence of Helen's father around the holidays is acute, and Helen does not want to be reminded of that any more than she already is. Though she cannot bring herself to attend Christmas lunch with Vivienne and her family, Helen does want to spend Christmas with others. Once again, Maxted depicts Helen attempting to achieve normalcy through domestic tasks; she tries to capture the holiday spirit by having Helen buy "turkey, a bag of potatoes, and a jar of cranberry sauce" for her own Christmas dinner (280). When her mother decides to go to Vivienne's and her grandmother makes plans with a friend, Helen discovers that her attempts at familiarizing the holiday in the absence of her father will not be realized. Instead, Maxted portrays Helen as combating the premier, domestic holiday by defiantly refusing to conform to it; she abandons her plans to cook and eats potato wedges dipped in cranberry sauce. Her act of eating, then, becomes an act of rebellion. Helen's ability to survive this important, family-centered holiday is the first sign of some emotional progress.

Though Christmas is dismal, the turn of events that follow are some of the most significant steps that Helen makes. Among these is Helen's decision to buy a flat. Helen looks at several places without much luck and then finally stumbles upon the perfect property. The flat, though in a state of disrepair, affects Helen: "I don't trust myself to speak . . . My heart is thumping and I feel hot with trepidation. I don't know why, but I want it" (289–290). Despite the fact that she makes an offer, she still has reservations about going through with the purchase. Helen desperately wishes her dad were around to advise her with the deal. And, upon moving in, the place seems lonely, which is why when Jasper, her ex-boyfriend, asks for a place to stay she kindly obliges.

What she discovers, however, is that not only does she not need the help of her father but that her home space is actually much more pleasant without the presence of Jasper. When Helen's solicitor asks her for a deposit of nine thousand pounds, Helen realizes that she has made an error, assuming the amount could be paid upon completion. Panicked, she calls her mother who not only fixes Helen's error but who also proves to be indispensable throughout the house buying and decorating process. Though initially Helen's mother is resentful of her moving out, when she realizes just how much Helen needs her to help with this purchase and to assist in her emotional healing, Helen's mother rises to the occasion. She contacts contractors and oversees the renovations of the flat. Additionally, she consults such magazines as *Elle Decoration* and *Living, Etc.* for decorating ideas. This moment is significant in terms of the larger plot. Though the home has been a contested space for Helen, here she is finally able to use domestic-advice manuals to help her not only decorate her flat but also heal herself. While Maxted shows Helen and her mother failing at domestic tasks like cooking at the start of the novel, in this scene the two work together to successfully create a home space for the first time without the guidance of Helen's father.

Maxted depicts this domestic creation as a positive act of healing for both Helen and her mother, even though Helen's home space is not traditional in the sense that it lacks a male presence. Instead of having Helen be immediately satisfied with her new flat, Maxted continues to explore the way in which Helen must come to terms with her decision to buy a flat on her own. Again, rather than neatly tying up the narrative, Maxted teases out this exploration. Though Helen sees that she and her mother can accomplish a significant task without the help of a man, Helen is unable to envision her life in the flat without a male presence. Upon moving in, Helen observes, "I expect moving in to feel ceremonial, but though I carry Fatboy [her cat] over the threshold, it doesn't" (313). Though Helen makes the bold and untraditional move into her own flat, Maxted shows the way in which she is still conditioned to think in terms of traditional marriage, citing the threshold ritual. Feeling ill at ease with her decision, Helen enthusiastically welcomes Jasper into her home when Louisa, his ex-girlfriend, kicks him out of hers. Jasper, she feels, might fill the void that her domestic space seems to lack.

Before long, however, Helen becomes annoyed with Jasper's presence, and the way that Maxted articulates this annoyance is by depicting Helen's resentment of Jasper's household items. He brings with him "two hideous wicker chairs," and he leaves his things lying about the apartment, never tidying up after himself (318). Helen views this as encroachment upon her home space. The final straw comes when Jasper asserts himself as her boyfriend to Tom; Helen kicks him out of her flat as a result. Again, the way in which Maxted portrays Helen's emotional catharsis is by having her rid her flat of Jasper's household items; Helen throws his possessions out the window, realizing that despite what society might encourage her to do she is actually better off on her own. By including this narrative action (moving in on her own, asking Jasper to move in, discovering Jasper unfit to live with), Maxted once again slows the narrative, giving added weight to Helen's important decision and her ability to come to terms with this decision. In allowing Helen time to process this move she has made in her life, Maxted stresses how difficult it might be for a woman to act out against the ideologies offered by domestic-advice manuals and create a home space in which she is truly happy. From this point, Maxted resolves the narrative. Helen makes peace with both her mother and her father's death, and she reunites with Tom. As *GirlTime* advised, it is only after Helen relinquishes the constructed idea of home, and, in turn, family, that her life can more clearly fit her.

Helen's decision to make a space for herself in a "pebble-dashed exception" filled with thrift store furniture flies in the face Martha Stewart's domestic ideology (287).[25] Rather, than emphasize a particular, perfected lifestyle,

Maxted instead depicts a character that takes the pieces of her already existent life and molds them into a space that will serve as her home. Her characterization, then, bears more of a similarity to British cooking show host and cook book author, Nigella Lawson, whose recent success has reinforced the idea that reality can be just as satisfying as fantasy.[26] Her cooking shows, *Nigella Bites* (2000), *Nigella Bites II* (2001), and *Forever Summer* (2002), have aired in both England and the United States and emphasize the fact that "cooking takes place in the context of everyday life" (Hollows 182). In "Feeling Like a Domestic Goddess: Postfeminism and Cooking," the first, and very important, critical study of Nigella Lawson and her productions, Joanne Hollows cites examples of the ways in which Lawson's "cooking style is carefully distanced from the prim and proper efficiency of the (female) home economist and from the decontexualized precision of the (male) professional chef" (182).

The cooking that takes place on Lawson's television shows directly contrasts to Martha Stewart's, ordered and precise version of cooking.[27] For instance, though Martha Stewart's television show is shot "largely at the Westport compound," these surroundings are extremely cultivated (Lippert 31). Lawson's *Nigella Bites*, by contrast, intersperses moments in Nigella's own kitchen with other areas of her much "lived in" west London home, such as her study and her pantry. As if reinforcing the "lived messiness" of her life, the show itself is shot in a frenetic fashion.[28] The camera constantly moves, following Nigella as she flits about the kitchen, and the short, cooking segments are interspersed with scenes of her picking up her children from school or entertaining guests. The television show, then, itself is constructed in such as way as to put emphasis on the hectic, hurried nature of everyday life.

Another notable difference between Stewart and Lawson is Lawson's disregard for cooking precision. Lawson often encourages viewers to estimate rather than carefully measure given amounts, noting that depending on your own personal preference you may want to season something more or less. She encourages viewers and readers to be aware of their likes and dislikes and to adjust recipes accordingly. For instance, in an "Easy Almond Cake" recipe contained in *How To Be a Domestic Goddess*, Lawson writes, "if you wanted to replace the vanilla extract with the zest of an orange, I wouldn't mind in the slightest" (6). As Hollows notes, Lawson's method of cooking also acknowledges that cooking is not an infallible art: "Potential failures are anticipated and the reader is assured that mistakes are not only 'normal', but also need not be read as failures" (Hollows 186). Referring again to the "Easy Almond Cake" recipe, Hollows observes that "a photograph of an 'Easy Almond Cake' that has been patched up after it stuck to the tin" (Hollows

186) accompanies the text because as Lawson notes, "these things happen to us all and I wanted to show it wasn't the end of the world . . . Life isn't lived in a lab" (Lawson 6). Lawson's television show and cookbooks de-emphasize perfection, focusing less on prescriptive recipes and more on the practical, end result.

One of the reasons that Lawson is less concerned with the exact steps to producing a food item is because her utmost concern is with the final product. Lawson, unlike many other cooking show hosts, revels in eating.[29] Frequently, during her shows, she is shown sampling food, and "the show customarily ends with her picking from the fridge or attaching a freshly cut piece of cake" (Hollows 183). Additionally, she made statements such as "All food is good for you" and "if it tastes good, eat it" during talk show appearances.[30] Her ability to enjoy food publicly is particularly important, given the complicated relationship that many women, including chick lit characters, have with food. This love of eating reinforces the fact that "the representation of cooking in Nigella's work starts from the importance of satisfying and caring for the self rather than others" (Hollows 184). While Lawson's television show does occasionally include advice concerning how to cook a meal for guests, her primary emphasis is not on entertaining, as is Stewart's. In fact, the episode "Home Alone" concentrated solely on things to cook for one, thus reinforcing her belief in the importance of feeding the self.

Another significant way that Lawson challenges the sentiments of domesticity is through her redefinition of the concept of family. Initially, when *Nigella Bites* aired, Lawson presented herself as a wife and mother. Following the death of her husband, British journalist John Diamond, the second series concentrated more on her role as a single parent. In *Forever Summer*, she exhibits a "carefree and newly-in-love partner in a reconstituted family" (182).[31] In terms of this chapter, this narrative is important because Nigella Lawson portrays shifting ideals of what her family is and what a family can be. Rather than clinging tightly to those standards set by the 1950s, Lawson's personal life, as exhibited in the show, presents alternative representations of the family.

Lawson's show, then, emphasizes that cooking, like life, is about making modifications. This lesson is one that many of the chick lit characters discussed here struggle to learn. Throughout the course of these novels, we see chick lit characters coming to terms with the "recipe" for life they have been given to follow and improvising in order to produce an end product that will ultimately fulfill them. When Jane Goodall's relationship with Ray fails, she moves in with her co-worker Eddie; though Jane can never see the two linked romantically, they form a bond, which contributes to the happiness

Jane now feels in her home place; horrified by her experience at Jolie's house, Carrie takes refuge with her girlfriends in Bowery Bar; and, when Bridget runs out of time to complete her shepherd's pie, her friends save the day and whisk her off to a restaurant. Bridget realizes, then, that it is not about the food but about the love her friends feel for her. To readers, characters such as Bridget, Helen, Jane, Carrie, and Elizabeth serve as examples of women who are able to come to terms with lives that do not meet society's standard that has been set for them. And, in creating these characters, chick lit authors deconstruct the potentially limiting ideologies imparted by domestic-advice manuals. These novelists depict female characters who ultimately realize that they can "cook up" a home even if they do not have the "essential" ingredients. All it takes is a little adjustment to the recipe.

Chapter Six
# Afterword

> As a feminist, I find the attack on chick-lit more than a bit disheartening. Is this where we are—one group of women writers mocking another, deeming its work irrelevant? Are women really criticizing one another about what they read?
>
> —Jennifer Coburn from *This Is Chick-Lit*,
> Edited by Lauren Baratz-Logsted (2006)

On June 10, 2002, I received an email invitation to Vivian Livingston's book signing for her soon to be published autobiography, *The Autobiography of Vivian Livingston*. Vivian wrote, "Not too sure what to expect actually . . . all I know is that I'm beyond nervous and the more friendly faces, the better!" (Livingston). Determined to support Vivian, I made plans to travel to New York City on Wednesday, June 26th in order to be present for her book signing at Barnes and Noble on 86th and to check out the after party at the bar Fitzpatrick's, which was just around the corner. After all, Vivian assured me that there would be free goody bags! How could I resist?

Book signings, as we all know, are not unusual in the least. But what I failed to mention here is that Vivian Livingston is not an actual person.[1] Rather, she is a cartoon character, living in cyberspace at the web address Vivianlives.com and making appearances in magazines such as *Elle*, *InStyle*, *Glamour*, and *Marie Claire* (Mack 6). I discovered her website while wandering lost one afternoon in the library, following a trail of other chick lit references. In reading about Vivian that afternoon, her importance to my topic became apparent. The launch of her website in 1999 occurred three years after the publication of *Bridget Jones's Diary* in England and one season after *Sex and the City* debuted in June of 1998 (Denitto). And, Vivianlives.com speaks to a remarkably similar audience; Vivian herself is a twenty-something who moved from Pennsylvania to New York City where she landed a job at

VH1 before being approached to be the model for a "Web site where you'd follow the life and times of a twenty-something young woman living in New York City" (Krantz 293).[2] Her website allows viewers to watch Vivian's daily activities (which range from dancing to rapper 50 Cent's "In Da Club" in her office to watching the latest romantic comedy to visiting the Hamptons for Mother's Day) via the "Vivcam" and to visit her Nolita apartment "where they can rifle through her wardrobe, [and] rummage through her refrigerator" (Mack 1).[3] Additionally, the website includes Vivian's diary where she can vent about disagreements with her boyfriend Jack or gush over Faith Hill's new album. The simultaneous success of the website and the rise of chick lit coincided with Sherrie Krantz's, Vivian's creator, decision to "co-write" an "autobiography" with Vivian, *The Autobiography of Vivian Livingston*, conveying the story of Vivian's life in traditional narrative form.[4]

Vivian's texts serve as an appropriate ending to this study because, historically, they are situated during an important time in "chick lit-erary" history. As noted above, Krantz's website came after the initial chick lit boom, following the success of Fielding's and Bushnell's works, and *The Autobiography of Vivian Livington* was published in 2002—a year after Doris Lessing's infamous comments about chick lit in 2001. Krantz's texts, then, are on the cusp of the early chick lit movement and the proliferation of chick lit texts that soon followed. The way in which Krantz constructs her empire, in fact, is indicative of her historical positioning. In many ways, Krantz relies on the conventions of the chick lit genre; in particular, she connects both her website and novel directly to her reading audience, and her novel, more specifically, encourages women readers to be discerning consumers, particularly when it comes to women's advice manuals. Yet, Krantz's texts speak to the new direction that chick lit texts are headed as well. Krantz enmeshes her texts in consumer culture in a way that early chick lit novelists like Helen Fielding and Candace Bushnell had not with their debut novels. For these reasons, it is fitting to conclude with Krantz's website and novels because, in fostering these connections with consumer culture mediums, texts like Krantz's force readers to renegotiate their understanding of the relationship between consumer culture and fiction while presenting their authors with new artistic and marketing challenges.

*The Autobiography of Vivian Livingston*, in many ways, previews the multiple off-shoots and subgenres that have flooded the literary marketplace—all in the name of chick lit. After the initial success of authors like Fielding and Bushnell, writers like Jane Green (*Jemima J*, 1999), Jennifer Weiner (*Good in Bed*, 2001), and Jenny Colgan (*Amanda's Wedding*, 1999) began publishing their first chick lit novels while previously established chick lit authors like Helen Fielding, Sophie Kinsella, Candace Bushnell, and Laura Zigman began writing both sequels to their bestsellers and/or other chick lit novels.[5] Many of these later chick lit authors, like Krantz, began to experiment with the conventions of chick lit, particularly in terms of expanding the target audience for the texts and in straying from the previously established narrative structures of these texts.

Though early chick lit novels have been narrowly defined, focusing primarily on single, white, heterosexual, British and American women in their late twenties and early thirties, living in metropolitan areas, more recently chick lit authors have begun broadening representations of their protagonists and, in turn, their target audience. In her article for the *Washington Post*, Alyson Ward discussed recent manifestations of the chick lit novel, which crossed race and age lines, including chick lit for Latinas (Alisa Valdes-Rodriguez, *The Dirty Girls Social Club*, 2003). And in the *New York Times*, Lola Ogunnaike reported on a newly emerging publishing trend in which black women writers are adapting chick lit to their experience (Charlotte Burley and Lyah LeFlore, *Cosmopolitan Girls*, 2004). Additionally, as Rachel Donadio reports in her article, "The Chick-Lit Pandemic," for the *New York Times*, ever since "Bridget Jones first hit the world stage . . . an international commuter train of women has been gathering speed close behind." Donadio's article references such books as Indian writer Swati Kaushal's *Piece of Cake*, Polish writer Malgorzata Warda's *Never to Paris*, and Italian writer Camilla Vittorini's *Something's Hot in the City*. And, Suzanne Ferriss and Mallory Young's critical collection *Chick Lit: The New Woman's Fiction* includes an essay by Nóra Séllei's entitled "Bridget Jones and Hungarian Chick Lit" where the author discusses *Állítsátok meg Terézanyut! (Stop Mammatheresa!)*. In a short amount of time, then, the genre has expanded, crossing racial and geographic boundaries.

Chick lit today also includes women protagonists at different stages of their lives. In her article, "Chick Lit: Is the Honeymoon Over?" Alyson Ward also notes that there is chick lit for teenagers (Louise Rennison, *Angus, Thongs and Full-Frontal Snogging: Confessions of Georgia Nicolson*, 1999) and for mothers (Allison Pearson, *I Don't Know How She Does It: The Life of Kate Reddy, Working Mother*, 2002). In fact, Lizzie Skurnick's article, "Chick Lit, the Sequel: Yummy Mummy" for the *New York Times* chronicles the onslaught of books by chick lit authors like Laura Zigman and Sophie Kinsella, written in much the same vein as their earlier chick lit texts, which now feature mothers as main characters. As Skurnick notes even "the puckish heroine Bridget Jones" has made a "recent journey to the delivery room [which] has been serialized in *The Independent* in Britain." Again, these sub-genres point to the way in which the demographic for chick lit has steadily been expanding.

Not only do these off-shoots represent different protagonists and target a different audience demographic, but many of them also challenge the clearly defined narrative strategies of early chick lit texts. Chick lit seems to have become a catch-all term for any text written by a female author about a female protagonist. For instance, Laura Weisberger's *The Devil Wears Prada* (2003) is a thinly veiled fictional autobiography chronicling Weisberger's time spent as an assistant to Anna Wintour, Editor in Chief of American *Vogue* (Quinn). Consistently, critics have labeled Weisberger's novel as chick lit; however, I would agree with *New York Times* writer Alex Kuczynski that a more appropriate label for this text be "gossip lit" ("Too Good Not to Be True" 1). This trend fictionalizes high-profile individuals and leaves readers guessing as to their identity. In this way, then, it differs significantly in its narrative aims from books like Fielding's or Bushnell's. Likewise, many autobiographical texts of late have been lumped into the category of chick lit. Former New Yorker, Stephanie Klein, who wrote about her adventures in dating on her blog, *Greek Tragedy*, recently published her memoir *Straight Up and Dirty* (2006), which the *Independent* noted was "Outrageous, outspoken and always honest . . . makes *Sex and the City* look passé."[6] Klein has become known as "the Carrie Bradshaw of New York bloggers."[7] And, more recently, writers from all genres have been capitalizing on the chick lit trend, adding a chick lit spin to their narratives. This past spring, a colleague of mine lent me *Undead and Unemployed* (2004) by MaryJanice Davidson. The description on the back of the 2004, paperback edition reads, "Nothing can make Betsy Taylor give up her shoe fetish—even dying and rising as the new Queen of the Vampires." The praise included on the book's back cover includes a quote by Catherine Spangler which describes the book as, "Chick lit meets vampire action." Even Ferriss and Young's anthology seems to embrace a less restrictive definition of the genre. Their anthology includes essays about nanny lit, mommy lit, and what author Joanna Webb Johnson deems "chick lit jr." The boundaries of the chick lit genre, as I have defined them here, have become decidedly blurred as more and more writers produce books that experiment with the literary conventions that early writers, like Fielding and Bushnell, established.

Krantz's text, in many ways, is representative of these off-shoots, which simultaneously align themselves with chick lit but which also transform the pioneering texts of the movement. Like other chick lit texts, *The Autobiography of Vivian Livingston* glamorizes life as a singleton. Krantz constructs a protagonist, not unlike Elizabeth West or Carrie Bradshaw, who lives an enviable life—complete with a chic New York City apartment and a closet filled with designer clothes. Though, according to her autobiography, Vivian struggles at first to find a niche in the Big Apple, she eventually lands her dream job at VH1—a job that includes the perk of riding in a racecar with Paul Newman. In glamorizing this lifestyle, Krantz validates, as other chick lit authors do, her protagonist's decision to live as a single woman in a big city, negotiating her career, her self, and her love life. Krantz's work seeks to redefine the often negative image of the spinster, which Betsy Israel in *Bachelor Girl: The Secret History of Single Women in the Twentieth Century* argues is epitomized by "the Dickensian sideshow freaks—the world-renowned bride, Miss Havisham, Miss Wade of *Little Dorrit*, and Rosa Dartle of *David Copperfield*," in exchange for the hipper and more fashionable singleton (17). Much like Helen Gurley Brown did with *Cosmopolitan* in the 1960s, Krantz's texts redefine their target audience—single, heterosexual women in their late twenties/early thirties. The demographic, as constructed by these texts, becomes not only socially acceptable but trendy; today, we see real women beginning to embrace the image of themselves being sold to them in fiction.

The women present that night at the signing evidenced this trend. That evening, the bookstore was filled with women looking as though they had shown up to audition for *Sex and the City* rather than to have a book signed. The women who attended seemed in many ways to possess qualities similar to Vivian and her creator—the flesh and bones version of the cyber model. Outwardly, the women appeared to be young, upwardly mobile, white, heterosexual (some were there with reluctant boyfriends in tow), and equipped with that New York City flair for fashion, decked out in their Manolo Blahniks and their DKNY skirts.[8] In their uniformity of dress, the women present seemed to be buying into those trends offered by various avenues of consumer culture, whether it be Vivian's book, HBO's *Sex and the City*, or women's magazines like *Cosmopolitan* and *Marie Claire*, cultivating the lifestyle upon which those avenues of consumer culture capitalize.

Though the life that Vivian leads borders on the fantastic, Krantz's novel is more than just escapism. Rather in the spirit of Ben Franklin's autobiography, Vivian's story presents readers with the tale of a girl from humble beginnings who moves to New York City where she works hard at earning a living and is eventually rewarded for that hard work with her dream job at VH1 and a contract to become a cyber model. Her book, at times, echoes Munroe Leaf's 1938 advice manual *Listen Little Girl Before You Come to New York*, a guide for women thinking of moving to the Big Apple. Leaf's book, he explains in the opening chapter, is for those women who had:

# Afterword

> ... been through a loop in New York that included the headaches, feetaches, the heartaches of selling in department stores, they had had their literary illusions blasted by Christmas selling in fashionable book shops, had dabbled in decorating, restaurant hostessing, flirted with modeling, they had cried in subways, danced in night clubs and crawled home to cheap two-room apartments where five girls shared their clothes and lives and the last girl home won the lumpy day-bed. (2)

Vivian's story (which includes "restaurant hostessing" and dancing in clubs), like Munroe's, serves as an advisory tale to women thinking of moving to New York. But while the premise of Leaf's book seems at times to discourage women's migrations to New York (his opening chapters concludes with "This book will stop no one, but whatever our faults and shortcomings, 'don't say we didn't try to tell you'"), the aim of Vivian's book is to encourage readers to be confident and pursue their dreams (10).[9] In the vein of these advice manuals, Vivian's book directly addresses the reader throughout; she repeatedly uses the personal pronoun "you" and often disseminates advice. The opening of Krantz's novel exemplifies this technique; she writes, "You know, it's funny ... my whole life I've never really been satisfied (1). She continues: "My drive, my spirit made me who I am today and will also make for some fine storytelling if I do say so myself. And that's when I'll touch you. When you realize that us average gals have a lot in common and when set free can live a life you can only read about" (2–3). Like other advice manuals, Krantz uses direct address in her narrative; however, instead of providing explicit and rigid instructions to her readers, her opening draws the reader in by directly addressing them while her casual, conversational tone creates the illusion of kinship with her audience.[10]

Krantz's narrative structure aims to establish a rapport with the reader and implies a companionship between the two by making it seem as though both are navigating this adventure together. Her text, at times, reads like a "how to" manual, advising readers on the best way to make their fortune in the big city. However, like other chick lit texts, Krantz's novel becomes the "anti-manual manual," encouraging readers to simultaneously embrace and interrogate the advice being offered to them by women's magazines, self-help books, romantic comedies, and domestic publications. *The Autobiography of Vivian Livingston* represents a protagonist enmeshed with consumer culture yet able to revamp those ideologies offered to suit her own needs. In the opening paragraph of her novel, Krantz's protagonist states her dissatisfaction with her life, going on to detail the ways in which she always believed that her life "was going to be my own movie, my own novel" (1). Yet, while she envisions her life lived as a movie or a novel, she emphasizes that that life will be "lived on [her] own terms with all the highs and lows I could fill it with" (1). Living one's life on one's own terms is a central theme of the novel. Though Vivian's fantasies frequently become her reality, she achieves her goals without sacrificing her sense of self and often because she has taken a chance. One such example occurs when Vivian wants to be promoted at VH1; she decides to approach her boss in a non-traditional way. Vivian comes up with the idea for her to be named a "special projects manager," arguing that she represents VH1's demographic and explaining that she would do a good job of developing programming that appealed to that demographic. Her boss questions her approach, mainly because he feels that someone who has put more time in than her should be promoted. When he asks her why he should not give the job to someone who put more time in, Vivian counters, "'Because I asked. I brought it to you. Maybe it's not the conventional way of doing things, but that doesn't make it undoable'" (175). Vivian stresses here that she is not one to follow "the rules," but, rather, she is someone who will take a chance to get what she wants. In constructing Vivian in such a way, Krantz presents her readers with another model for resisting and/or revising advice offered, and her protagonist imparts to readers that it is possible to love consumer culture and still be critical of it. Vivian works within the system yet is still able to remain an active, rather than a passive, reader and consumer.

Though remarkably similar to the other chick lit texts discussed here, what became immediately evident to me at Barnes and Noble that evening was the principle way in which Krantz's texts differed from chick lit written just a few years earlier. Vivian Livingston's empire, unlike many chick lit texts, has connected itself to multiple aspects of consumer culture—illustrated that evening by everything from the pre-event publicity to the free promotional products for those in attendance. Like other book signing events, Vivian's book launch was promoted in the traditional ways; however, Vivian's association with *Marie Claire* and her connections to the World Wide Web provided additional event exposure. As Frances Kelly, the coordinator for this Barnes and Noble event, noted in a telephone interview, the general public received word about Krantz's signing through several different venues. Kelly explained that event promotions for bookstore signings operate on two levels—the store level and the corporate level. Normally, book signings such as Krantz's are advertised through window displays, the Barnes and Noble in store calendar, and press releases, which are distributed to a variety of New York publications such as *Time Out New York, New York, The New York Press*, and *The Village Voice*. At the corporate level, Barnes and Noble usually runs a full page advertisement in the *New York Times*, detailing its upcoming events at all stores.[11] Kelly remarked, however, that she felt Krantz had done a large amount of publicizing on her own. In fact, Krantz had publicized the event on Vivianlives.com, posting it on her site and sending out email reminders, like the one I received, to her mailing list. In addition to this publicity, other websites devoted to readings in and around New York listed Krantz's signing on their websites.

Vivian's association with *Marie Claire* magazine provided additional exposure. Since February 2001, Vivian has appeared in issues of *Marie Claire*, promoting products such as Clairol Herbal Essences, Cingular Wireless, Betsey Johnson, and Audi TT® Roadsters ("Vivian Subscribes to Mag" 29).[12] In turn, *Marie Claire* magazine appears in various forms on Vivianlives.com; copies of it lie around Vivian's virtual apartment while virtual cutouts from the magazine are pasted in Vivian's online journal, accompanied by Vivian's comments on the clothing: "I Want Her: Coat!!! how decadent!!! And those bell sleeves—perfection!!!!"[13] And, that evening further cemented the association. Each person present received a Nautica goody bag, complete with a host of products like those advertised on the pages of *Marie Claire*—Clarins Normalizing Facial Mask, Bourjois mascara, and Noodé facial cleanser. In addition, those in attendance received postcards with an image of Vivian on one side and, on the other side, the announcement that a CD of her favorite songs would be released in August 2002.

Each aspect of the evening reinforced the increasing potential for the interconnectedness between consumer culture and fiction and revealed new possibilities now open to authors. With globalization comes the potential for authors to distribute their work to a larger audience, and as seen earlier, some popular fiction authors have admittedly used the World Wide Web to their advantage.[14] Krantz was among one of the first chick lit authors to use these consumer resources is such multifaceted ways. Krantz has had significant experience with the promotion of consumer goods; she formerly worked as a publicist for Calvin Klein and Donna Karan before she founded Forever After Inc., "the parent company to Vivianlives.com" (Mack 6). Like the magazines which showcase Calvin Klein's and Donna Karan's products, Krantz's website and her book contain a multitude of references to consumer culture mediums from movies to television shows to popular songs to products. In some ways, these connections are not new. Like other chick lit texts, Vivianlives.com showcases products that Vivian uses and finds to be exceptional, and her novel mentions Hollywood movies such as *Top Gun* and *The Breakfast Club*. However, in other ways, Krantz has taken this interconnectedness to another level, Krantz's company, Forever After Inc., earns money from product placement (Manning-Schaffel). So, while Becky Bloomwood may mention reading *Cosmopolitan* and may talk of purchasing Clarins neck cream, Vivian Livingston *appears* in Marie Claire, wearing a Betsey Johnson dress, holding a Nokia 3300 series phone, and her creator and company receive compensation for featuring Pantene Products on her website.[15]

Krantz's chick lit, then, is different from the other chick lit authors texts examined here. Rather than existing purely in written, or sometimes visual, forms, Krantz's chick lit heroine's activities are chronicled in novels, in magazines, and on her website, thus blurring the line between what is considered "literature," "popular fiction," and "blogs." And, Krantz's receipt of kickbacks for product placement further confuses what is "literature" and what is "advertising." And, as evidenced that evening in New York, the reaction of Krantz's fans to her texts further blur the distinction between "heroines," "readers," and "consumers." Krantz's text is also important because it points the ways in which contemporary global society may alter the consumption of all fiction—chick lit and otherwise.

While Krantz may have begun this experimentation with the boundaries of the novel and the use the World Wide Web, more recently, other chick lit writers have also encouraged their readers to connect with them via homepages and blogs. Philadelphia author Jennifer Weiner includes a letter at the back of her 2001 paperback edition of *Good In Bed* which directly addresses her readers, thanking them for reading her book and encouraging them to visit her website and email her directly at jen@jenniferweiner.com. Her website contains direct links to Amazon and Barnes and Noble where visitors can buy her book, and she includes an online journal for readers interested in reading more of Weiner's work while in between Weiner novels. Additionally, authors like Weiner, Laura Zigman, and Alisa Valdes-Rodriguez have set up MySpace pages, which allow them to interact with readers on another level. MySpace, the virtual community which was established in November 2003, allows visitors to create pages about themselves. Participants can post music, photos, videos, and blogs; they can add virtual friends; and they can post messages on one another's pages. Writers like Weiner have used this site to their advantage. In many cases, the pages of chick lit writers are part personal, part professional. Weiner, Zigman, and Valdes-Rodriguez include information about their chick lit books, but they also integrate personal information. For instance, Valdes-Rodriguez has a picture slideshow, which contains shots of the covers of her novels alongside childhood photos of herself and pictures of her family. Additionally, on these pages, these authors often include other chick lit novelists in their "top friends." That way, visitors can easily access the pages of other authors and make a friend request, becoming virtual friends with the authors of their favorite books.

# Afterword

Sites like MySpace add another layer to the interactions that can occur between authors and their readers.

Chick lit writers are finding other creative ways for readers to become active participants in the creation of chick lit texts as well. Candace Bushnell has gone so far as to elicit the help of readers in writing her next novel. In March 2003, Bushnell was asked by Montblanc, the pen maker, to participate in a promotional event in which Bushnell would write the first line of a love story, with "the company's Meisterstuck Solitaire Royal diamond fountain pen, which has 4,810 pave diamonds set in 18-karat gold" (Ligos 2). At the Madison Avenue store, "customers . . . [were] invited to add their own lines to continue the story" (Ligos 2). The "1,000-page blank book that stands two feet tall" will then travel to eight other cities to gain more entries (Ligos 2). This move by Montblanc and Bushnell mirrors already existent policies in the soap opera industry, which frequently relies on viewer input to determine their storylines. Literary experimentation like this has obvious implications for the history of the novel as globalization produces an even larger, and more accessible, audience and forces writers to re-examine their creative process, adjusting to the technological advances currently available to them.

Though these off-shoots and sub-genres of chick lit, whether written by chick lit novices or already established authors, are outside the immediate scope of this project, they are fertile ground for future, scholarly examination. Like the chick lit texts that are examined here, they, too, point to the continued and varied ways that chick lit seeks to connect itself to consumer culture. In many ways, the questions asked at the beginning of *Cosmopolitan Culture and Consumerism in Chick Lit* need to be revisited with this new wave of chick lit in mind, noting whether these off-shoots and sub-genres continue in the vein of their "foremothers" to challenge the consumer industry to which they are linked or whether they simply reproduce many of these ideologies offered by women's advice manuals. Most importantly, we should consider how these new forms of technology will affect our perception and consumption of the novel.

The web address of Vivian Livingston's website not only speaks to the ways in which Sherrie Krantz attempts to connect with her readers, but it is also representative of the multiple ways that the contemporary women's popular fiction examined here strives to cross previously fixed fictional boundaries. The address—Vivianlives.com—is a multi-layered one, referencing the many lives affected by Krantz's texts. Vivian "lives" both at this web address and within the pages of *Marie Claire* and Krantz's novel, occupying multiple consumer spaces. And, in turn, tracking Vivian's life becomes a way for her readers to live, purchasing goods that Vivian has recommended, accepting her advice, and mimicking the behavior of this cyber role model. Vivian, then, lives both in our literary (and cyber) imagination and through the lives enacted everyday by readers affected by her texts. And, Krantz's texts, like the work of her chick lit contemporaries, points to the way in which an age-old literary form is still very much alive, as its creators adjust and adapt their medium to meet the needs of an audience increasingly enmeshed in contemporary consumer culture.

# Notes

**NOTES TO CHAPTER ONE**

1. Fielding, Helen. *Bridget Jones's Diary*. London: Picador, 1998. All subsequent citations will be from this edition unless otherwise noted.
2. It is important to acknowledge that Cris Mazza initially coined the term "chick-lit" when titling her co-edited volumes, *Chick-Lit: Postfeminist Fiction* (1995) and *Chick-Lit 2 (No Chick Vics)* (1996). In her essay, "Who's Laughing Now?: A Short History of Chick-Lit and the Perversion of a Genre," for Suzanne Ferriss and Mallory Young's *Chick Lit: The New Woman's Fiction*, Mazza explains that the term was later adopted by the popular press to label these texts about young, single women in the city. In this essay, Mazza makes it quite clear that her intention for the term is at odds with what the term has come to mean. Thus, it is important not to confuse the "chick-lit" of Mazza's anthologies with "chick lit" like *Bridget Jones's Diary*. Chick lit, as I discuss it here, is more in line with the popular press's definition than Mazza's.
3. As Imelda Whelehan notes in her book *Helen Fielding's* Bridget Jones's Diary: *A Reader's Guide*, there is some debate about the evolution of what the media has commonly deemed "chick lit." She notes, "American critics pointed out that Candace Bushnell's 'Sex and the City' column in the *New York Observer* predates Fielding's column in the *Independent* by a year and therefore might more appropriately be seen as the *ur-text* of what came to be defined as 'chick lit'" (57–58). However, I would argue against these critics, as Whelehan does, noting that Fielding's novel was published two years prior to Bushnell's. Furthermore, Fielding's novel was initially more heavily reviewed and received much more media attention than Bushnell's novel.
4. Here, Ferriss and Young reference Kate Zernike's article, "Oh, to Write a 'Bridget Jones' for Men: A Guy Can Dream" published in the *New York Times* on February 22, 2004. In this article, Zernike uses the term "commercial tsunami."
5. Chick lit's off-shoots and sub-genres are discussed more in the final chapter.

6. See Betts, Hannah. "Be Honest With Me, Do My Literary Pretensions Look Big in This?" *Times* 25 Aug. 2001. *LexisNexis*. Univ. of Delaware Morris Library, Newark, DE. 22 July 2003. <http://web.lexis-nexis.com.proxygw.wrlc.org>. Also, see Colgan, Jenny. "Real Lives: We Know the Difference Between Foie Gras and Hula Hoops, Beryl, but Sometimes We Just Want Hula Hoops." *Times* 25 Aug. 2001. *LexisNexis*. Univ. of Delaware Morris Library, Newark, DE. 22 July 2003. <http://web.lexis-nexis.com.proxygw.wrlc.org>.
7. For this article, see McCartney, Jenny. "No Wonder Beryl's Cross. Bainbridge et al Wanted Boadiceas. Instead They've Got Posh Spice." *Sunday Telegraph*. 26 Aug. 2001: 21. *LexisNexis*. Univ. of Delaware Morris Library, Newark, DE. 22 July 2003. <http://web.lexis-nexis.com.proxygw.wrlc.org>.
8. Anna Weinberg's fellow train passenger makes this comment when he spots Weinberg reading Anna Maxted's hot-pink, covered *Behaving Like Adults* while he, on the other hand, is reading "a Nelson DeMille thriller."
9. *Cosmopolitan Culture and Consumerism in Chick Lit* began as my dissertation project. When I first began working on this project in 2002, there had been little scholarly work done on the genre.
10. See Fraz, Ulrike. "Voices and Characterization in *Bridget Jones's Diary*: A Comparitive Study." Masters Thesis. University of Manchester, Institute of Science and Technology, 2001; Regules, Anne. "Working Women and Re-Working the Romance: Chick-Lit from Kate Chopin to Jennifer Weiner to *Sex and the City*." Masters Thesis. University of Texas at San Antonio, 2006; and Chan, Ka-ling. Evolution of a Heroine: From *Pride and Prejudice* to *Bridget Jones's Diary*." Chinese University of Hong Kong, Masters Thesis. 2004.
11. I adopt Sarah A. Leavitt's use of the term "domestic-advice manuals" as used in *From Catharine Beecher to Martha Stewart: A Cultural History of Domestic Advice*. Leavitt uses this term to delineate a wide variety of domestic advice ranging from books to magazines to television shows.
12. Fielding, Helen. *Bridget Jones's Diary*. London: Ted Smart, 1998.
13. The transcript for this interview can be found at: http://www.time.com/time/community/transcripts/chattr061698.html.
14. Wells's essay primarily concerns itself with distinguishing the nineteenth-century novels of Brontë and Austen from the chick lit of today. She notes, "While wit is undeniably abundant in chick lit, however, the genre can hardly be said to be overflowing in either taste or genius, even allowing for changes in the meaning of these terms since Austen's day. Chick lit amuses and engrosses, but it does not richly reimagine in literary form the worlds that inspire it" (67).
15. This quote comes from the book jacket of Johnson's paperback edition of the sequel to *Le Divorce—Le Mariage* (2000).

16. In general, the distinction between consumer industries is blurring. For example, the Hearst Corporation, a major publisher of magazines, is also involved in the television industry, operating Hearst Entertainment and Syndication (*The Hearst Corporation*). Additionally, in November 2004, Simon & Schuster, the book publishers, partnered with ABC's *Good Morning America* for "The Story of My Life Contest," a competition which asks viewers to write their life stories (*Simonsays.com: Simon & Schuster, Inc.*).
17. These product promotions appeared in the June 2002 issue of *Marie Claire* in an advertisement for Herbal Essences True Intense Color by Clairol.
18. Anna Maxted was a consistent contributor in the late nineties, writing such articles as "Sex and Shopping: The Orgasmic Connection" (December 1996).
19. In an interview with Christina Nunez entitled "Meet the Writers: Sophie Kinsella" found on Barnesandnoble.com, Kinsella indicates that she has also published books under the pen name Madeleine Wickham.
20. James Playstead Wood, in his book *Magazines in the United States*, traces the evolution of women's magazines, noting that as early as April 1709 in England *The Tatler*, though not a magazine targeted specifically at women, devoted space to women's issues. It was not until the nineteenth century, however, that women proved to be a viable demographic in both England and America. At this time, publications aimed specifically at women grew.
21. Foster uses the term conduct literature to refer to texts that address issues of "etiquette, manners, dress, behavior, and charm" (vii). To me, Foster's umbrella term is synonymous with etiquette books or advice manuals. Foster's choice of terms, however, emphasizes how these texts direct readers' behaviors.
22. Sophie Kinsella's first novel was published in England under the title *The Secret Dreamworld of a Shopaholic* in 2000. When published in America, the title was changed to *Confessions of a Shopaholic* and certain sections of the text were changed.
23. In her book *Love and Ideology in the Afternoon: Soap Opera, Women, and Television Genre*, Laura Stempel Mumford provides an excellent definition of what is meant by "dominant ideology." She writes: "*dominant ideology*, refers to the various tightly intertwined economic, social, political, religious, cultural, and other systems and practices that define, express, and maintain the existing power structure . . . Dominant ideology is necessarily conservative in the broadest sense, in that it strives to maintain itself and the status of those in power. But it is also conservative in a more specific sense, identifying and perpetuating a narrow range of 'correct' choices in the political, economic, sexual, familial, and other spheres of life" (10–11).
24. Radford's book is a collection of essays that critically interrogates the evolution of the romance, from the Greek ages to the 1980s; Radway examines the reading strategies of romance readers.

25. In addition to this heavy criticism, women writers themselves have begun to either embrace or distance themselves from the chick lit label. For example, in 2005, Lauren Baratz-Logsted published *This Is Chick-Lit*. Elizabeth Merrick responded in 2006 with her edited collection *This Is Not Chick Lit: Original Stories by America's Best Women Writers*.
26. Examples of such publications are: Blumenthal, Dannielle. *Women and Soap Opera: A Cultural Feminist Perspective*. Westport, Connecticut: Praeger, 1997.; Geraghty, Christine. *Women and Soap Opera: A Study of Prime Time Soaps*. Cambridge, UK: Polity Press, 2001.; Miner, Madonne M. *Insatiable Appetites: Twentieth-Century American Women's Bestsellers*. Westport, Connecticut: Greenwood Press, 1984.
27. Radway comments, "Because readers are presented in this theory as passive, purely receptive individuals who can only consume the meanings embodied within cultural texts, they are understood to be powerless in the face of ideology . . . In this theory of mass culture, ideological control is thought to be all-pervasive and complete as a consequence of the ubiquity of mass culture itself and of the power of the individual artifacts or texts over individuals who can do nothing but ingest them" (6).
28. These product promotions appeared in the June 2002 issue of *Marie Claire*. Herbal Essence Hair Color sponsored a contest in which contestants would log onto their website (www.herbalessencescolor.com), enter their UPC code from their package of Herbal Essences color, and be registered to win a variety of prizes. Grand prize was an Audi TT® Roadster while additional prizes were a $2000 Betsey Johnson shopping spree and free Cingular Wireless services for a year.

## NOTES TO CHAPTER TWO

1. In this chapter, all references to the women's magazines mentioned are to the British editions of those magazines unless otherwise noted.
2. In March 1995, *Cosmopolitan* contained a section "The Power of Single" while in June 1995 the magazine contained an article by Jenny Firth Cozens entitled "The New Traditionalism: Four Weddings and a Funeral?". The tag line for that article reads, "More like four million weddings and a funeral. Suddenly, *everyone* [my emphasis] is embracing the traditional ritual of the long engagement and the grand, white wedding" (36).
3. There are several important studies that detail the history of women's magazines; these texts will be referenced later in this chapter. Some important content analyses of women's magazines are as follows. Joke Hermes gives an excellent summary of this type of criticism written about women's magazines in her introduction to *Reading Women's Magazines* (1995). She mentions texts such as Ros Ballaster, Margaret Beetham, Elizabeth Frazer and Sandra Hebron's *Women's Worlds: Ideology, Femininity and Women's Magazines*;

Jacqueline Blix's "A Place to Resist: Reevaluating Women's Magazines"; and Janice Winship's *Inside Women's Magazines*. I would also add to this list such texts as Marjorie Ferguson's *Forever Feminine: Women's Magazine and the Cult of Femininity*; Ellen McCracken's *Decoding Women's Magazines: From Mademoiselle to Ms.*; and Nancy Walker's two books: *Shaping Our Mothers' Worlds: American Women's Magazines* and *Women's Magazines, 1940–1960: Gender Roles and the Popular Press*.

4. Kinsella's text was originally published in England under this title. The title of the American edition of Kinsella's text is *Confessions of a Shopaholic*.

5. The term "reduce" was a popular during the 1950s and was frequently used in American women's magazines to refer to dieting strategies. For instance, the July 1953 issue of American *Mademoiselle* offered an article by Bernice Peck entitled "Diet with Dessert: The New Reducing Theory That Lets You Have Your Cake and Figure Too" (66).

6. For a more complete discussion of the history of magazines in both England and the United States, see Theodore Peterson's *Magazines in the 20th Century* and James Playstead Wood's *Magazines in the United States*.

7. For a more complete discussion of the history of women's magazines in England see Cynthia White's *Women's Magazines: 1693–1968*. For more information regarding the history of women's magazines in the United States, see Mary Ellen Zuckerman's *A History of Popular Women's Magazines in the United States: 1792–1995*.

8. For a more complete discussion of twentieth-century women's magazines in both England and America, see David Reed's *The Popular Magazine in Britain and the United States: 1880–1960* (Toronto: University of Toronto Press, 1997) and for a more complete discussion of twentieth-century women's magazines in the United States, see Mary Ellen Zuckerman's *A History of Popular Women's Magazines in the United States, 1792–1995* (Westport, Connecticut: Greenwood Press, 1998).

9. Of the remaining four articles, three do not credit an author. The fourth, "75 Sex Tricks," is written by Dan Kraus.

10. Anna Maxted was a consistent contributor in the late nineties while Jane Green published "Help! I'm a N.E.W. (Never Enough Woman)!" in August 1998.

11. Interestingly enough, the *Cosmo* diary is red with lettering on the front that reads "*Cosmopolitan*" with the word "diary" underneath and 1995 off to the side. The appearance of the diary, particularly because of its red color, is very similar to the diary used in the film adaptation of *Bridget Jones's Diary* released in 2001. This is not the only direct correlation to *Cosmopolitan*. Additionally, in reviewing the 1995 editions of *Cosmopolitan*, I discovered many connections between the articles written that year and Fielding's text. The March 1995 edition contained a special section on single life entitled "The Power of Single" while the July 1995 edition contained an article by

Jane Laidlaw entitled "Oh, To Be in Edinburgh," the festival that Bridget attends in the novel. Also, in November of 1995 there was an article on feng shui ("Feng Shui Introduction"), a home decorating practice that Bridget engages in, and in December of that same year, there was a piece by Laura Marcus entitled "In Praise of Bossy Mothers." In subtly referencing these articles, Fielding shows an additional way that women's magazines inform her novel.

12. Kinsella, Sophie. *The Secret Dreamworld of a Shopaholic*. London: Black Swan, 2000. All subsequent citations will be from this edition unless otherwise noted.

13. The January 2000 edition of *Marie Claire* contains a fashion article entitled "*Friends* Trends," detailing clothing that consumers can buy that is similar to those clothes worn by the women on the American sitcom *Friends*. Both Jigsaw and French Connection are mentioned here. Additionally, page 306 of the September 2000 edition of *Marie Claire* contains a promotion for Agnés B make-up.

14. The September 2001 American issue of *Glamour* magazine featured a photo spread by Walter Chin on actress Bridget Moynahan entitled "Bridget's Diary;" the subtitle reads, "No, not that Bridget," referencing Fielding's protagonist. The article "It's in the dictionary, d'oh!" from BBC News online comments that popular culture inspired words have been added to the *Oxford English Dictionary*. Among them is the phrase "bad hair day:" "Helen Fielding's novel and the subsequent film may have inspired a generation of women but it is also having an effect on English. 'Bad hair day' is an expression that has been around for years, but it was the chardonnay-swilling Bridget's use of the phrase that caused it to be included" (2).

15. See Young, Suzanne. "*Confessions of a Shopaholic*." *Booklist* 1 Jan. 2001: 918. Also, see Rev. of *Confessions of a Shopaholic*. *Publishers Weekly* 18 Dec. 2000: 53.

16. Fielding concludes her narrative with a list of summary of Bridget's activities for the year, so the narrative effectively ends with the line, "An *excellent* year's progress" (310). Her diary, itself, though, ends with this assertion about motherly advice.

17. A comparison between Jane Austen's novels and Helen Fielding's text is particularly apt, as critics of Fielding's novel have noted. Most obviously, her character Mark Darcy is decidedly similar to Mr. Darcy of *Pride and Prejudice*. Also, Bridget and her friends continually watch the BBC's production of *Pride and Prejudice* in their spare time. For more on this comparison, see Salber, Cecelia. "Bridget Jones and Mark Darcy: Art Imitating Art . . . Imitating Art." *Persuasions On-Line* 22.1 (2000). 2 June 2004 <http://www.jasna.org/pol04/salber.html>.

## NOTES TO CHAPTER THREE

1. See Gerston, Jill. "So Many Rules, So Little Time." *New York Times* 23 October 1996: B1. Also, see Esselman, Mary. "Altar Girls: How to Get a Man? Sherrie Schneider and Ellen Fein Say Just Follow The Rules." *People Weekly* 11 November 1996: 170–73. The duo appeared on *Dateline* segment entitled "Here Comes the Brides" on October 25, 1996 and made two appearances on *The Oprah Winfrey Show* ("Dating Rules," October 11, 1996 and "*The Rules* Backlash," June 19, 1997).
2. Though the book was published in 1995, it was not until Oprah invited Fein and Schneider on her October 11, 1996 show that the book began to receive extensive media attention.
3. After having Fein and Schneider on her October 11, 1996 show, Oprah had the pair return on June 19, 1997 in a show entitled "*The Rules* Backlash." Here, Oprah's audience debated the publication, raising many of the issues that I have detailed above.
4. The back of the 1995 edition of *The Rules* contains a form for readers to fill out and send in so that they can find out more information about *The Rules* seminars. Additionally, Fein and Schneider advertise phone and email consultations on their website: http://www.therulesbook.com/.
5. Simonds offers a very detailed analysis of the critical reception of self-help books about gender in her chapter entitled "The Tangled Web: Self-Help Books about Gender."
6. I use the term "popular fiction works" here deliberately because Melissa Bank's book is technically not a novel. Rather, *The Girls' Guide to Hunting and Fishing* is a collection of short stories, many of which appeared in various publications such *as The North American Review, Another Chicago Magazine, Chicago Tribune, Other Voices,* and *Zoetrope: All-Story* before being collected in this book.
7. There have been few book length studies of self-help literature; however, many newspapers and magazines have devoted time to studying the genre. See: Forest, James J. "Self-Help Books." *American Psychologist* July 1988: 599; Goleman, Daniel. "Feeling Gloomy? A Good Self-Help Book May Actually Help." *New York Times* 6 July 1989: B6; Hinds, Michael deCourcy. "Coping with Self-Help Books." *New York Times* 16 January 16 1988: 33; MacDonald, Dwight. "Howtoism." *New Yorker*, 22 May 1954, 82–109; Reiff, David. "Victims All?: Recovery, Co-dependency, and the Art of Blaming Someone Else." *Harper's* October 1991: 49–56.
8. For her book, Simonds conducted interviews with a variety of female, self-help readers between May 1988 and February 1989.
9. Though Fein and Schneider's book focuses primarily upon the action that needs to be taken during the courtship phase, they do devote sections

of their book to life with Mr. Right, specifically "Rule 26: Even if You're Engaged or Married, You Still Need The Rules" and "Rule 35: Be Easy to Live With."

10. These reviews appear on the opening pages of the 1999 paperback edition of Wolper's text.

11. Wolper, Carol. *The Cigarette Girl*. New York: Riverhead, 1999. All subsequent citations will be from this edition unless otherwise noted.

12. Bank's fourth short story, "The Best Possible Light," and her sixth short story, "You Could Be Anyone," do not center on the character of Jane. "The Best Possible Light" is the only story not directly connected to Jane, though she is mentioned casually in a conversation between two characters as the woman who lives in the upstairs apartment building. In it, a woman named Nina has an impromptu reunion with her children Barney, P.K, and Isabelle at which time Barney announces that his ex-wife and his new wife are both pregnant with his children. Though Jane is not mentioned in "You Could Be Anyone," the story serves an important purpose in terms of the way that Bank's critiques self-help books and will be discussed later in this chapter.

13. These texts mentioned by Bank are often cited in critical analyses of self-help books. Starker devotes considerable time to Friedan's book while Simonds discusses both Friedan and J.

14. See Susan McCabe's *Elizabeth Bishop: Her Poetics of Loss*. The Pennsylvania State University Press: University Park, PA: 1994 and Robert Dale Parker's *The Unbeliever: The Poetry of Elizabeth Bishop*. University of Illinois Press: Urbana, 1988.

15. Robert and Jane go to watch a performance of one acts entitled *Mere Mortals* by David Ives. Jane's favorite of the night is a story "about two mayflies on a date; they watch a nature documentary about themselves and discover their life span is only one day long—after mating, they'll die" (256).

16. Like Bank, Zigman names her main character, Jane.

17. Zigman, Laura. *Animal Husbandry*. New York: Delta, 1998. All subsequent citations will be from this edition unless otherwise noted.

18. Some of these titles include W.S. Gilbert's *Princess Ida*, *The Kama Sutra*, Otto Kernberg's *Borderline Conditions*, Stendhal's *Love*, Friedrich Nietzsche's *Human, All Too Human*, Charles Darwin's *The Expressions of the Emotions in Man and Animals*, Jane Goodall's *In the Shadow of Man*, *National Geographic*, and *The New York Post*.

19. How to "Live Your Best Life" is a frequent theme in both Winfrey's magazine and her television show. However, this particular phrase appears in the March 2004 edition of her magazine.

**NOTES TO CHAPTER FOUR**

1. Brown was editor-in-chief of *Cosmopolitan* from 1965–1996 (Plotz).

2. Rubinfeld's work deconstructs Hollywood romantic comedies from 1970–1999. His study, which follows on the heels of work by such scholars as David Shumway and Stanley Cavell, provides readers with a very detailed look at the way in which romantic comedies rely on traditional assumptions concerning gender in order to succeed at the box office. Stanley Cavell's *Pursuits of Happiness: The Hollywood Comedy of Remarriage* (Cambridge: Harvard, 1981) takes a critical look at comedies of remarriage made in Hollywood between 1934 and 1949 while David Shumway's article "Screwball Comedies: Constructing Romance, Mystifying Marriage" (from *Film Genre Reader II*. Ed. Barry Keith Grant. Austin: University of Texas, 1995) directly opposes Cavell's argument, noting "Where Cavell goes wrong—and it is hardly a peripheral place—is his position that the screwball comedies succeed in enlightening us about marriage itself. My argument is that they do just the opposite: they mystify marriage by portraying it as the goal—but not the end—of romance" (381). Rubinfeld contributes greatly to discussions of romantic comedies because he seeks to deconstruct the romantic comedy; he not only identifies, defines, and charts the overarching plots and themes, but he also details what these plots and themes convey to audiences concerning gender.
3. Though Jeffries also appeared in *The Buccaneer* (1958) and *The Pink Panther* (1964) prior to her role as Gretchen, in the 1965 movie poster, Jeffries's name is not highlighted as the other five stars' names are ("*Sex and the Single Girl*"). Furthermore, on the VHS video box, Jeffries's name is also overlooked.
4. Arguably, some romantic comedies of the last few years have made attempts to resist the conventions of the genre. The 2003 movie *Down With Love*, starring Renée Zellweger and Ewan McGregor, spoofs the romantic comedy industry, particularly the films of the late 1950s and early 1960s like the 1959 film *Pillow Talk*. More recently, in 2006, Jennifer Aniston and Vince Vaughn starred in the film, *The Break-Up*, which did not provide its viewers with an ending that resulted in the lead characters' coupling. The film, as evidenced by reader reviews on Amazon.com, received heavy criticism. Viewers on Amazon.com seemed disappointed with the ending and deemed it "a very serious, very boring, very unpleasant drama" as well as "a pointless waste of time."
5. The second scene of the film shows Cameron Diaz dancing up the streets of San Francisco to the song "Sexual Revolution" by Macy Gray. The inclusion of Gray's song, which discourages women from repressing their sexuality, reinforces the idea that this film is about women's sexual freedom.
6. In *Bound to Bond*, Mark D. Rubinfeld labels one of the four romantic comedy plots as "the prick foil plot." I use the term prick here in the same spirit that Rubinfeld does, though his "prick" is more narrowly defined as "a romantic rival who is economically and/or socially better positioned than the hero, knows it, and flaunts" (34).

7. The film continually makes Cameron Diaz (5'9") ("Cameron Diaz Image Gallery, Card Gallery, Biography") and Christina Applegate (5'5") ("Christina Applegate: Biography, Filmography, Pictures, Comments") appear decidedly taller than Selma Blair (5'5") ("Selma Blair"). In several scenes, Diaz and Applegate flank Blair, drawing attention to her petite nature and consistently implying a childlike innocence in comparison to the "authority" figures that surround her.
8. I use the term "New Woman" deliberately here to call to mind the type of women this term initially referred to and to establish a connection between unconventional women of the past and present. In her book, *Bachelor Girl: The Secret History of Single Women in the Twentieth Century*, Betsy Israel explains the history behind the term "New Woman." She comments that "the precise meaning of 'new woman,' like that of the contemporaneous term 'free love,' has become impossibly blurry" (114). The term initially referred to women who at the start of the twentieth century "derived from Henry James and his irreverent moderns Daisy Miller and Isabel Archer" (114). The New Woman's "attitudes and beliefs were descended from elite early feminists;" they attended college and sometimes graduate school (114). As Israel explains, "But the new woman was most famous for her refusal or, rather, polite disinclination, to marry" (115). For these reasons, it seems appropriate to evoke this term here.
9. It is interesting to note that the only characters who do not end up happily coupled in this film are Jane and Peter's brother. Once again, the film serves to admonish Jane for her reckless sexual acts, again reinforcing the idea that women who have sex like Jane cannot achieve a Hollywood happily ever after ending. It also calls to mind Gretchen's fate from *Sex and the Single Girl*.
10. The following films produced from 1995–1999 are listed in Rubinfeld's "The 'Top' 155 Hollywood Romantic Comedies: Plots, Genre Types, and Themes" table: *While You Were Sleeping, French Kiss, Forget Paris, Nine Months, Something to Talk About, The American President,* and *Sabrina* (1995); *The Truth About Cats and Dogs, Multiplicity, Tin Cup, The Mirror Has Two Faces, The Preacher's Wife, Jerry Maguire, One Fine Day,* and *Michael* (1996); *Fools Rush In, Grosse Pointe Blank, Addicted to Love, My Best Friend's Wedding, Picture Perfect, For Richer or Poorer,* and *As Good As It Gets* (1997); *The Wedding Singer, The Object of My Affection, Hope Floats, Six Days, Seven Nights, There's Something About Mary, The Parent Trap, How Stella Got Her Groove Back, Practical Magic, Shakespeare in Love,* and *You've Got Mail* (1998); *She's All That, Blast From the Past, The Other Sister, Forces of Nature, 10 Things I Hate about You, The Out-of-Towners, Never Been Kissed, Notting Hill, An Ideal Husband, Runaway Bride, For Love of the Game, Drive Me Crazy, The Story of Us, The Best Man,* and *The Bachelor* (1999).

11. I want to emphasize the fact that, in their works, chick lit authors are responding to the portrayals of white women in romantic comedies. As Patricia Hill Collins notes in *Black Feminist Thought: Knowledge, Consciousness, and the Politics of Empowerment* (1991), there are controlling images specific to black women. These images differ from the way that white women have traditionally been portrayed, and it is important to note that the chick lit books discussed here respond only to white women's representations.
12. The presence of Zellweger's son complicates the virgin/whore paradigm because, admittedly, Zellweger's character is clearly not a virgin. However, in contrast to Preston's character, Dorothy Boyd keeps her sexuality in check. Unlike Avery who gives her love more freely, Dorothy's decision to have sex with Jerry comes about because she seems convinced that there is a spiritual connection between the two of them.
13. *Sex and the City* evolved from Bushnell's *Observer* columns. The HBO series, which began in June of 1998, was then adapted from this collection. Bushnell's collection contains a cast of characters, among them Carrie and Samantha who also appear, true to Bushnell's original form, in the series. Though Miranda appears in the written text, she is fleshed out by HBO, and the character of Charlotte, absent from the book, is an entirely new creation. The series does retain some of the original themes. In the first season, episode two, "Models and Mortals," revolves around a group of men obsessed with dating models while episode eight, "Three's a Crowd," explores the concept of threesomes. Furthermore, episode ten, "The Baby Shower," seems to evolve from the women's experiences at Jolie Bernard's wedding shower.
14. Bushnell, Candace. *Sex and the City*. New York: Warner, 1996. All subsequent citations will be from this edition unless otherwise noted.
15. The Internet Movie Database site offers this summary of Barry Levinson's film, written by Jeremy Perkins: "With his company about to merge, a happily married and successful computer expert is expecting a promotion. Instead the job goes to a woman from another plant with whom he had an affair in his bachelor days. His new boss, not only dangerously sexy but equally dangerously ambitious, tries to pick up where they left off but he just about manages to resist. As his position at work comes under increasing pressure he decides to file charges of sexual harassment. This is the last thing the company needs."
16. Admittedly, the HBO series ended in a way much more consistent with the conventions of the Hollywood romantic comedy. In the final two episodes, "An American Girl in Paris, Part Une" and "Part Deux," which aired in February 2004, we find Samantha and Smith facing Samantha's battle with breast cancer together; Miranda and Steve have moved to a brownstone in Brooklyn, resolute in caring for Steve's aging mother; and Charlotte and Harry have just received news that they've been approved to adopt a baby

from China. In turn, Carrie and Mr. Big end up together, after Big flies to Paris to save her from the temperamental artist Petrovsky. The final scene of the series shows Carrie walking down the streets of Manhattan; her cell phone rings, and she looks at the screen which reads, "John," ostensibly Mr. Big's name.

17. Interestingly enough, Bushnell herself didn't seem to believe in the "happily-ever-after" of her own text's ending. In the 2001 edition of *Sex and the City*, Bushnell revised the ending, adding two chapters in which Carrie and Mr. Big break-up. She concludes this version of the text with the statement, "Mr. Big is happily married. Carrie is happily single" (289).
18. Wolper, Carol. *The Cigarette Girl*. New York: Riverhead, 1999. All subsequent citations will be from this edition unless otherwise noted.
19. Like Wolper's heroine, the heroines of *The Sweetest Thing* philosophize about their own Mr. Maybes whom they deem Mr. Right Now—a notable intersection between texts.

## NOTES TO CHAPTER FIVE

1. The December 2003 edition of *Living* contained an article by Jonathan Hayes in which instructions were given for making marshmallow snowflakes.
2. In this chapter, I adopt Sarah A. Leavitt's use of the term "domestic-advice manuals" as used in *From Catharine Beecher to Martha Stewart: A Cultural History of Domestic Advice*. Leavitt uses this term to delineate a wide variety of domestic advice ranging from books to magazines to television shows.
3. In *The Martha Stewart Cookbook: Collected Recipes for Every Day*, Stewart writes, "I use mason jars with screw-on or clap tops to store sugars" (xii). She continues, listing those sugars needed to complete a cupboard: "granulated, rose geranium, vanilla, dark brown, light brown, confectioners', brown rock, French coffee cubes pralines (nut sugars), honey, molasses, corn syrup (light and dark), maple syrup" (xii). She acknowledges that "The listings below may at first seem intimidating" but encourages readers to "keep in mind that this is an ultimate list that includes ingredients that will allow you to cook a variety of ethnic and regional dishes" (xii).
4. For additional critical commentary on Martha Stewart, see the "Martha Stewart Roundtable" in the summer 2001 edition of *American Studies*. This edition contains a variety of essays on such topics as Martha Stewart and Kmart, Martha Stewart and whiteness, and the historical precedents for Martha Stewart's publications. More specifically, in the introduction to this section, entitled "Martha Stewart and Taste Cultures," Jay Mechling notes the way in which Martha Stewart's publications encourage a specific type of performance. He writes, "Through these essays we see that Martha belongs to a long tradition of domestic advice literature, and we see precisely how

the advice is aimed at helping readers and viewers 'perform' a white, middle-class gentility through the careful arrangements of the commodities—the props, sets, and costumes—essential to the performance" (68).
5. Stewart includes a recipe for pink cucumber soup on page 139 of *The Martha Stewart Cookbook*.
6. In *Shaping Our Mothers' Worlds: American Women's Magazines*, Nancy A. Walker holds a similar definition of domesticity, noting it "also includes family and social relationships, child-rearing practices, personal well-being, purchasing habits, recreation, schools and neighborhoods, gardening, civic involvement, food preferences, health, and personal appearance" (viii). Likewise, in the introduction to her book *Kitchen Culture in America: Popular Representations of Food, Gender, and Race*, Sherrie A. Inness identifies "kitchen culture" as "the various discourses about food, cooking, and gender roles that stem from the kitchen but that pervade our society on many levels" (3). All three of these authors stress that domesticity extends beyond the goods and behaviors to the feelings, or sentiments, that accompany proper household management.
7. For a more comprehensive discussion of Martha Stewart's American predecessors see Sarah A. Leavitt's *From Catharine Beecher to Martha Stewart: A Cultural History of Domestic Advice*.
8. For a comprehensive history of American housekeeping manuals, see Glenna Matthew's *"Just a Housewife": The Rise and Fall of Domesticity in America*. Additionally, Kathleen Anne McHugh's book *American Domesticity: From How-to Manual to Hollywood Melodrama* historically examines the concept of domesticity in America by reading representations of domesticity in a variety of texts. McHugh acknowledges her debt to Nancy Armstrong's *Desire and Domestic Fiction: A Political History of the Novel*, a book similar to hers in methodology and which analyzes domesticity in British nineteenth century texts. Armstrong also contributed an essay entitled "The Rise of the Domestic Woman" to the collection *The Ideology of Conduct: Essays on Literature and the History of Sexuality* which deals with similar subject matter. For a history of housekeeping manuals in America prior to the nineteenth century, see Sarah E. Newton's book *Learning to Behave: A Guide to American Conduct Books Before 1900*.
9. Tebbel and Zuckerman do not provide starting dates for the publications mentioned in this quotation although their text does include the date that the *Ladies' Home Journal* began. Theodore Peterson's *Magazines in the Twentieth Century* includes the inception dates of the other three magazines on pages 202, 165, and 166 respectively.
10. For more information on the domestic science movement, see Barbara Ehrenreich and Deirdre English's *For Her Own Good: 150 Years of the Experts' Advice to Women*. Also, see Laura Shapiro's book *Perfection Salad: Women and Cooking at the Turn of the Century* and Sarah A. Leavitt's chapter

entitled "The Rise of the Domiologist: Science in the Home" in her book *From Catharine Beecher to Martha Stewart: A Cultural History of Domestic Advice*.

11. In *The Feminine Mystique*, Betty Friedan discusses the dissatisfaction that many American women of the 1950s were feeling about their roles as housewives and mothers while in her article "Do Women Like to Cook?" Laura Shapiro discusses how state-of-the-art kitchen appliances and packaged foods forced women to renegotiate their relationships to their kitchens. And, in *The Way We Never Were: American Families and the Nostalgia Trap*, Stephanie Coontz reexamines the era of the 1950s, deconstructing popular perception of that time period.

12. Friedan herself purported this in her closing chapter entitled "A New Life Plan for Women."

13. It is interesting to note that Faludi observes, "This happens to be the same verdict *Newsweek* reached when it last investigated female discontent—at the height of the feminine-mystique backlash. 'American women's unhappiness is merely the most recently won of women's rights,' the magazine reported then" (78). Additionally, it is important to note that Wasserstein's 1990 Pulitzer Prize winning play is a serious comment on what Wasserstein perceives to be the gains and losses of the feminist movement. In the play, Wasserstein examines the sacrifices that Heidi Holland has made in choosing to privilege her career over her personal life and in refusing to compromise her ideals and "settle" into an unsatisfying marriage. The play is as much a comment upon men's inability to adjust to women's changing gender roles as it is upon women's dilemmas as a result of their newly gained freedoms.

14. For a more comprehensive discussion of the man shortage, see Faludi's chapter "Man Shortages and Barren Wombs: The Myths of the Backlash."

15. Martha Stewart's approach to household management has incited much discussion among contemporary scholars. Though Stewart clearly exploits societal anxieties about women's separation from the home, the implications of her enterprise are not as easy to read. It can be argued that Stewart is not furthering the split between job and home; in actuality, she fuses the two by making her career center on improving the home. However, it can also be argued that she is in some ways exacerbating superwoman syndrome by encouraging her reading public, among which a high percentage of these readers and viewers work outside the home, to make perfecting the home a fulltime job. In "Discipline—It's a 'Good Thing': Rhetorical Constitution and Martha Stewart Living Omnimedia," Cynthia Duquette Smith cites Yvonne Moran's statistics: "85 % of Stewart's catalog customers are college-educated, home-owning women in their forties with an average income of $70,000. Three-quarters of these women are married, and three-quarters of these women work outside the home' (338). Though these statistics refer to

catalog readers only, it is safe to assume that demographic for Stewart's magazines and television shows is similar. While these issues are interesting to consider and worth noting, however, they are not the focus of this chapter. For more on this debate, see Ann Mason and Marian Meyers's article "Living With Martha Stewart Media: Chosen Domesticity and the Experience of Fans."

16. Certainly, Martha Stewart is not the first cook to exploit visual media. In her article "Vicarious Consumption: Food, Television, and the Ambiguity of Modernity," Pauline Adema discusses the history of cooking shows, noting James Beard, Dionne Lucas, and Julia Child to be pioneers in the field. Where Martha Stewart differs from these individuals and where she also differs from her contemporaries is in her comprehensive approach to marketing domesticity. Not only does she cover cooking, gardening, and household management in her publications, but she also transmits that message through print, television, radio, and the web, exploiting all contemporary consumer culture mediums.

17. Magazines, cookbooks, catalogs, cooking shows, and home decorating shows are admittedly different in form from one another. In particular, catalogs from Williams-Sonoma and Pottery Barn are less prescriptive than magazines, cookbooks, cooking shows, and home decorating shows, which give explicit, how-to instructions. However, each of these mediums emphasizes either household products or behaviors central to the home.

18. These advertisements all appeared in the September 1997 edition of *Living*.

19. Laura Shapiro notes that Stewart once commented, "'Without those pictures, the books would be useful but not as fabulous'" ("The Art of Showing Off: What Makes Martha Stewart Cook?" (66). I would argue that the text in Stewart's publications is equally important and complements her photographs to complete her vision. For instance, to return to the dish-towel curtain project, the photograph and text work together to invoke a warm summer day and the feelings connected to that type of day. The photograph shows the finished dish-towel curtains: the white linen curtains outlined in red are artfully arranged in front of the window adding elegance to the seemingly stark space. The text to the right of the photograph reads: "Made from vintage linen dish towels, these casual curtains are the perfect cover-up for windows in a kitchen or a bare summer rental" and follows with detailed instructions (106). The idea to decorate a "summer rental" with these curtains is reinforced by the photograph; on the window sill rests two seashells. In the background, through the window framed by dark wood much like that found in an old restored farmhouse, one can see lush, out of focus green trees and grass. The photograph and text, then, work to support the same association.

20. Martha Stewart, the personality, is mentioned in American texts *The Cigarette Girl* and *Sex and the City* and the British text *Getting Over It*.

Additionally, chick lit texts mention home decorating magazines, like *Elle Decoration*, which are different from *Living* in terms of content but which put an equal emphasis on home decorating. Chick lit texts also occasionally mention catalogs such as Williams-Sonoma, "the catalog for cooks." Again, though these publications are different from one another, they are similar in so far as they encourage the consumption of goods in order to achieve a particular, and again often times more affluent, lifestyle.

21. Stewart continues to expand her empire. In September 2005, Stewart launched her own talk show, *The Martha Stewart Show* ("Martha Stewart"). The same year, she also starred in the reality television show, *The Apprentice*.
22. Fielding further mocks this notion in her construction Magda's marriage, which is in serious danger of ending due to her husband's infidelity.
23. Maxted, Anna. *Getting Over It*. London: Arrow, 2000. All subsequent citations will be from this edition unless otherwise noted.
24. Helen literally meets Tom accidentally. On the way to her father's funeral, she rear-ends the car in front of her which belongs to Tom's vet tech, Celine. Noticing the commotion, Tom comes out to help the two resolve the problem and ends up driving Helen to the funeral.
25. The house that Helen eventually ends up buying differs dramatically from the others on the block. While the rest are white, Helen's home is a "pebble-dashed exception," which again underscores the fact that Helen's decision to buy it and inhabit it alone is unexpected, like the house itself.
26. In her article for *Time*, Marion Hume asks "Who Will Be the Next Domestic Diva?" The subtext reads: "With Martha Stewart mired in legal troubles, a cadre of successors is lining up to take her place. The good thing: perfect is passé" (52). She proceeds to list those women and men who are beginning to change the Martha Stewart aesthetic by presenting readers and viewers with more realistic and less time consuming projects. Martha Stewart herself has even addressed the limitations of her early cookbooks by launching the magazine *Everyday Foods*, which includes recipes with easy to find ingredients that one can cook in a limited amount of time.
27. Unlike Lawson, Martha Stewart very rarely improvises in her recipes. Additionally, her cookbooks, more often than not, call for unusual ingredients which one may not have lying about the house. For instance, *The Martha Stewart Cookbook: Collected Recipes for Every Day* contains a recipe for "Oriental Five-Spice Hens," which calls for "2 small Cornish hens," ginger, coarse kosher salt, sesame oil, and guava jelly (213). Though subtitled "Collected Recipes for Every Day," these ingredients do not seem as though they would be ones that would readily be on hand.
28. Leslie Heywood and Jennifer Drake use the term "lived messiness" in *Third Wave Agenda: Being Feminist, Doing Feminism* to describe the contradictions that define Third Wave feminism (7–8). I invoke the term here because

Nigella Lawson and her cultural productions embrace contradictions in a way that is compliant with Third Wave feminism.

29. On his talk show *So Graham Norton*, Norton held up the British edition of Lawson's book *How To Be a Domestic Goddess*. On the front was a picture of a perfectly cooked cupcake; on the back, was the cupcake wrapper. These cover photographs work to support Lawson's philosophy that cooking is really about eating—a direct contrast to Stewart's idea that presentation is more important than the actual consumption.

30. Lawson made the first statement during her April 24, 2003 appearance on *Live with Regis and Kelly*. The second statement was made during her visit to Jay Leno's *The Tonight Show* (April 29, 2003).

31. Nigella Lawson married art collector and advertising executive Charles Saatchi in 2003 ("Who'd be a goddess?").

## NOTES TO CHAPTER SIX

1. In fact, this was one of the initial reasons I decided to attend the book signing. I was curious as to how Krantz would solve the problem of her promise to have Vivian, a cyber character, actually *sign* books. Krantz solved this dilemma by having Vivian deliver a videotaped message to the group gathered for the evening, sending her apologies and assuring everyone that they were in good hands with Krantz. Krantz, then, signed books that evening, asking each person if they'd like her signature, Vivian's signature, or both.

2. Krantz, Sherrie. *The Autobiography of Vivian Livingston*. New York: Ballantine, 2002. All subsequent citations will be from this edition unless otherwise noted.

3. Through the web cam, I viewed Vivian engaged in each of these activities on her website at various times from 2002–2004. Since the time that I first began this project, Vivian's website has changed a bit. Among the changes made, it no longer contains a web cam, and the online journal has been discontinued.

4. In her article "New York, New York," Emily DeNitto reports that since the launch of Vivian's website in 1999 the site receives an average of "an impressive 1 million hits a month."

5. Fielding and Kinsella both wrote subsequent novels that featured their popular heroines (*Bridget Jones: The Edge of Reason*, 2001 and *Shopaholic Takes Manhattan*, 2002, *Shopaholic Ties the Knot*, 2003, *Shopaholic and Sister*, 2004, and *Shopaholic and Baby*, 2007). Bushnell and Zigman, however, have written books in the same vein but with different leading ladies (*Four Blondes*, 2000, *Trading Up*, 2003, *Lipstick Jungle*, 2005, and *Dating Big Bird*, 2001, *Her*, 2002, *Piece of Work*, 2006). Kinsella has also written books that

do not feature Becky Bloomwood (*Can You Keep a Secret?*, 2003 and *The Undomestic Goddess*, 2005).
6. Klein used to live in New York City. She currently resides in Austin, Texas. This quote comes from the back of the hardcover, 2006 edition of Klein's memoir.
7. This quote also comes from the back of the hardcover, 2006 edition of Klein's memoir.
8. Manolo Blahniks shoes are the brand of shoes that Carrie Bradshaw (played by Sarah Jessica Parker) often wears on HBO's *Sex and the City*.
9. Throughout the book, Krantz emphasizes repeatedly how "average" Vivian is. A major theme of the novel then becomes that the "everyday" girl can go out and achieve her dreams, just like Vivian, if she puts her mind to it.
10. Krantz and her associates maintain this tone in her emails as exhibited in the email quoted earlier. This technique is being utilized more and more in the consumer industry. In her article "Discipline—It's a 'Good Thing'" Rhetorical Constitution and Martha Stewart Living Omnimedia," Cynthia Duquette Smith analyzes the way in which Martha Stewart's company uses a similar approach in her electronic correspondence.
11. Kelly could not tell me for sure if Krantz's signing appeared in the *New York Times*. I searched the publication myself, but I found no record of it.
12. These product promotions appeared in the June 2002 issue of *Marie Claire*. Herbal Essence Hair Color sponsored a contest in which contestants would log onto their website (www.herbalessencescolor.com), enter their UPC code from their package of Herbal Essences color, and be registered to win a variety of prizes. Grand prize was an Audi TT® Roadster while additional prizes were a $2000 Betsey Johnson shopping spree and free Cingular Wireless services for a year.
13. Vivian recorded this comment in her online journal (www.Vivianlives.com) on January 8, 2002.
14. Jennifer Weiner's book *Good in Bed* (2001) contains a letter from the author on the closing page of its paperback edition that encourages readers to visit her website or email her directly. Weiner's website, www.jenniferweiner.com, contains links to her books as well as her upcoming tour dates and her online journal.
15. Again, this advertisement appeared in the June 2002 edition of *Marie Claire*.

# Bibliography

Adema, Pauline. "Vicarious Consumption: Food, Television, and the Ambiguity of Modernity." *Journal of American and Comparative Cultures* 23.3 (2000): 113–24.
Adams, Mary Elizabeth. "Female Fear: The Body, Gender, and the Burdens of Beauty." Diss. U of Oklahoma, 2001.
"An American Girl in Paris, Part Deux." *Sex and the City*. Writ. Michael Patrick King. Dir. Tim Van Patten. HBO. 22 Feb. 2004.
"An American Girl in Paris, Part Une." *Sex and the City*. Writ. Michael Patrick King. Dir. Tim Van Patten. HBO. 15 Feb. 2004.
Armstrong, Nancy. *Desire and Domestic Fiction: A Political History of the Novel*. Oxford: Oxford University, 1987.
———. "The Rise of the Domestic Woman." *The Ideology of Conduct: Essays on Literature and the History of Sexuality*. Ed. Nancy Armstrong and Leonard Tennenhouse. New York: Methuen, 1987.
Austen, Jane. *Northanger Abbey*. New York: The Modern Library, 2002.
"The Baby Shower." *Sex and the City*. Writ. Terri Minsky. Dir. Susan Seidelman. HBO. 9 Aug. 1998.
"Bainbridge denounces chick-lit as 'froth.'" *Guardian* 23 Aug. 2001. 24 June 2003 <http://books.guardian.co.uk/bookerprize2001/story/0,1090,541335,00.html>.
Ballaster, Ros, Margaret Beetham, Elizabeth Frazer and Sandra Hebron. *Women's Worlds: Ideology, Femininity and Women's Magazines*. Basingstoke: Macmillan, 1991.
Bank, Melissa. *The Girls' Guide to Hunting and Fishing*. New York: Viking, 1999.
Baratz-Logsted, Lauren, ed. *This Is Chick-Lit*. Dallas, Texas: Benbella Books, 2005.
Barrientos, Tanya. "Sassy, kicky 'Chick Lit' is the hottest trend in publishing." *Philadelphia Inquirer* 23 May 2003. 2 June 2003 <http://www.philly.com/mld/inquirer/entertainment/5937712.htm?1c.>.
Beecher, Catharine Ester. *A Treatise on Domestic Economy*. 3rd ed. New York: Harper & Brothers, 1858.

Beetham, Margaret and Kay Boardman. *Victorian Women's Magazines: An Anthology.* Manchester: Manchester University Press, 2001.

Beeton, Isabella Mary. *The Book of Household Management.* London: Ward, Lock, and Tyler, 1869.

Bellefante, Ginia. "Birds Do It, Creeps Do It." *Time* 12 Aug. 1996: 66.

Bernard, Sarah. "Success and the Single Girl." *New York* 26 April 1999: 32–37.

Bethman, Brenda. "Chick Lit 101." *NWSAction* 18.1 (Fall 2006): 12.

Betts, Hannah. "Be Honest With Me, Do My Literary Pretensions Looks Big in This?" *Times* 25 Aug. 2001. *LexisNexis*. Univ. of Delaware Morris Library, Newark, DE. 22 July 2003 <http://web.lexis-nexis.com.proxygw.wrlc.org>.

Blix, Jacqueline. "A Place to Resist: Reevaluating Women's Magazines." *Journal of Communication Inquiry.* 16.1 (1992): 56–71.

Blumenthal, Dannielle. *Women and Soap Opera: A Cultural Feminist Perspective.* Westport, Connecticut: Praeger, 1997.

Bolotin, Susan. "Women Who Read Too Much: Current Self-Help Books Trap Women in a Vicious Cycle of Man-Hating and Self-Hating." *Vogue* Feb. 1987: 246, 254.

Bordo, Susan. *Unbearable Weight: Feminism, Western Culture, and the Body.* Berkley: University of California Press, 1993.

*The Break-Up.* Dir. Peyton Reed. Perf. Jennifer Aniston and Vince Vaughan. Mosaic Media Group, 2006.

"The Break-Up." *Amazon.com* 30 May 2007 <http://www.amazon.com/Break-Up-Widescreen-Vince-Vaughn/dp/B000HCPS94/ref=pd_bbs_sr_1/102-2196247-0397731?ie=UTF8&s=dvd&qid=1172971883&sr=8-1>.

*Bridget Jones's Diary.* Dir. Sharon Macguire. Perf. Renée Zellweger, Colin Firth, and Hugh Grant. Miramax, 2001.

"*Bridget Jones's Diary.*" *Internet Movie Database.* 19 June 2004 <http://www.imdb.com/title/tt0243155>.

Brown, Helen Gurley. *Sex and the Single Girl: The Unmarried Woman's Guide to Men, Careers, the Apartment, Diet, Fashion, Money and Men.* New York: Bernard Geis Associates, 1962.

Burley, Charlotte and Lyah LeFlore. *Cosmopolitan Girls.* New York: Broadway Books, 2004.

Bushnell, Candace. *Four Blondes.* New York: Atlantic Monthly Press, 2000.

———. *Lipstick Jungle.* New York: Hyperion, 2005.

———. *Sex and the City.* New York: Warner, 1996.

———. *Sex and the City.* New York: Warner, 2001.

———. *Trading Up.* New York: Hyperion, 2003.

"Cameron Diaz Image Gallery, Card Gallery, Biography." 22 June 2003 <http://www.celebwelove.com/Cameron_Diaz/>.

Caperton, Katie. "*Vogue* The Younger." *Folio: The Magazine for Management* 1 March 2003: NA.

Carter, Steven and Julia Sokol. *Men Who Can't Love: When a Man's Fear Makes Him Run From Commitment (and What a Smart Woman Can Do About It)*. New York: Berkley, 1987.

Case, Alison. "Authenticity, Convention, and *Bridget Jones's Diary*." *Narrative* 9.2 (2001): 176–81.

Cavell, Stanley. *Pursuits of Happiness: The Hollywood Comedy of Remarriage*. Cambridge: Harvard, 1981.

Chan, Ka-ling. Evolution of a Heroine: From *Pride and Prejudice* to *Bridget Jones's Diary*." Chinese University of Hong Kong, Masters Thesis. 2004.

Chin, Walter, photographer. "Bridget's Diary." *Glamour* (US) Sept. 2001: 282–87.

"China's Child Sports Slaves." *Marie Claire* (UK) Feb. 1995: 30+.

"Christina Applegate: Biography, Filmography, Pictures, Comments." *Celebrities Station: The Ultimate Station for Celebrities Info*. 22 June 2003 <http://www.celebstation.org/actresses/christina_applegate.php>.

ckelly@ed.ac.uk. "Absolutely fab—EVERY WOMAN HAS BEEN THERE!: Review of *Animal Husbandry* by Laura Zigman." *Amazon.co.uk*. 1999 Dec. 4 <http://www.amazon.co.uk/exec/obidos/ASIN/0099248522/quid%3D1088801596/ref/202-5495644-6947012>.

Colgan, Jenny. *Amanda's Wedding*. London: HarperCollins, 2000.

———. "Real Lives: We Know the Difference Between Foie Gras and Hula Hoops, Beryl, but Sometimes We Just Want Hula Hoops." *Guardian* 24 Aug. 2001. 22 July 2003 <http://www.guardian.co.uk/g2/story/0,3604,541637,00.html>.

———. *West End Girls*. London: Time Warner, 2006.

Collins, Patricia Hill. *Black Feminist Thought: Knowledge, Consciousness, and the Politics of Empowerment*. New York: Routledge, 1991.

Conway, Amy. "A Pumpkin Carving Party." *Martha Stewart Living* Oct. 1999: 200–07.

———. "A Weekend Project: Footstools." *Martha Stewart Living* Sept. 1997: 166–71.

Cool and Collected: Jaeger London Collection. Advertisement. *Marie Claire* (UK) April 1995: 102.

Coontz, Stephanie. *The Way We Never Were: American Families and the Nostalgia Trap*. New York: Basic, 1992.

"*Cosmo*'s Passion Package: A Raunchy Guide to Living Your Lust-Life to the Fullest." *Cosmopolitan* (US) Feb. 2002: 86–90.

"*Cosmopolitan*." *The Hearst Corporation* 30 May 2007 <http://www.hearstcorp.com/magazines/property/mag_prop_cosmo.html>.

*Cosmopolitan* (US) June 2007.

Cowan, Connell and Melvyn Kinder. *Smart Women, Foolish Choices: Finding the Right Men, Avoiding the Wrong Ones*. New York: Signet, 1985.

Cozens, Jenny Firth. "The New Traditionalism." *Cosmopolitan* (UK) June 1995: 36+.

Dam, Robina. "Love Bites." *Marie Claire* (UK) Feb. 2000. 172+.

"Dating Rules." *The Oprah Winfrey Show*. ABC. 11 Oct. 1996. Transcript. 1–28.

Davidson, MaryJanice. *Undead and Unemployed*. New York: Berkley Sensation, 2004.

Davis, Kenneth C. *Two-Bit Culture: The Paperbacking of America*. Boston: Houghton Mifflin, 1984.

Denitto, Emily. "Outfoxing the Competition." *Crain's New York Business* 21 Aug. 2000: 6. *LexisNexis*. Univ. of Delaware Morris Library, Newark, DE. 29 April 2003 <http://web.lexis-nexis.com.proxygw.wrlc.org>.

"Dick and Jane School Books: History and Information." *Tagnwag Children's Books*. 7 July 2004 <www.tagnway.com/dick_and_jane_books.html>.

"Disclosure." *Internet Movie Database*. 28 July 2004 <http://www.imdb.com/title/tt0109635>.

Donadio, Rachel. "The Chick-Lit Pandemic." *New York Times*. 3 March 2006. 25 May 2007 <http://www.nytimes.com/2006/03/19/books/review/>.

*Down With Love*. Dir. Peyton Reed. Perf. Renée Zellweger, Ewan McGregor, and Sarah Paulson, and David Hyde Pierce. Epsilon Motion Pictures, 2003.

Ehrenreich, Barbara and Deirdre English. *For Her Own Good: 150 Years of the Experts' Advice to Women*. Garden City, New York: Anchor Press, 1978.

Eliot, George. "Silly Novels by Lady Novelists." *Westminster Review* 10 (1856): 442–61. 17 June 2003. *Literature Online*. Chadwyck-Healy. Univ. of Delaware Morris Library, Newark, DE. 17 June 2003 <http://lion.chadwyck.com>.

Esselman, Mary. "Altar Girls: How to Get a Man? Sherrie Schneider and Ellen Fein Say Just Follow *The Rules*." *People Weekly* 11 Nov. 1996: 170–73.

The Essential *Cosmo* Diary. Advertisement. *Cosmopolitan* (UK) Jan. 1995. 15.

Faludi, Susan. *Backlash: The Undeclared War Against American Women*. New York: Anchor Books, 1991.

Fein, Ellen and Sherrie Schneider. *The Rules: Time-tested Secrets for Capturing the Heart of Mr. Right*. New York: Warner, 1995.

"Feng Shui Introduction." *Cosmopolitan* (UK) Nov. 1995: 59.

Ferguson, Marjorie. *Forever Feminine: Women's Magazine and the Cult of Femininity*. London: Heinmann, 1983.

Ferriss, Suzanne and Mallory Young, eds. *Chick Lit: The New Woman's Fiction*. New York: Routledge, 2006.

Fielding, Helen. *Bridget Jones's Diary*. London: Picador, 1998.

———. *Bridget Jones's Diary*. London: Ted Smart, 1998.

———. *Bridget Jones's Edge of Reason*. London: Picador, 1999.

———. *Bridget Jones's Guide to Life*. New York: Penguin, 2001.

———. "Sex and the Single Girl." *Vogue* May 1998: 276–79.

Forest, James J. "Self-Help Books." *American Psychologist* July 1988: 599.

*Forever Summer*. Channel Four, London. 2002.

Forward, Susan and Joan Torres. *Men Who Hate Women and the Women Who Love Them: When Loving Hurst and You Don't Know Why*. New York: Bantam Books, 1986.

Foster, Gwendolyn Audrey. *Troping the Body: Gender, Etiquette, and Performance.* Carbondale: Southern Illinois University Press, 2000.
Fraz, Ulrike. "Voices and Characterization in *Bridget Jones's Diary*: A Comparitive Study." Masters Thesis. University of Manchester, Institute of Science and Technology, 2001.
Friedan, Betty. *The Feminine Mystique.* New York: W.W. Norton, 1963.
"*Friends* Trends." *Marie Claire* (UK) Jan. 2000.
Geraghty, Christine. *Women and Soap Opera: A Study of Prime Time Soaps.* Cambridge, UK: Polity Press, 2001.
Gerston, Jill. "So Many Rules, So Little Time." *New York Times* 23 Oct. 1996: B1.
Gleick, Elizabeth. "Playing Hard to Get." *Time* 30 Sept. 1996. 58.
Goleman, Daniel. "Feeling Gloomy? A Good Self-Help Book May Actually Help." *New York Times* 6 July 1989: B6.
*Good Things: A Collection of Inspired Household Ideas and Projects.* New York: Martha Stewart Living Omnimedia LLC, 1997.
Gray, John. *Men Are From Mars, Women Are From Venus: A Practical Guide for Improving Communication and Getting What You Want in Your Relationships.* New York: HarperCollins, 1992.
Gray, Macy. "Sexual Revolution." *The Id.* Sony, 2001.
*Greek Tragedy.* <http://stephanieklein.blogs.com/>.
Green, Jane. "Help! I'm a N.E.W. (Never Enough Woman)!" *Cosmopolitan* (UK) Aug. 1998: 133–34.
———. *Jemima J.* New York: Broadway, 2001.
Hamilton, William L. "Lanterns." *Martha Stewart Living* July and Aug. 1996: 104–111.
Handelman, David. "One-Stop Shopping: *Lucky* Wins Readers and Advertisers With the Simplest of Premises; Tell Them What to Buy and Where to Buy It." *Mediaweek* 4 March 2002: SR37.
Hantman, Melissa. "Helen Gurley Brown." *Salon* 26 Sept. 2000 25 May 2007 <http://archive.salon.com/people/bc/2000/09/26/contest_winner_brown/>.
Harzewski, Stephanie. "Tradition and Displacement in the New Novel of Manners." Ferriss and Young 29–46.
Hayes, Jonathan. "Woodland Sweets." *Martha Stewart Living* Dec. 2003: 152–59.
Herbal Essences True Intense Color by Clairol. Advertisement. *Marie Claire* (US) June 2002. 68.
"Here Come the Brides." *Dateline.* NBC. 25 Oct. 1996.
Hermes, Joke. *Reading Women's Magazines.* Cambridge, MA: Polity Press, 1995.
Heywood, Leslie and Jennifer Drake. *Third Wave Agenda: Being Feminist, Doing Feminism.* Minneapolis: University of Minnesota Press, 1997.
Hinds, Michael deCourcy. "Coping with Self-Help Books." *New York Times* 16 Jan. 16 1988: 33.
Hodson, Phillip. "How To Change Your Life: New Year's Revolutions." *Cosmopolitan* (UK) Jan. 1995: 18–23.

Hollows, Joanne. "Feeling Like a Domestic Goddess: Postfeminism and Cooking." *European Journal of Cultural Studies* 6.2 (2003): 179–202.

Holt, Pat. "What It Means When Authors 'Get Back' Letters." *Holt Uncensored* 21 Aug. 2003. 21 Aug. 2003 <http://www.holtuncensored.com/members/column373.html>.

"Home Alone." *Nigella Bites*. E! Entertainment Network. 04 Dec. 2000.

Hume, Marion. "Who Will Be the Next Domestic Diva?" *Time* 16 Feb. 2004: 52.

Inness, Sherrie A. *Kitchen Culture in America: Popular Representations of Food, Gender, and Race*. Philadelphia: University of Pennsylvania Press, 2001.

Interview with Helen Fielding. *Time* 16 June 1998: 7 pp. 30 May 2007 <http://www.time.com/time/community/transcripts/chattr061698.html>.

Israel, Betsy. *Bachelor Girl: The Secret History of Single Women in the Twentieth Century*. New York: William Morrow, 2002.

"It's in the dictionary, d'oh!" *BBC News Online*. 11 Oct. 2002 <http://news.bbc.co.uk/1/hi/entertainment/1387335.stm>.

*Jennifer Weiner*. 19 June 2004 <www.jenniferweiner.com>.

Jennings, Luke. "Bad Boy in the Kitchen." *New Yorker* 27 April 1998: 136–41.

*Jerry Maguire*. Dir. Cameron Crowe. Perf. Tom Cruise, Cuba Gooding, Jr., Kelly Preston, Renée Zellweger. TriStar Pictures, 1996.

Jewell, Lisa. *Thirtynothing*. London: Penguin, 2000.

Johnson, Diane. *Le Divorce*. New York: Plume, 1998.

———. *Le Mariage*. New York: Plume, 2000.

Johnson, Joanna Webb. "Chick Lit Jr.: More Than Glitz and Glamour for Teens and Tweens." Ferriss and Young 141–57.

Kakutani, Michiko. "It's Like Really Weird: Another Bad-Luck Babe." *New York Times* 26 May 1998: E8.

Kelly. "Quick and light . . .: Review of *Animal Husbandry* by Laura Zigman." *Amazon.com*. 27 May 2001 <http://www.amazon.com/gp/product/customer-reviews/0385319037/ref=cm_rev_next/104-5962380-0841534?%5Fencoding=UTF8&customer-reviews.sort%5Fby=-SubmissionDate&n=283155&customer-reviews.start=21&me=ATVPDKIKX0DER>.

Kelly, Frances. Personal interview. 15 June 2002.

Kenmore. Advertisement. *Martha Stewart Living* Sept. 1997. 121.

Kilbourne, Jean. *Deadly Persuasion: Why Women and Girls Must Fight the Addictive Power of Advertising*. New York: The Free Press, 1999.

———. *Killing Us Softly 3*. Media Education Foundation, 2000.

———. *Killing Us Softly: Advertising's Image of Women*. Cambridge Documentary Films, 1979.

———. *Slim Hopes*. Media Education Foundation, 1995.

———. *Still Killing Us Softly*. Cambridge Documentary Films, 1987.

Kinsella, Sophie. *Can You Keep a Secret?* London: Black Swan, 2003.

———. *Confessions of a Shopaholic*. New York: Delta, 2001.

———. *The Secret Dreamworld of a Shopaholic*. London: Black Swan, 2000.

———. *Shopaholic Abroad*. London: Black Swan, 2001.
———. *Shopaholic and Baby*. London: Bantam, 2007.
———. *Shopaholic and Sister*. London: Bantam, 2004.
———. *Shopaholic Ties the Knot*. London: Black Swan, 2002.
———. *The Undomestic Goddess*. London: Bantam, 2005.
Klein, Stephanie. *Straight Up and Dirty*. New York: Regan, 2006.
Krantz, Sherrie. *The Autobiography of Vivian Livingston*. New York: Ballantine, 2002.
Kuczynski, Alex. "Dear Diary: Get Real." *New York Times* 14 June 1998, Sunday Styles: 1, 6.
———. "Too Good Not to Be True." *New York Times* 25 April 2004, late ed., sec. 9: 1.
Laidlaw, Jane. "Oh, To Be in Edinburgh." *Cosmopolitan* July 1995: 190+.
Landi, Ann. "Smart Women, Foolish Books." *Mademoiselle* Oct. 1987: 180–81, 245–57.
Lawson, Carol. "Women, Success, and Romantic Advice." *New York Times* 25 August 1986: C26.
Lawson, Nigella. *How To Be A Domestic Goddess: Baking and the Art of Comfort Cooking*. New York: Hyperion, 2001.
Leaf, Munroe. *Listen Little Girl Before You Come to New York*. New York: Stokes, 1938.
leahy2j. "great chick-lit for rainy afternoons." *Amazon.co.uk*. 12 Sept. 2001 <http://www.amazon.co.uk/exec/obidos/tg/listmania/list-browse/-/1PURQ6SNBZ1WK/qid=1088432081/sr=5-8/ref=sr_5_11_8/026-1134032-5417214>.
Leavitt, Sarah A. *From Catharine Beecher to Martha Stewart: A Cultural History of Domestic Advice*. Chapel Hill: The University of North Carolina Press, 2002.
———. "It Was Always a Good Thing: Historical Precedents for Martha Stewart." *American Studies* 42.2 (2001): 129.
Ligos, Melinda. "A Love Story With a Few Co-Co-Co Authors." *New York Times* 28 March 2004, sec. 3: 2.
*Live With Regis and Kelly*. WPVI, Philadelphia. 24 April 2003.
Livingston, Vivian. "Re: Book Signing." E-mail to the author. 10 June 2002.
Lippert, Barbara. "Our Martha, Ourselves." *New York* 28.20 (1995): 26–33.
MacDonald, Dwight. "Howtoism." *New Yorker*, 22 May 1954, 82–109.
Mack, Ann M. "Viva Vivian." *Brandweek* 42.2 (2001): 6.
Magnolia, Tiffany. "Martha and the Many Loaves: The Savior of Domesticity at the End of the Twentieth Century." *The Image of Europe in Literature, Media, and Society: Selected Papers from the 2001 Conference of the Society for the Interdisciplinary Study of Social Imagery* Pueblo, Co.: The Society, 2001. 28–32.
Manning-Schaffel, Vivian. "Vivian Lives Virtually." *Brand Features Profile on Brand channel.com*. 25 Feb. 2001. 7 Sept. 2004 <http://www.brandchannel.com/features_profile.asp?pr_id=58>.
*Marie Claire* (UK) May 2007.

"*Marie Claire*: 'For Women of the World.'" *iVilliage: Solutions for Women.* 25 Aug. 2004 <http://magazines.ivillage.com/marieclarie/print/0,,441086,00.html>.

"*Marie Claire*." *The Hearst Corporation* 30 May 2007 <http://www.hearstcorp.com/magazines/property/mag_prop_mc_2000.html>.

"Martha Stewart Roundtable." *American Studies* 42.2 (2001): 67–138.

"The Martha Yearbook." *Newsweek* 15 March 2004: 35.

Mason, Ann and Marian Meyers. "Living With Martha Stewart Media: Chosen Domesticity and the Experience of Fans" *Journal of Communication* 51.4 (2001): 801–25.

Massie, Alex and Camillo Fracassini. "The Old Girl Network." *Scotland on Sunday* 26 Aug. 2001: 11. *LexisNexis*. Univ. of Delaware Morris Library, Newark, DE. 22 July 2003 <http://web.lexis-nexis.com.proxygw.wrlc.org>.

Matthews, Glenna. *"Just a Housewife": The Rise and Fall of Domesticity in America.* New York: Oxford University Press, 1987.

Maxted, Anna. *Getting Over It.* London: Arrow, 2000.

———. "Sex and Shopping: The Orgasmic Connection." *Cosmopolitan* Dec. 1996: 155+.

Mazza, Cris. "Who's Laughing Now? A Short History of Chick Lit and the Perversion of a Genre." Ferriss and Young 17–28.

Mazza, Cris and Jeffrey DeShell, eds. *Chick-Lit: Postfeminist Fiction.* Normal, Illinois: Fiction Collective 2, 1995.

Mazza, Cris, Jeffrey DeShell, and Elizabeth Sheffield, eds. *Chick-Lit 2 (No Chick Vics).* Normal, Illinois: Fiction Collective 2, 1996.

McCabe, Susan. *Elizabeth Bishop: Her Poetics of Loss.* University Park, Pa: The Pennsylvania State University Press, 1994.

McCartney, Jenny. "No Wonder Beryl's Cross. Bainbridge et al Wanted Boadiceas. Instead They've Got Posh Spice." *Sunday Telegraph.* 26 Aug. 2001: 21. *Lexis-Nexis*. Univ. of Delaware Morris Library, Newark, DE. 22 July 2003 <http://web.lexis-nexis.com>.

McCracken, Ellen. *Decoding Women's Magazines: From* Mademoiselle *to* Ms. New York: St. Martin's Press, 1993.

McDaniel, Patricia. "Shrinking Violets and Caspar Milquetoasts: Shyness and Heterosexuality from the Roles of the Fifties to *The Rules* of the Nineties." *Journal of Social History.* 34.3 (2001): 547–68.

McDonald, Marci. "The New Cosmo Girl: Canadian Bonnie Fuller Is Remaking a Feminine Icon." *Maclean's* 17 Feb. 1997: 60–64.

McHugh, Kathleen Anne. *American Domesticity: From How-To Manual to Hollywood Melodrama.* Oxford: Oxford University Press, 1999.

Mabry, A. Rochelle. "About a Girl: Female Subjectivity and Sexuality in Contemporary 'Chick' Culture." Ferriss and Young 191–206.

Marcus, Laura. "In Praise of Bossy Mothers." *Cosmopolitan* Dec. 1995: 135.

Marsh, Kelly A. "Contextualizing Bridget Jones." *College Literature* 31.1 (2004): 52–72.

Mechling, Jay. "Introduction: Martha Stewart and Taste Cultures." *American Studies* 42.2 (2001): 67–69.
"*Men Are From Mars, Women Are From Venus.*" Amazon.com 10 Oct. 02 <http://www.amazon.com/exec/obidos/ASIN/006016848X/qid=1091028337/sr=2-1/ref=sr 2 1/104-5962380-0841534>.
Merkin, Daphne. "The Marriage Mystique." *New Yorker* 3 Aug. 1998: 70+.
Merrick, Elizabeth, ed. *This Is Not Chick Lit: Original Stories by America's Best Women Writers*. New York: Random House Trade Paperbacks, 2006.
Miner, Madonne M. *Insatiable Appetites: Twentieth-Century American Women's Bestsellers*. Westport, Connecticut: Greenwood Press, 1984.
"Models and Mortals." *Sex and the City*. Writ. Darren Star. Dir. Alison Maclean. HBO. 6 June 1998.
Modleski, Tania. *Loving with a Vengeance: Mass-Produced Fantasies for Women*. New York: Methuen, 1982.
Morrison, Toni. *The Bluest Eye*. New York: Washington Square Press, 1972.
Mumford, Laura Stempel. *Love and Ideology in the Afternoon: Soap Opera, Women, and Television Genre*. Bloomington: Indiana University Press, 1995.
"The National Magazine Company." *Marketing* 26 April 2001: 11.
Nautica Home Collection. Advertisement. *Martha Stewart Living* Sept. 1997. 6–7.
Nehring, Cristina. "Books: Mr. Goodbar Redux: Illusions. Affections. Lies." *Atlantic Monthly* Jan. 2002: 141+.
Neuhaus, Jessamyn. "The Way To a Man's Heart: Gender Roles, Domestic Ideology, and Cookbooks in the 1950s." *Journal of Social History* 32.3 Spring 1999: 529–55.
Newton, Sarah E. *Learning to Behave: A Guide to American Conduct Books Before 1900*. Westport, Connecticut: Greenwood Press, 1994.
*Nigella Bites*. Channel Four, London. 2000.
*Nigella Bites II*. Channel Four, London. 2001.
Norwood, Robin. *Women Who Love Too Much: When You Keep Wishing and Hoping He'll Change*. New York: Pocket, 1985.
Nunez, Christina. "Meet the Writers: Sophie Kinsella." *Barnes and Noble*. 25 May 2007 <http://www.barnesandnoble.com/writers/writerdetails.asp?z=y&cid=1020738#interview>.
*O: The Oprah Magazine* March 2004.
Ogunnaike, Lola. "Black Writers Seize Glamorous Ground Around 'Chick-Lit.'" *New York Times* 31 May 2004: A1.
*The Parent Trap*. Dir. Nancy Meyers. Perf. Lindsay Lohan, Dennis Quaid, and Natasha Richardson. Disney, 1998.
Parker, Robert Dale. *The Unbeliever: The Poetry of Elizabeth Bishop*. Urbana: University of Illinois Press, 1988.
Pearson, Allison. *I Don't Know How She Does It: The Life of Kate Reddy, Working Mother*. London: Vintage, 2003.

Peck, Bernice. "Diet With Dessert: The New Reducing Theory That Lets You Have Your Cake and Figure Too." *Mademoiselle* July 1953: 66–71.

Perrick, Penny. "Sex and the Single Girl." *Sunday Times* 20 Oct. 1996. *LexisNexis*. Univ. of Delaware Morris Library, Newark, DE. 22 July 2003 <http://web.lexis-nexis.com.proxygw.wrlc.org>.

Peterson, Theodore. *Magazines in the 20th Century*. Urbana: University of Illinois Press, 1964.

Peyser, Marc. "Paging Doctor Phil: Stop Your Whining!" *Newsweek* 2 Sept. 2002. 50.

Pfaltzgraff. Advertisement. *Martha Stewart Living* Sept. 1997. 127.

*Pillow Talk*. Dir. Michael Gordon. Perf. Doris Day, Rock Hudson, and Tony Randall. Arwin, 1959.

Plath, Sylvia. *The Bell Jar*. New York: Harper & Row, 1971.

Plotz, David. "Helen Gurley Brown: The *Cosmo* Girl at 78." *Slate* 7 April 2000 25 May 2007 <http://www.slate.com/id/78865/>.

Pogrebin, Robin. "Time Inc.'s Take on Teen-Agers: Yes, From the House that Luce Built, A Girls' Magazine." *New York Times* 8 Jan. 1998: C1.

Pollack, Judann. "Martha Stewart, Kmart form strategic alliance." *Advertising Age* 24 Feb. 1997: 83.

"The Power of Single." *Cosmopolitan* March 1995: 104–115.

Prisant, Carol. "Three-Generation Birthday Party." *Martha Stewart Living* Sept. 1997: 172–179.

Quinn, Anthony. "How To Woo A New Yorker." *Guardian* 9 Nov. 2003. 2 Dec. 2003 <http://observer.guardian.co.uk/foodmonthly/story/0,9950,1078132,00.html>.

Radford, Jean. Introduction. *The Progress of Romance: The Politics of Popular Fiction*. Ed. Radford. New York: Routledge & Kegan Paul, 1986. 1–20.

Radway, Janice A. *Reading the Romance: Women, Patriarchy, and Popular Literature*. Chapel Hill, N.C.: University of North Carolina Press, 1984.

A reader from Memphis, Tennessee. "A MUST-READ for all single women: Review of *Animal Husbandry* by Laura Zigman." *Amazon.com*. 17 May 1999 <http://www.amazon.com/gp/product/customer-reviews/0385319037/ref=cm_rev_next/104-5962380-0841534?%5Fencoding=UTF8&customer-reviews.sort%5Fby=-SubmissionDate&n=283155&customer-reviews.start=51&me=ATVPDKIKX0DER>.

Reed, David. *The Popular Magazine in Britain and the United States, 1880–1960*. Toronto: University of Toronto Press, 1997.

Regules, Anne. "Working Women and Re-Working the Romance: Chick-Lit from Kate Chopin to Jennifer Weiner to *Sex and the City*." Masters Thesis. University of Texas at San Antonio, 2006.

Reiff, David. "Victims All?: Recovery, Co-dependency, and the Art of Blaming Someone Else." *Harper's* Oct. 1991: 49–56.

Rennison, Louise. *Angus, Thongs and Full-Frontal Snogging: Confessions of Georgia Nicolson*. London: Scholastic, 2001.
Rev. of *Confessions of a Shopaholic*. *Publishers Weekly* 18 Dec. 2000: 53.
Rosen, R.D. Psychobabble: *Fast Talk and Quick Cure in the Era of Feeling*. New York: Antheneum, 1977.
Rubinfeld, Mark D. *Bound to Bond: Gender, Genre, and the Hollywood Romantic Comedy*. Westport: Praeger, 2001.
"*The Rules* Backlash." *The Oprah Winfrey Show*. ABC. 19 June 1997. Transcript. 1–28.
*The Rules from Ellen and Sherrie*. 30 May 2007 <http://www.therulesbook.com>.
Salber, Cecelia. "Bridget Jones and Mark Darcy: Art Imitating Art . . . Imitating Art." *Persuasions On-Line* 22.1 (2000). 2 June 2004 <http://www.jasna.org/pol04/salber.html>.
Séllei, Nóra. "Bridget Jones and Hungarian Chick Lit." Ferriss and Young 173–188.
"Selma Blair." *Absolutepictures.com*. 22 June 2003 <http://www.absolutepictures.com/b/blair selma>.
*Sex and the Single Girl*. Dir. Richard Quine. Perf. Lauren Bacall, Tony Curtis, Mel Ferrer, Henry Fonda, Fran Jeffries, Natalie Wood. Warner Brothers, 1964.
"*Sex and the Single Girl*." *Internet Movie Database*. 19 June 2003 <http://www.imdb.com/title/tt0058580>.
Shapiro, Laura. "The Art of Showing Off: What Makes Martha Stewart Cook?" *Newsweek* 1 Dec. 1986: 66–67.
———. "Do Women Like to Cook?" *Granta* 52 (1995): 153–62.
———. *Perfection Salad: Women and Cooking at the Turn of the Century*. New York: Farrar, Straus, and Giroux: 1986.
Shulman, Alix. "A Marriage Agreement." *Up From Under* Aug.-Sept. 1970: 5–8.
Shumway, David. "Screwball Comedies: Constructing Romance, Mystifying Marriage." *Film Genre Reader II*. Ed. Barry Keith Grant. Austin: University of Texas, 1995.
Siegel, Carol. *New Millennial Sexstyles*. Bloomington, IN: Indiana University Press, 2000.
Simonds, Wendy. *Women and Self-Help Culture: Reading Between the Lines*. New Brunswick, NJ: Rutgers, 1992.
*Simonsays.com: Simon & Schuster, Inc.* 27 Jan. 2005 <http://www.simonsays.com/content/index.cfm?sid=33>.
Skurnick, Lizzie. "Chick Lit, The Sequel: Yummy Mummy." *New York Times*. 17 Dec. 2006. 25 May 2007 <http://www.nytimes.com/2006/12/17/fashion>.
Smith, Cynthia Duquette. "Discipline—'It's a Good Thing:' Rhetorical Constitution and Martha Stewart Living Omnimedia." *Women's Studies in Communication* 23.3 (2000): 337–66.
*So Graham Norton*. Comedy Central. 14 Nov. 2003.
Sohn, Amy. Sex and the City: *Kiss and Tell*. New York: Pocket Books, 2002.

*Someone Like You.* Dir. Tony Goldwyn. Perf. Ashley Judd, Hugh Jackman, and Greg Kinnear. 20th Century Fox, 2001.
"*Someone Like You.*" *Internet Movie Database.* 19 June 2004 <http://www.imdb.com/title/tt0244970/>.
Starker, Steven. *Oracle at the Supermarket: The American Preoccupation with Self-Help Books.* Transaction: New Brunswick, NJ 1989.
Stewart, Martha. "A Letter From Martha." *Martha Stewart Living* Dec. 2003: 8.
———. *The Martha Stewart Cookbook: Collected Recipes for Everyday.* New York: Clarkson Potter, 1995.
"Streets Ahead." *Marie Claire* (UK) Dec. 2000: 172+.
"*Suburban Girl.*" *Internet Movie Database.* 30 May 2007 <http://www.imdb.com/title/tt0428579/>.
*The Sweetest Thing.* Dir. Roger Kumble. Perf. Christina Applegate, Jason Bateman, Selma Blair, Cameron Diaz, Thomas Jane. Columbia Pictures, 2002.
"*The Sweetest Thing.*" *Internet Movie Database.* 19 June 2003 <http://www.imdb.com/title/tt0253867>.
"Table of Contents." *Marie Claire* (UK) Feb. 1995: 3.
Tebbel, John and Mary Ellen Zuckerman. *The Magazine in America, 1741–1990.* New York: Oxford University Press, 1991.
Thomas, Scarlett. "The great chick lit conspiracy." *Independent* 4 Aug. 2002. 2 June 2003 <http://enjoyment.indepedent.co.uk/low res/story.jsp?story=321729&host=5&dir=497>.
"Three's a Crowd." *Sex and the City.* Writ. Jenny Bicks. Dir. Nicole Holofcener. HBO. 26 July 1998.
*The Tonight Show With Jay Leno.* WCAU, Philadelphia. 29 April 2003.
UnamunoChk@aol.com. "Buy it and laugh without guilt: Review of *Animal Husbandry* by Laura Zigman." *Amazon.com.* 9 April 1998 <http://www.amazon.com/exec/obidos/tg/detail/-/0385319037/104-5962380-0841534?v=glance>.
Valdes-Rodriguez, Alisa. *The Dirty Girls Social Club.* New York: St. Martin's Press, 2003.
———. MySpace Homepage. 5 May 2007 <http://www.myspace.com/alisavaldesrodriguez>.
Van Slooten, Jessica Lyn. "Fashionably Indebted: Conspicuous Consumption, Fashion, and Romance in Sophie Kinsella's Shopahlic Trilogy." Ferriss and Young 219–38.
———. "A Truth Universally (Un)Acknowledged: *Ally McBeal, Bridget Jones's Diary,* and the Conflict Between Romantic Love and Feminism." *Searching the Soul of Ally McBeal: Critical Essays.* Ed. Elwood Watson. Jefferson, NC: McFarland, 2006. 36–54.
*Vivian Lives.* 8 June 2002 <www.vivianlives.com>.
"Vivian Subscribes to Mag." *Brandweek* 15 Jan. 2001: 29.
Walker, Nancy A. *Shaping Our Mothers' Worlds: American Women's Magazines.* Jackson: University Press of Mississippi, 2000.

———. *Women's Magazines, 1940–1960: Gender Roles and the Popular Press*. Boston: Bedford/St. Martin's, 1998.
Walsh, Catherine. "Perspectives." *America* 23 Nov. 1996. 9.
Ward, Alyson. "Chick Lit: Is the Honeymoon Over?" *Washington Post* 14 Sept. 2003: D5.
Wasserstein, Wendy. *The Heidi Chronicles*. New York: Dramatists Play Service, 1991.
Weinberg, Anna. "She's Come Undone: Chick Lit Was Supposed To Be the Bright Light of Postfeminist Writing. What Happened?" *Book* July-Aug. 2003. 1 July 2004 <http://www.bookmagazine.com/issue29/chicklit.shtml>.
Weiner, Jennifer. *Good In Bed*. New York: Washington Square Press, 2001.
———. *In Her Shoes*. New York: Atria, 2002.
———. MySpace Homepage. 5 May 2007 <http://www.myspace.com/uncanniegirl>.
Weisberger, Lauren. *The Devil Wears Prada*. New York: Doubleday, 2003.
Wells, Juliette. "Mothers of Chick Lit? Women Writers, Readers, and Literary History." Ferriss and Young 47–70.
Wharton, Edith. *The House of Mirth*. New York: Oxford University Press, 1994.
*When Harry Met Sally*. Dir. Rob Reiner. Perf. Billy Crystal, Carrie Fisher, Meg Ryan. Columbia Pictures, 1989.
Whelehan, Imelda. *Helen Fielding's Bridget Jones's Diary: A Reader's Guide*. New York: Continuum, 2002.
———. *The Feminist Best Seller: From* Sex and the Single Girl *to* Sex and the City." New York: Palgrave Macmillan, 2005.
———. "Sex and the Single Girl: Helen Fielding, Erica Jong, and Helen Gurley Brown." *Contemporary British Women Writers*. Woodbridge, England: Brewer, 2004. 16–27.
White, Cynthia. *Women's Magazines: 1693–1968*. London: Joseph, 1970.
Whitehead, Barbara Dafoe. "The Plight of the High-Status Woman." *Atlantic Monthly* 284.6 (1999): 120–24.
"Who'd be a goddess?" *Guardian* 16 Oct. 2004. 28 Jan. 2005 <http://books.guardian.co.uk/departments/houseandgarden/story/0,6000,1328538,00.html>.
*Williams-Sonoma: The Catalog for Cooks* Spring 2001.
Wilson, Melissa. "The Singleton Life." *Amazon.com*. 10 Oct. 02 <http://www.amazon.com/exec/obidos/tg/listmania/list-browse/-/LD4IZ6MAPP5M/ref=cm_lm_dp_l_3/104-6167886-1879159>.
Winship, Janice. *Inside Women's Magazines*. London: Pandora, 1987.
Wolf, Naomi. *The Beauty Myth: How Images of Beauty Are Used Against Women*. New York: W. Morrow, 1991.
Wolper, Carol. *The Cigarette Girl*. New York: Riverhead, 1999.
Wood, James Playstead. *Magazines in the United States*. New York: Ronald Press, 1971.
"The World According to Oprah." *Newsweek* 8 Jan. 2001: 43.
Young, Suzanne. "*Confessions of a Shopaholic*." *Booklist* 1 Jan. 2001: 918.

Zahn, Susan Brown. "Martha Stewart's Intimate Invitations To e-commerce." *Popular Culture Review* 12.1 (2001): 53–66.
Zanzinger, Jaimee. "Bridget's Diary." *Glamour* (US) Sept. 2001: 284.
Zigman, Laura. *Animal Husbandry*. New York: Delta, 1998.
———. *Dating Big Bird*. New York: Dial Press, 2000.
———. *Her*. New York: Alfred A. Knopf, 2002.
———. MySpace Homepage. 5 May 2007 <http://profile.myspace.com/index.cfm?fuseaction=user.viewprofile&friendid=159945500>.
———. *Piece of Work*. New York: Warner, 2006.
Zuckerman, Mary Ellen. *A History of Popular Women's Magazines in the United States, 1792–1995*. Westport, CT: Greenwood Press, 1998.

# Index

## A

*Amanda's Wedding* (Colgan), 3, 135.
Amazon.com, 10, 46, 69, 70, 142.
*American Domesticity: From How-To Manual to Hollywood Melodrama* (McHugh), 102–103, 110, 115.
*Amy Vanderbilt's Complete Book of Etiquette: A Guide to Gracious Living*, 1, 55.
*Animal Husbandry*, 52. See also Laura Zigman.
  Critique of domestic-advice manuals, 102, 104, 111, 113, 117–118, 119–20.
  *Critique* of self-help books, 16–17, 47–48, 65–73.
  Film adaptation, *Someone Like You*, 10, 71.
  Reader reviews of, 70.
  Sequels to, 136.
"The Art of Showing Off: What Makes Martha Stewart Cook" (Shapiro), 108–10.
Austen, Jane, 43.
*The Autobiography of Vivian Livingston*, 3, 6, 9, 18–19, 135–36, 137–40. See also Sherrie Krantz.
  Appearance in *Marie Claire*, 9, 11, 18, 134–42.
  Book signing, 134, 138, 140–42.
  Consumer culture connections, 11.
  Website, Vivianlives.com, 3, 8–9, 134–35, 141–42, 143–44.

## B

*Bachelor Girl: The Secret History of Single Women in the Twentieth Century* (Israel), 24, 75, 138.
*Backlash: The Undeclared War Against American Women* (Faludi), 107.
Bainbridge, Beryl, 3, 4.
Bank, Melissa, 6. See also *The Girls' Guide to Hunting and Fishing*.
*The Beauty Myth* (Wolf), 21.
*The Bell Jar* (Plath), 8.
*The Bluest Eye* (Morrison), 8.
*The Book of Household Management* (Beeton), 104–03, 108.
Bordo, Susan, 30.
*Bound to Bond: Gender, Genre, and the Hollywood Romantic Comedy* (Rubinfeld), 87–88.
  "Bitch foil plot," 85–86.
  Gendered behaviors in, 13.
  "Social regeneration through coupling," 76–77, 80.
  "Temptress foil plot," 86–87.
*Bridget Jones's Diary*. See also Helen Fielding.
  Author photograph, 7.
  Connection to *Pride and Prejudice*, 7, 43.
  Consumer culture connections, 11.
  Critique of domestic-advice manuals, 17–18, 102, 103–04, 111, 112–15, 118–19, 121–23, 123–24.
  Critique of self-help books, 62–63.
  Critique of women's magazines, 1–2.

*177*

*Bridget Jones's Diary (continued)*
    Film adaptation, *Bridget Jones's Diary*, 3, 10, 40–41.
    *Independent* column, 9–10, 27–28, 40, 136.
    Reviews of, 3, 40–42.
    Referenced in women's magazines, 9.
    Sequels to, 135–36.
*Bridget Jones's Guide to Life* (Fielding), 101–02.
Brown, Helen Gurley, 4. See also *Sex and the Single Girl*.
    *Cosmopolitan*, Editor-in-Chief of, 24–25, 26–27, 45, 74, 138.
Bushnell, Candace 3, 17, 102, 143. See also *Sex and the City*.

## C
Chick lit
    Adaptations, film and television, 9–10.
    Audience for, 7.
    Connections to popular culture, 8–9.
    Consumer culture references in, 11.
    Criticism of, 3–4.
    Critique of domestic-advice manuals, 17–18, 101–33.
    Critique of romantic comedies, 17, 74–100.
    Critique of self-help books, 13–14, 16–17, 45–73.
    Critique of women's magazines, 14–15, 16, 20–44.
    Definition, 2, 137–38.
    History of, 6–7.
    Scholarship on, 4–5
    Subgenres, 18–19, 135–37.
*Chick Lit: The New Woman's Fiction* (Ferris and Young), 2, 5, 6, 136, 137.
*The Cigarette Girl*, 5. See also Carol Wolper.
    Consumer culture connections, 11.
    Critique of domestic-advice manuals, 103, 104, 120–21, 123, 133.
    Critique of self-help books, 52–54.
    Critique of romantic comedies, 17, 76, 94–100.
Colgan, Jenny, 10.
Conduct literature, 12–13. See also etiquette books and women's advice manuals.
"*Cosmo* girls," 24–25, 27, 34. See also Helen Gurley Brown.
*Cosmopolitan*. 9, 16, 20, 28–29, 31, 108, 109, 138. See also Helen Gurley Brown and women's advice manuals; women's magazines.
    Body image, 29–30.
    Constructed reader, 27.

## D
*Deadly Persuasion: Why Women and Girls Must Fight the Addictive Power of Advertising* (Kilbourne), 21.
*Decoding Women's Magazines: From Mademoiselle to Ms.* (McCracken), 18, 30, 35, 38–40, 102.
*The Devil Wears Prada* (Weisberger), 137.
*Le Divorce* (Johnson), 8.
Domestic science movement, 106.

## E
Eliot, George, 4.
*Englishwoman's Domestic Magazine* (Beeton), 105.
Etiquette books, 12–13, 51, 56, 80, 101. See also conduct literature and women's advice manuals.

## F
*Fear of Flying* (Jong), 8.
"Feeling Like a Domestic Goddess: Postfeminism and Cooking," (Hollows), 131–32.
Fein, Ellen and Sherrie Schneider. See *The Rules: Time-tested Secrets for Capturing the Heart of Mr. Right*.
*The Feminine Mystique* (Friedan), 21, 55, 59, 123.
*The Feminist Bestseller: From* Sex and the Single Girl *to* Sex and the City (Whelehan), 4, 8.
Fielding, Helen, 36. See also *Bridget Jones's Diary*.

# Index

Friedan, Betty, 107. See also *The Feminine Mystique.*

## G

*Getting Over It*, 10. See also Anna Maxted.
  Consumer culture connections, 11.
  Critique of domestic-advice manuals, 5, 17–18, 102, 104, 124–33.
*The Girls' Guide to Hunting and Fishing.* See also Melissa Bank.
  Critique of self-help books, 4, 13–14, 16–17, 47–48, 52, 54–65, 73.
  Film adaptation, *Suburban Girl*, 10.
*Good In Bed* (Weiner), 6, 135, 142.
Gothic fiction, 8, 15, 23.
Gossip literature, 137.

## H

Hawthorne, Nathaniel, 4.
*The Heidi Chronicles* (Wasserstein), 107.
*Helen Fielding's* Bridget Jones's Diary: *A Reader's Guide* (Whelehan), 4, 9, 27, 28, 40.
Heroine-centered novels 2, 7. See also nineteenth-century novels and sentimental novels.
*A History of Popular Women's Magazines in the United States, 1792–1995* (Zuckerman), 24.
Household management books, 104–05. See also women's advice manuals; domestic-advice manuals.
*The House of Mirth* (Wharton), 8.

## I

*In Her Shoes* (Weiner), 6.

## J

*Jane Eyre* (Brontë), 7.
*Jemima J* (Green), 26, 135.
*Jerry Maguire*, 86–87.

## K

Keyes, Marian, 10.
Kilbourne, Jean, 22, 30.
*Killing Us Softly 3* (Kilbourne), 21.
*Killing Us Softly: Advertising's Image of Women* (Kilbourne), 21.
Kinsella, Sophie, 9. See also *The Secret Dreamworld of a Shopaholic.*
Klein, Stephanie, 137.
Krantz, Sherrie, 6–7. See also *The Autobiography of Vivian Livingston.*
Kuczynski, Alex, 137.
  Review of *Bridget Jones's Diary* 3, 42–43.

## L

Lawson, Nigella
  *Forever Summer*, 131, 132.
  *How To Be a Domestic Goddess: Baking and the Art of Comfort Cooking*, 115, 131–32.
  *Nigella Bites*, 12, 131, 132.
  *Nigella Bites II*, 131.
Lessing, Doris, 3, 135.
*Loving With a Vengeance: Mass-Produced Fantasies for Women*, 15–16.

## M

McBeal, Ally, 11, 41.
*The Magazine in America 1741–1990* (Zuckerman and Tebbel), 26.
*Magazines in the United States* (Wood), 23.
*Marie Claire*, 11–12, 25, 26, 27, 33, 38, 134, 138. See also women's advice manuals; women's magazines and *The Autobiography of Vivian Livingston.*
  Body image, 30
*Martha Stuart's Better Than You at Entertaining* (Connor and Downey), 101.
Maxted, Anna, 9, 26. See also *Getting Over It.*
*Men Are From Mars, Women Are From Venus: A Practical Guide for Improving Communication and Getting What You Want in Your Relationships* (Gray), 46, 52, 65, 121.
*Men Who Can't Love: When a Man's Fear Makes Him Run from Commitment (and What a Smart Woman Can Do About It)* (Carter and Sokol), 49, 51, 66.

*Men Who Hate Women and the Women Who Love Them: When Loving Hurts and You Don't Know Why* (Forward and Torres), 49.
Modleski, Tania, 5.
Mommy lit, 5, 137.
MySpace.com, 142.

**N**

The "New Woman," 83–84.
Nineteenth-century novels, 2, 4, 7. See also heroine-centered novels and sentimental novels.
*Northanger Abbey* (Austen), 7, 8.

**O**

"One Art," (Bishop), 55–56, 69.
*Oracle at the Supermarket: The American Preoccupation with Self-Help Books* (Starker), 48–49, 67.

**P**

The Parent Trap, 13, 87.
*Perfection Salad: Women and Cooking at the Turn of the Century* (Shapiro), 106.
Pocket Books, 9, 48.
*Pride and Prejudice* (Austen), 72.
*Pride and Prejudice*, BBC adaptation, 28.
*The Progress of Romance: The Politics of Fiction* (Radford), 4, 15.
*Psychobabble: Fast Talk and Quick Cure in the Era of Feeling* (Rosen), 48.

**R**

*Reading the Romance: Women, Patriarchy, and Popular Literature* (Radway), 15–16.
Romance novels, 4, 7–8, 15–16, 42, 75–76, 94.
    Downtown Press, 9.
    Harlequin Enterprises Inc., 9, 15.
    Red Dress Ink, 9.
*The Rules: Time-tested Secrets for Capturing the Heart of Mr. Right*, 12, 45, 52, 55, 64, 75. See also Ellen Fein and Sherrie Schneider.
    Critical reception of, 45–46.
    Relationship advice, 51–52.
    Sexual etiquette, 53.

**S**

*The Secret Dreamworld of a Shopaholic*. See also Sophie Kinsella.
    American edition, *Confessions of a Shopaholic*, 35, 40.
    Consumer culture references, 11.
    Critique of domestic-advice manuals, 111.
    Critique of women's magazines, 14–15, 16, 22–23, 34–40, 43–44.
    Reviews of, 40–43.
    Sequels to, 136.
    Series, 5, 13.
*Self-Help Culture: Reading Between the Lines* (Simonds), 46–47, 48, 49–50, 67.
*The Sensuous Woman* (J), 55, 59, 75–76.
*Sex and the City*, 4, 8, 18, 134, 135–36, 137, 138. See also Candace Bushnell.
    Consumer culture references, 11.
    Critique of domestic-advice manuals, 17–18, 102, 103, 104, 115–17, 118, 133.
    Critique of romantic comedies 17, 76, 88–94, 95, 100.
    HBO series, 3, 10, 88, 138.
    *New York Observer* column, 10, 17.
    Referenced in women's magazines, 9.
*Sex and the Single Girl*, 24, 45, 74–76. See also Helen Gurley Brown.
    Female sexuality, 78.
    Film adaptation, 17, 74, 76, 77–80, 82–83.
"Sex and the Single Girl: *Helen Fielding, Erica Jong, and Helen Gurley Brown*" (Whelehan), 4.
Sentimental novels, 4, 23. See also heroine-centered novels and nineteenth-century novels.
"Shrinking Violets and Caspar Milquetoasts: Shyness and Heterosexuality From the Roles of Fifties to *The*

# Index

*Rules* of the Nineties" (McDaniel), 51, 65.
*Shaping Our Mothers' Worlds: American Women's Magazines* (Walker), 19, 103, 104.
Shapiro, Laura, 107.
*Smart Women, Foolish Choices: Finding the Right Men, Avoiding the Wrong Ones* (Cowan and Kinder), 49, 51, 64.
Soap operas, 15–16, 143.
Stewart, Martha. 107–08, 114. See also women's advice manuals; domestic-advice manuals.
   *Good Things: A Collection of Inspired Household Ideas and Projects*, 109, 110–11.
   *Martha Stewart Living* magazine, 12, 105, 108–11, 115–11, 122–23.
*Still Killing Us Softly* (Kilbourne), 21.
*The Sweetest Thing*, 17, 76, 77, 80–85.

# T

*Thirtynothing* (Jewell), 10.
*This Is Chick-Lit* (Baratz-Logsted), 134.
*A Treatise on Domestic Economy* (Beecher), 104.
*Two-Bit Culture: The Paperbacking of America* (Davis), 48.

# U

*Unbearable Weight: Feminism, Western Culture, and the Body* (Bordo), 21–22.

# V

Valdes-Rodriguez, Alisa. 136.

# W

"The Way to a Man's Heart: Gender Roles, Domestic Ideology, and Cookbooks in the 1950s" (Neuhaus), 103.
Weiner, Jennifer, 10, 142.
*West End Girls* (Colgan), 3.
Wharton, Edith, 88–89.

White, Marco Pierre, 112.
   Referenced in chick lit, 11, 102, 115, 121–22.
Winfrey, Oprah
   *O: The Oprah Magazine*, 25, 72.
   *The Oprah Winfrey Show*, 45.
   "Dating Rules," 53, 67, 72–73.
   "*The Rules* Backlash," 73.
Wolper, Carol, 9, 52. See also *The Cigarette Girl*.
*Women Men Love, Women Men Leave* (Cowan and Kinder), 49.
*Women Who Love Too Much: When You Keep Wishing and Hoping He'll Change* (Norwood), 45, 49, 51.
Women's advice manuals, 143. See also conduct literature and etiquette manuals.
   Domestic-advice manuals
      Definition of, 12.
      Chick lit's critique of, 5–6, 11, 16, 17–18, 19, 102–04, 111–31, 132–33, 139–40.
      History of, 104–08.
      Magazines, 105–06.
         *Good Housekeeping*, 21, 23, 37.
         *Ladies' Home Journal*, 21, 23, 105, 106
         *McCall's*, 21, 105.
   Romantic comedies
      As advice manuals, 12–13, 77–78.
      Chick lit's critique of, 5–6, 11, 16, 17, 19, 88–100, 139–40.
      Of the chick lit era, 85–88.
   Self-help books.
      Audience for, 50–51.
      As advice manuals, 11–12
      Chick lit's critique of, 5–6, 11, 13–14, 16–17, 19, 47–48, 52–73, 139–40.
      Gendering of, 49–50.
      History of, 48–50.
      Scholarly criticism of, 46–47.
   Women's magazines, 1, 9.
      Chick lit's critique of, 5–6, 11, 14–15, 16, 19, 22–23, 27–44, 138, 139–40.

Women's advice manuals (*continued*)
   Women's magazines (*continued*)
      Constructed reader, 26–27, 34, 38.
      Construction of, 20–21.
      *Glamour*, 9, 18, 25, 134.
      History of, 23–25.
      Scholarly criticism of, 21–22.
      *Vogue*, 9, 14, 37, 40, 47, 49, 50, 137.
      Women writing for, 25–26.
   *Women's Magazines 1940–60: Gender Roles and the Popular Press* (Walker), 26.
World Wide Web, 3, 10, 140, 141, 142.

## Z

Zigman, Laura, 6, 142. See also *Animal Husbandry*.

CPSIA information can be obtained at www.ICGtesting.com
Printed in the USA
LVOW081729250313

325925LV00004B/825/P